Turn to Page 101 3104

STATE OF THE ART PROGRAM

Portfolios

Robyn Montana Turner

BARRETT KENDALL PUBLISHING, LTD.
AUSTIN, TEXAS

CREDITS

EDITORIAL

Project Director: *Sandy Stucker Blevins*

Senior Development Editor: *Sandra Mangurian*

Editorial Support: *Lorrie Tenos*

Copy Editor: *Susan Sandoval*

Administrative Manager: *Mark Blangger*

Administrative Support: *Kathy Blanchard*

DESIGN, PRODUCTION, AND PHOTO RESEARCH

Project Director: *Pun Nio*

Designers: *Leslie Kell Designs, Jane Thurmond Designs, Pun Nio*

Design and Electronic Files: *Leslie Kell Designs, Jane Thurmond Designs, Isabel Garza, Rhonda Warwick*

Photo Research: *Laurie O'Meara*

Photo Art Direction: *Laurie O'Meara*

Illustrations: *Holly Cooper, Leslie Kell, Mike Krone, Jane Thurmond, Rhonda Warwick*

Cover Design: *Leslie Kell Designs; Art Director, Pun Nio; Student Art: Crayons – Michelle, Corbett Junior High School; King Tut – Catherine, Collins Intermediate; Zebra Feathers – James, Oak Crest Middle School; Cheerleader sculpture – Stephanie, Collins Intermediate; Portrait – Margeaux, Collins Intermediate; Blue-jean sculpture – Lauren, Collins Intermediate; Background – Brushworks Photo Disc, Inc.*

Copyright © 2001 by BARRETT KENDALL PUBLISHING, LTD.
All rights reserved. No part of this publication may be reproduced or transmitted in any form or by any means, electronic or mechanical, including photocopy, recording, or any information storage retrieval system, without permission in writing from the publisher. Requests for permission to reproduce or transmit any part of this publication should be mailed to: Permissions, Barrett Kendall Publishing, Ltd., 3106 Longhorn Blvd., Austin, Texas 78758.

Printed in the United States of America

ISBN 1-889105-63-5   4 5 6 7 8 9 10   RD   06 07 09 05 04 03 02 01

Consultants

Doug Blandy, Ph.D.
Director
Arts and Administration Program
University of Oregon
Eugene, Oregon

Cindy G. Broderick, Ph.D.
Art Faculty
Alamo Heights Junior School
Alamo Heights Independent School District
San Antonio, Texas

Georgia Collins, Ph.D.
Professor Emeritus
Department of Art
University of Kentucky
Lexington, Kentucky

Deborah N. Cooper, M.Ed.
Coordinating Director
Curriculum and Instruction
Charlotte-Mecklenburg Schools
Charlotte, North Carolina

Sandra M. Epps, Ph.D.
Project Director
PS-36 Multicultural Arts Collaborative
Columbia University Teachers College
New York, New York

Diane C. Gregory, Ph.D.
Associate Professor of Art Education
Department of Art and Design
Southwest Texas State University
San Marcos, Texas

Susan M. Mayer, M.A.
Senior Lecturer of Art
The University of Texas at Austin
Austin, Texas

Aaronetta Hamilton Pierce
Art Consultant, Lecturer
African American Art and Artists
San Antonio, Texas

Contributing Writers

Studios
Sara Chapman, M.A.
Visual Arts Coordinator
Alief Independent School District
Houston, Texas

Studios
James Clarke, M.A.
Consultant, Art Education
Houston, Texas

What Have You Learned?
Renee Sandell, Ph.D.
Professor, Department of Art Education
Maryland Institute, College of Art
Baltimore, Maryland

Art Links
Tamim Ansary
Educational Writer and Editor
San Francisco, California

Reviewers

Linda Catlin
Art Educator
Metropolitan School District of Washington Township
Indianapolis, Indiana

Jeannette L. Clawson
Art Educator
Sandy Springs Middle School
Fulton County School District
Atlanta, Georgia

Joey Doyle
Program Director for Visual Arts
Aldine Independent School District
Houston, Texas

Dean Johns
Visual Arts Specialist
Charlotte-Mecklenburg Schools
Charlotte, North Carolina

Sean Wells
Art Educator
Marshall Middle School
San Diego Unified School District
San Diego, California

Iris Williams
Art Educator
Webb Middle School
Austin Independent School District
Austin, Texas

CONTENTS

UNIT 1 The Language of Art 6

LESSON 1 Line 8
  Studio: *Experimenting with Line*

LESSON 2 Studio: **Creating a Contour Drawing** 10
  Studio Option: *Contour Resist Drawing*

LESSON 3 Shape 12
  Studio: *Sketches Using a Viewfinder*

LESSON 4 Studio: **Creating a Composition with Shapes** 14
  Studio Option: *Drawing of a Detail*

LESSON 5 Form 16
  Studio: *Clay Forms and Contour Drawings*

LESSON 6 Space 18
  Studio: *Drawings Showing Deep Space*

LESSON 7 Studio: **Creating a Perspective Drawing** 20
  Studio Option: *Drawing a Long, Straight Road*

LESSON 8 Value 22
  Studio: *Creating a Value Scale/Drawing*

LESSON 9 Color 24
  Studio: *Creating Your Own Color Wheel*

LESSON 10 Color and Colorists 26
  Studio: *Experimenting with Colors*

LESSON 11 Texture 28
  Studio: *Rubbing and Drawing to Show Tactile Texture*

LESSON 12 Balance 30
  Studio: *Drawings Showing Balance*

LESSON 13 Emphasis 32
  Studio: *Drawing with Emphasis*

LESSON 14 Proportion 34
  Studio: *Drawing Proportion*

LESSON 15 Studio: **Drawing Altered Proportions** 36
  Studio Option: *Collage of Body Proportions*

LESSON 16 Rhythm and Pattern 38
  Studio: *Drawing Patterns*

LESSON 17 Studio: **Showing Emotions with Pattern and Rhythm** 40
  Studio Option: *Pattern and Rhythm with Computer Tools*

LESSON 18 Studio: **Unity and Variety** ... 42
  Studio Option: *Design with Unity and Variety*

Talk About Art: Vincent van Gogh 44
  Studio: *Impasto Brushstrokes*

Portfolio Project: Painting an Impasto Landscape 46

ARTLINKS Music, Dance, Theatre, Literature .. 48

What Have You Learned? Unit Review 50

UNIT 2 The Creative Art Process 54

LESSON 1 Drawing 56
  Studio: *Drawing in Ink*
LESSON 2 Studio: Gesture Drawing 58
  Studio Option: *Gesture Flipbook*
LESSON 3 Painting 60
  Studio: *Experimenting with Watercolor*
LESSON 4 Studio: Painting a Landmark ... 62
  Studio Option: *Textured Painting*
LESSON 5 Printmaking 64
  Studio: *Making a Monoprint*
LESSON 6 Studio: Making a Relief Print .. 66
  Studio Option: *Foam-Block Relief Print*
LESSON 7 Collage 68
  Studio: *Collage*
LESSON 8 Textiles and Fiber Art 70
  Studio: *Textile Design*
Lesson 9 Sculpture 72
  Studio: *Paper Sculpture*
LESSON 10 Studio: Making a Relief Sculpture 74
  Studio Option: *Metal Relief Sculpture*
LESSON 11 Architecture 76
  Studio: *Architectural Plan*
LESSON 12 Studio: Making an Architectural Model 78
  Studio Option: *Interior Design of a School*
LESSON 13 Computer Art 80
  Studio: *Computer Design*
LESSON 14 Still Photography 82
  Studio: *Photographic Collage*
LESSON 15 Studio: Creating a Storyboard . 84
  Studio Option: *Storyboard Comic Strip*

Talk About Art: M.C. Escher 86
  Studio: *Sketches for a Print*

Portfolio Project: Making a Tessellation .. 88

ARTLINKS Music, Dance, Theatre, Literature ... 90

What Have You Learned? Unit Review 92

UNIT 3 A World of Art and Artists 96

LESSON 1 Mysteries of Long Ago 98
  Studio: *Cave Painting*
LESSON 2 Art of Ancient Egypt 100
  Studio: *Mummy Case*
LESSON 3 Studio: Designing Your Own Throne 102
  Studio Option: *Crown*
LESSON 4 Art of Ancient Greece 104
  Studio: *Poster for the Olympics*
LESSON 5 Art of Ancient Rome 106
  Studio: *Animal Mosaic*
LESSON 6 Studio: Designing a Model with Arches 108
  Studio Option: *Restaurant Design*
LESSON 7 Art of the Middle Ages 110
  Studio: *Medieval Design*
LESSON 8 Studio: Creating an Illuminated Storybook 112
  Studio Option: *Stained-Glass Window*

LESSON 9 Architecture in the Early Americas 114
Studio: *Combining Old and New Designs*

LESSON 10 Art of the Renaissance in Europe 116
Studio: *Renaissance Mural*

LESSON 11 Eastern Art of Long Ago 118
Studio: *Banner*

LESSON 12 Western Art of the Nineteenth and Twentieth Centuries 120
Studio: *Comparison of Art Styles*

LESSON 13 Studio: Creating an Abstract Collage 122
Studio Option: *Abstract Design*

Talk About Art: African Artists 124
Studio: *Symbol of Celebration*

Portfolio Project: Creating a Clay Object About History 126

ARTLINKS *Music, Dance, Theatre, Literature* .. 128

What Have You Learned? *Unit Review* 130

UNIT 4 A World of Subjects and Styles 134

LESSON 1 People as Subjects 136
Studio: *Light Sources*

LESSON 2 Proportion and Full Figures .. 138
Studio: *Wire Sculpture*

LESSON 3 Proportion and Faces 140
Studio: *Drawing Faces*

LESSON 4 Studio: Creating a Self-Portrait 142
Studio Option: *Past, Present, and Future Self-Portrait*

LESSON 5 Animals as Subjects 144
Studio: *Animal Subject*

LESSON 6 Studio: Making a Ceramic Animal Vessel 146
Studio Option: *Drawing an Imaginary Animal*

LESSON 7 Still Life as a Subject 148
Studio: *Still Life*

LESSON 8 Studio: Creating a Cubist Still Life 150
Studio Option: *Cubist Portrait*

LESSON 9 Landscape as a Subject 152
Studio: *Landscape with Watercolor*

LESSON 10 Studio: Creating a Pointillist Seascape 154
Studio Option: *Watercolor Resist*

LESSON 11 Impressionism 156
Studio: *Impressionist Painting*

LESSON 12 Studio: Drawing as an Impressionist 158
Studio Option: *Impressionist Portrait*

LESSON 13 Expressionism 160
Studio: *Expressive Painting*

LESSON 14 Surrealism 162
Studio: *Surrealist Scene in Mixed Media*

LESSON 15 Studio: Making a Surrealist Painting 164
Studio Option: *Fantasy Animal Drawing*

LESSON 16 Pop Art 166
Studio: *Pop Art Sculpture*

Talk About Art: Frida Kahlo 168
Studio: *Self-Portrait*

Portfolio Project: Developing Individual Style 170

ARTLINKS *Music, Dance, Theatre, Literature* .. 172

What Have You Learned? *Unit Review* 174

3

UNIT 5 A World of Places and Objects 178

LESSON 1 Murals as Visual Stories in Communities 180
Studio: *Mural*

LESSON 2 Mosaics as Objects of Expression 182
Studio: *Mosaic Mural*

LESSON 3 Outdoor Sculptures as Objects of Adornment 184
Studio: *Outdoor Sculpture*

LESSON 4 Studio: Creating a Maquette for a Bronze Sculpture 186
Studio Option: *Papier Mâché Maquette*

LESSON 5 Furniture as Art 188
Studio: *Furniture Design*

LESSON 6 Design of Everyday Objects .. 190
Studio: *Designing a Product*

LESSON 7 Studio: Creating a Model for a Prototype 192
Studio Option: *Paper Model*

LESSON 8 Found-Object Assemblages ... 194
Studio: *Found-Object Robot*

LESSON 9 Studio: Creating a Combine Painting 196
Studio Option: *Combine Sculpture*

LESSON 10 Pottery as a Global Artform . 198
Studio: *Pottery Vessel*

LESSON 11 Art as Clothing Design 200
Studio: *Clothing Design*

LESSON 12 Studio: Creating a Repoussé Wall Hanging 202
Studio Option: *Tooling Copper*

LESSON 13 Art as Functional Decoration . 204
Studio: *Decorative Art*

Talk About Art: Henri Matisse 206
Studio: *Sequel to an Artwork*

Portfolio Project: Creating a Triptych ... 208

ARTLINKS Music, Dance, Theatre, Literature .. 210

What Have You Learned? Unit Review 212

UNIT 6 A World of Expression and Meaning .. 216

LESSON 1 Expression Through Nature .. 218
Studio: *Colors and Shapes*

LESSON 2 Expression of Self 220
Studio: *Self-Portrait in Mixed Media*

LESSON 3 Expressive Points of View ... 222
Studio: *Worm's-Eye View*

LESSON 4 Studio: Creating an Abstract Cityscape 224
Studio Option: *Cityscape Collage*

LESSON 5 Expression Through Commercial Arts 226
Studio: *Poster*

LESSON 6 Expression Through Symbols . . 228
  Studio: *Totem Sculpture*
LESSON 7 Masks for Expression 230
  Studio: *Mosaic Mask*
LESSON 8 Studio: **Creating a Papier Mâché Animal Mask** 232
  Studio Option: *Paper Mask for a Festival*
LESSON 9 Expression Through Humor . . 234
  Studio: *Cartoon Strip*
LESSON 10 Studio: **Creating a Caricature** . 236
  Studio Option: *Caricature of a Famous Person*

LESSON 11 Art Museums and Galleries . . 238
  Studio: *Model of an Art Gallery*
Talk About Art: Georgia O'Keeffe 240
  Studio: *Creating a Swirl Painting*
Portfolio Project: Creating an Art Exhibition 242
ARTLINKS Music, Dance, Theatre, Literature . . 244
What Have You Learned? Unit Review 246

Think Safety 250
Technique Handbook 251
Glossary 267
Color Wheel 285
Elements of Art 286
Principles of Design 288
List of Art and Artists 290
Careers in Art 300
Art History Timeline 306
Index 314
Acknowledgments 320
Photo/Illustration Credits 321

Unit 1

Vincent van Gogh. (Detail) *Enclosed Field with Rising Sun*, 1889. Oil on canvas, 27 2/3 by 35 1/3 inches. Private collection.

The Language of Art

When you communicate an idea or a feeling, you usually do it with a sign. Signs can be body gestures, as in dance and theatre. They can be musical, as in the notes of your favorite guitar melody. Signs can be oral or written, as in your tone of voice or the words of poetry and novels. This book is about visual signs, known as works of art, or *artworks,* and the language used to discuss them. Artworks are all around you. You may see them as designs in nature, such as stripes on a zebra's back or ripples in a puddle. They can also be created by people, as in an artist's design, known as a *composition.* Artists plan the composition of their artworks to help them communicate their ideas and feelings. This painting of a vibrant scene shows how artist Vincent van Gogh felt about the sunrise.

Special words, such as *line* and *shape* or *pattern* and *rhythm,* help artists talk about their compositions. Line and shape are two of the **elements of art,** or basic parts and symbols of artworks. What other elements do you recognize in the list at the right? Pattern and rhythm are two **principles of design,** or guidelines to organize the elements in a composition. How have these and other principles helped you plan your compositions?

Elements of art are to a visual artist what words are to a writer or numbers are to a mathematician. They are the basic signs, or symbols, used to construct ideas. Principles of design are to a visual artist what sentences and paragraphs are to a writer or operations and formulas are to a mathematician. They govern the way the elements are used to convey ideas and feelings.

This unit introduces you to elements of art and principles of design. You will learn to use them to express your thoughts, feelings, and imagination. You can practice using them separately and together, and soon they will become a part of your everyday vocabulary. Your understanding of these words, along with a host of other art terms in this book, will serve you throughout your life. You may use this understanding as you plant a garden or arrange furniture in a room. You may also use the language of art as you respond to a fireworks display or a work of art in a museum. You may even use it in expressing yourself—as a full-time artist!

line
shape
form
space
value
color
texture

balance
emphasis
proportion
pattern
rhythm
unity
variety

 **At a Glance**

Does this painting remind you of a particular time or place? Explain.

Does it seem calm, peaceful, friendly, angry, frightening, or does it portray a totally different mood? Explain.

What visual signs help you understand the painting?

Lesson 1

ELEMENTS OF ART

Line

What Is Line?

Look around you to find something that is *not* made of lines. Your desk, your chair, the threads in your clothing—everything around you has lines. They appear as branches on a winter tree. They define musical instruments, rooftops, and mountains. Even the words you are reading are made of lines. Artists see line as an important element of art in any composition. To an artist, **line** is the path of a dot moving through space.

Line Quality

Artists pay close attention to **line quality**—the special character of any line. They notice whether a line is thick or thin, smooth or rough. They strive to create these and other special qualities with their tools—for example, by pressing down to make a thick line or applying less pressure for a thinner one. To create a slightly rough edge, they might use a crayon, chalk pastel, or charcoal stick. What tool could you use to create a smooth line? Some other qualities of lines artists notice and create are broken - - - or continuous ———, dark ▬▬▬ or light ——— . How many kinds of lines can you find in **A** and **B**?

Types of Lines

Artists notice that a line moves as it goes through space. Lines travel up, down, or across. Some travel in straight paths, while others do not. Each type of line gives the viewer a message that may evoke specific feelings and ideas about the artwork. As you read about these different types of lines, look for examples of them in **A** and **B**.

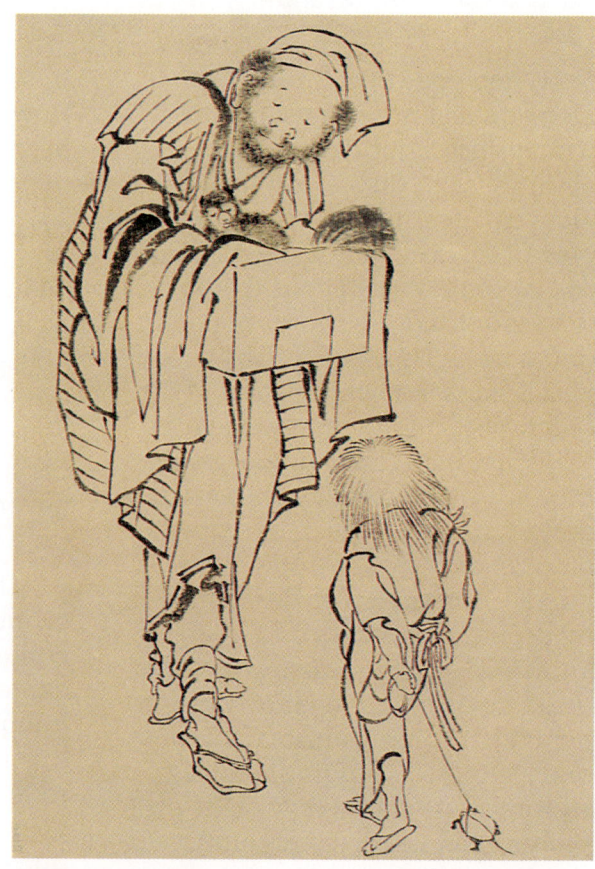

A How would you describe the types of lines in this drawing?

Katsushika Hokusai. *Man and Boy*, Edo period (1658–1868). Ink on paper, $12^{11}/_{16}$ by $8^{11}/_{16}$ inches. Freer Gallery of Art.

Vertical lines run up and down. A flagpole forms a vertical line, as do buildings, rockets blasting off, and giant redwood trees. Vertical lines appear strong and powerful. What message do the vertical lines in **A** convey?

Horizontal lines run across, from side to side. A tabletop makes a horizontal line, and so does your lap. The ocean meets the sky at the *horizon*—another horizontal line. Horizontal lines appear peaceful and calm.

B

Many artists come to understand line by drawing. Often they draw a **sketch** to record what they see, explore an idea, or plan another artwork. They carry a **sketchbook** filled with blank pages. Sketching helps you learn more about the language of art. As you draw, think about different ways you can use line creatively. Draw sketches every day, and write about them in a sketchbook of your own.

Experimenting with Line

To help you with this Studio, refer to pages 252, 253, and 254.

Look around your classroom and identify different types of lines. Create a **Technique Sheet** by dividing a paper into six or eight equal spaces. Draw different types and directions of lines. Experiment with a variety of drawing tools, such as pencils, felt-tip pens, colored pencils, markers, crayons, and oil pastels. Look again at the people in **A**. Imagine yourself interacting with a favorite person, and create a drawing that shows a variety of techniques you have learned about line.

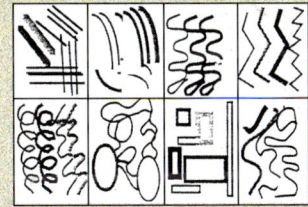

Label each line with its quality and direction. Label the kinds of drawing tools you used. Store your Technique Sheet in your *Portfolio*, the container you use to organize your artworks.

Diagonal lines stand at a slant. Your body forms a diagonal line when you lean forward to race, suggesting a sense of movement and excitement.

Zigzag lines are made of a series of diagonal lines moving in different directions that come together at sharp angles. A zigzag line itself can move vertically, horizontally, or diagonally. Zigzag lines create a feeling of confusion, nervousness, or excitement.

Curved lines change direction gradually, expressing movement in a graceful way, as a snake wiggling through water. Circles and spirals have curved lines. Point out some curved lines in **A** and **B**.

Actual and Implied Lines

Most lines are called **actual lines** because they are real; you can actually see them. The artworks on these pages show actual lines. **Implied lines** are not actually seen; they are imagined. The placement of other lines, shapes, and colors helps you imagine implied lines. Study **A** to find an implied line.

Sketchbook/Journal

Draw a variety of qualities and directions of lines that you see in your classroom or at home. Write about your favorite kinds of drawing tools and ways in which they can help you express your ideas and feelings.

Line 9

Lesson 2: Creating a Contour Drawing

Get the Picture

Artists draw **contours,** or edges of an object, by looking closely at the object as they slowly move their drawing tool. Their eyes stay fixed on the edges of the object as their hand guides the drawing tool. Some say it feels as though their hand becomes their eyes.

The drawing in **A** shows the contour of a woman who is apparently deep in thought. Observe how artist Henri Matisse used thin, delicate lines to show details and one heavy bold line to show contrast. As the disconnected shapes on the model's necklace indicate, Matisse picked up his drawing tool to draw each heart. Which lines in the drawing show that he kept his eye on his model?

As you create your own contour drawing, keep in mind the qualities and types of lines available to you. Be prepared to observe your chosen object keenly as you draw your composition.

 Contour drawings are sometimes done as sketches for a painting or sculpture. As in this line drawing, they may stand alone as finished artworks.

Henri Matisse. *Girl with Gold Necklace*, 1944.
Ink on paper, 20 1/4 by 15 1/8 inches.
The University of Arizona Museum of Art.

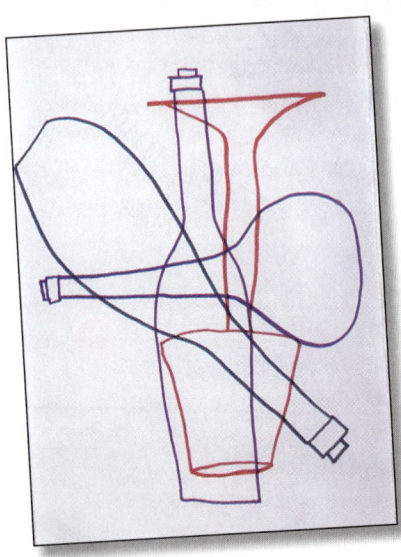

 Samantha, Agnew Middle School. *Untitled.* Markers on paper, 12 by 18 inches.

Get Set

 **Materials you will need:**

- 12" x 18" white drawing paper
- masking tape
- drawing tools, such as pencils, black felt-tip pens, markers, crayons, oil pastels, or charcoal
- an object with interesting lines to draw, such as a shoe, plastic bottle, stapler, or trash can

How to Create a Contour Drawing

To help you with this Studio, refer to page 255.

1. Sit close to an object to draw. Tape your drawing paper to your desk.

2. Practice drawing by imagining where the contour lines will go on your paper. Then practice with your drawing tool in the air.

3. Draw all the lines—inside and outside—as you look at the lines of the object. Do not lift your pencil from your paper, and keep your eyes on the lines of the object you are drawing at all times.

4. Rotate your drawing paper, and draw the same or another object with another drawing tool. Repeat and overlap your contour drawings.

Creating a Contour Resist Drawing

Use light-colored crayons or oil pastels to draw four or five of your favorite objects. Show different angles and rotate the paper. Paint over the finished drawings with dark watercolor paints. Discover how the oil in the crayons or oil pastels resists the water in the paints.

Sketchbook/Journal

Draw several of your favorite objects. Describe the process you used in creating your contour drawings.

Be an Art Critic!

1. **Describe** What types of lines make up your drawing? Which qualities do they show?
2. **Analyze** How does the technique of contour drawing affect the arrangement of your lines?
3. **Interpret** What feeling does your drawing convey? Why does it convey that feeling?
4. **Judge** What is best about your drawing? Explain.

Creating a Contour Drawing

Lesson 3

Shape

How do these organic shapes differ from geometric shapes?

John Storrs. *Genesis*, 1932. Oil on board, 32 by 25 1/8 inches. Courtesy of SBC Communications Inc.

What Is Shape?

What would you say if someone asked you how a tablecloth, a sheet of paper, and the shadow of a basketball are alike? As an artist, you might respond that each one is a shape. A **shape** is a flat, two-dimensional area with height and width. It might have an edge, or an outline, around it. Or you might know it by its area, as in the shape of a shadow. Shape is an element of art.

Types of Shapes

Artists think of shape as being a flat area created when actual or implied lines meet to surround a space. Shapes can be grouped into two types: *geometric* and *organic*.

Geometric shapes are precise, mathematical shapes. The basic and most common geometric shapes are the circle, square, and triangle. All other geometric shapes, such as the oval and rectangle, are variations of the basic shapes. Most geometric shapes look like the shapes you might draw with a ruler; they are regular and even, unlike shapes you find in nature. Name the geometric shapes in **B**, **C**, and **D**.

Organic shapes, sometimes referred to as "free-form," are irregular and uneven. They are often found in nature, although you can make them yourself. Organic shapes often form natural curves or zigzags. The shapes of a leaf, a flower, and a cloud are organic. Notice the organic shapes in **A**.

As you create sketches of shapes you observe, think about the elements that define them. Are the lines actual or implied? Does color help you see them? Then ask yourself how the shapes—geometric and organic—enhance your composition.

C

Some Geometric Shapes

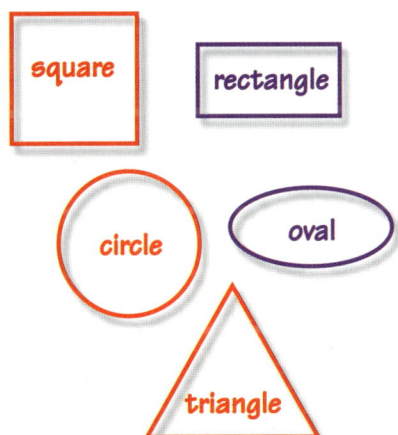

D This artwork shows geometric shapes: an oval, triangles, squares, and rectangles.

Jennifer, Zachry Middle School. *Untitled.* Tempera on paper, 18 by 12 inches.

Creating Thumbnail Sketches Using a Viewfinder

Fold a paper in half and then in fourths. Cut a small rectangle or square (about one inch) on the corner of the fold. Open it and look through your **viewfinder** to find combinations of shapes around you. Draw what you see by making several *thumbnail sketches* the size of your viewfinder.

Some Organic Shapes

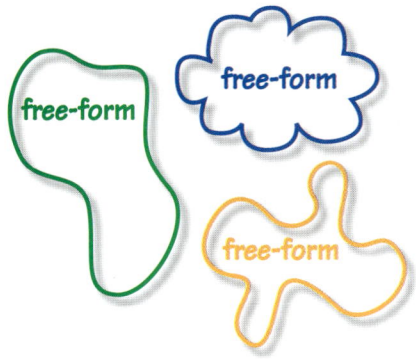

Sketchbook/Journal

Make some thumbnail sketches of shapes you see inside or outside your home. Explain why these shapes are interesting to you. Record notes about shapes that you observe through your viewfinder.

Shape 13

Lesson 4: Creating a Composition with Shapes

Get the Picture

In 1936, artist Sonia Terk Delaunay secured a commission to decorate the Air and Railroad Pavilions for the Paris Exposition of 1937. *Study for Portugal* (detail), in **A**, is a part of her composition for that monumental public work. This **detail**, a small part of the larger artwork, shows only one of the four scenes in the study. Point out geometric and organic shapes in the arches of the railroad viaduct, buildings, village people, and oxen of Portugal. Notice how the artist's use of colored shapes with few outlines, or *contours*, creates many implied lines in the composition.

To plan your own composition, first think about an overall scene that holds special meaning to you. Perhaps it is a city you have visited or a peaceful place in nature. Then consider how you might convey the feelings you have for your scene with organic and geometric shapes.

 A detail shows a part of the larger artwork.
Sonia Terk Delaunay. (Detail) *Study for Portugal*, ca. 1937. Gouache on paper, 14 1/4 by 37 inches. The National Museum of Women in the Arts.

 Jordan, Austin Elementary School. *City Lights*. Cut colored paper on paper, 9 by 12 inches.

Get Set

Materials you will need:
- 12" x 18" white drawing paper
- colored construction paper
- wallpaper samples
- scissors
- glue or gluestick

Lesson 4

How to Create a Composition with Shapes

1. On white drawing paper, make a sketch of a special place you have been. Include only basic lines and shapes, without details.

2. Cut out shapes from colored paper and wallpaper samples to help you express your feelings about your scene.

3. Arrange and rearrange the shapes on your paper. Trim them, and cut out more shapes until the white paper is filled and you are satisfied with your composition.

4. Glue your shapes onto the white paper.

Making a Drawing of a Detail

Arrange a group of objects on a table, and select a part of them to sketch. Draw the composition on white paper, and add color with chalk pastels, colored pencil, and colored markers.

Sketchbook/Journal

Using your viewfinder, draw several thumbnail sketches of interesting shapes in your larger composition. Label each shape as geometric or organic. Then describe the feeling you intended to convey about your special place.

Be an Art Critic!

1. **Describe** What shapes appear in your artwork? Which shapes are geometric? organic?
2. **Analyze** Cover up a part of your artwork with a sheet of blank paper. Does this change the artwork? If so, how?
3. **Interpret** What feeling did you want to convey about your special place? What about your artwork creates that feeling? How does the meaning change when you see only a part of the artwork?
4. **Judge** Where will you display your composition? Why?

Creating a Composition with Shapes

Lesson 5 — Form

 The artist observes his glass forms.
Dale Chihuly. *Isola di San Giacomo in Palude Chandelier*, 1996. Blown-glass, 9 by 7 feet. Venice, Italy.

What Is Form?

A **form** is an object with three dimensions—height, width, and depth. A basketball is a form. Like a flat circle, the ball has height and width, but it also has depth. Like some forms, the ball is empty, whereas other forms are full. In order to fully understand a form, you can examine the front, sides, and back of it. For example, you can hold a basketball in your hands and dribble it, go around it, toss it, catch it. Sometimes you can even examine the interior of a form, as you might explore the inside of a building.

Types of Forms

Basic **geometric forms** are the sphere, cube, and pyramid, the contours of which resemble a circle, square, and triangle, respectively. All other geometric forms, such as the cylinder and the cone, are variations of the basic forms. Skyscrapers, barrels, and hot-air balloons are geometric forms. Notice some geometric forms around you.

Like organic shapes, **organic forms,** often called "free-forms," have irregular and uneven edges and are often found in nature. Unlike organic shapes, however, these forms have depth, as do apples, trees, and animals. Find some organic forms on these pages.

 Which shapes are closely related to these forms?

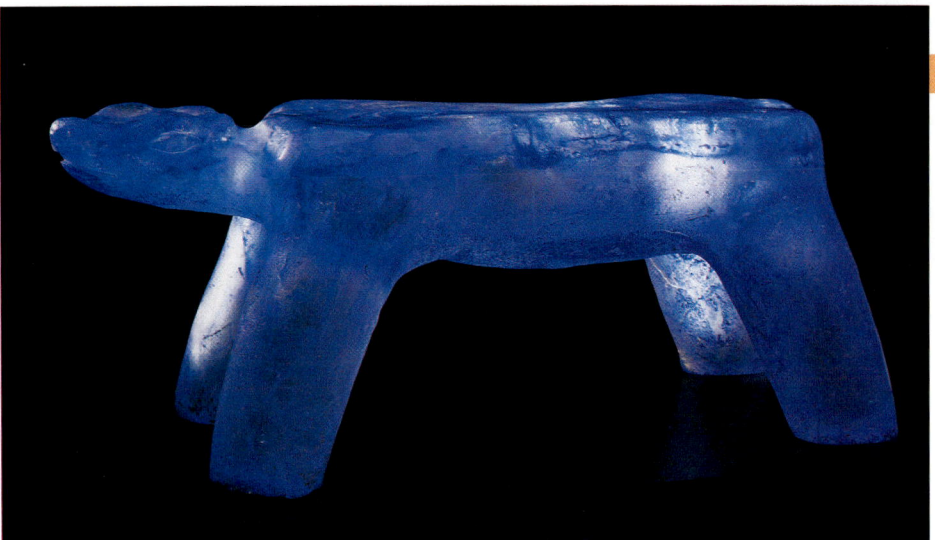

"It's the interplay of texture, color, and light that I like with glass."
—Isabel De Obaldía, 1997

Isabel De Obaldía. *Sebastian's Beast,* 1997. Kiln cast glass, 6 3/4 by 17 by 6 inches. Courtesy of Mary-Anne Martin/Fine Art, New York.

Career Link

Dale Chihuly and Isabel De Obaldía

Artists plan and create their artworks in many ways. The artist of **A**, Dale Chihuly, leads a team of artists to create the organic glass forms you see. First he creates a plan for the forms. Then he closely supervises his trained assistants, who make the glass forms according to his plans.

The artist of **C**, Isabel De Obaldía, also creates three-dimensional glass forms, but primarily on her own. She does not strive for decorative and detailed effects in her plans. Instead, she contends to show the power and force of her figures through fundamental organic forms.

Artists, such as Chihuly and De Obaldía, prefer to show form in three-dimensional compositions. But you can also show three-dimensional forms in two-dimensional compositions. Think about how contour drawing can help you show form.

Creating Clay Forms and Contour Drawings

Identify several forms in your classroom, including spheres, cubes, cylinders, and cones, as well as a variety of organic forms. With modeling clay, make one or two models of each of these various forms. Choose your favorite model for each form.

Create a Technique Sheet by dividing a paper into six equal spaces. In each space, draw three contours of a specific form, using your favorite model of the form as your guide. As you draw, think about what your three-dimensional model and two-dimensional representation have in common. How does making a contour drawing help you understand this relationship?

Sketchbook/Journal

Draw sketches of spaceships, space stations, planets, moons, and other forms in outer space. Describe the relationship between shape and form in your drawings.

Form 17

Lesson 6

Space

 Find positive and negative spaces in this three-dimensional artwork.

Barbara Hepworth. *Merryn,* 1962. Alabaster, 13 by 11 1/2 by 8 1/4 inches. The National Museum of Women in the Arts.

What Is Space?

"Space" means many things to many people. It can mean anything from the blank area between words and lines in a sentence to the vast outer limits of the universe. In the language of art, **space** can describe empty or full areas, areas that are far away or nearby, and areas that are huge or small. Space is an element of art.

Positive and Negative

The form of your body is called a **positive space** because it fills a space. The empty space around you is called **negative space.** Artists think of shapes and forms as being either positive or negative spaces. Notice the negative space in **A**, by sculptor Barbara Hepworth. A trademark of her work is holes, which create centers of interest. Arranging a composition without much negative space, as did artist Pierre-Auguste Renoir, in **B**, makes a painting or drawing appear busy.

Techniques

Look again at **B**, which is a two-dimensional artwork. The artist used several techniques to show the illusion of deep space, or **depth,** on a two-dimensional plane. You may wish to try some of these techniques:

Foreground The artist places objects appearing larger toward the bottom of the artwork. Objects in this part seem nearest to you.

Background The artist places objects appearing smaller toward the top of the artwork. Objects in this part seem farthest away.

Middle Ground The artist places objects appearing mid-size between the top and bottom of the artwork. This space appears to be between near and far.

Detail The artist uses crisp and clear line and shape to show close-up detail. More detail is added to close objects, less detail and/or fuzziness to distant objects.

Overlapping The artist partly covers faraway shapes and forms with nearer ones. This technique helps the artist show distance.

Linear Perspective The artist sets guidelines, as in **C**, to help position shapes to appear near or far away. Faraway objects seem smaller, creating the *illusion,* or appearance, of depth. The guidelines designate a **horizon line,** where earth and sky meet. They set a point on the

B Where did the artist paint detail? How does this help you understand negative space?

Pierre-Auguste Renoir. *Le Moulin de la Galette,* 1876. Oil on canvas, 68 by 51 inches. Musée d'Orsay, Paris.

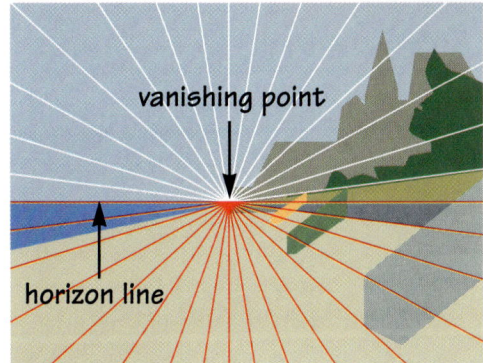

Linear perspective

horizon, the **vanishing point,** to which your eye is led by following slanted lines. This technique of linear perspective helps artists show railroads, highways, and other paths that seem to fade into the distance.

Atmospheric Perspective The artist may use this technique to create the illusion of air and space in a scene. Artists often use muted colors and large portions of white paint to show faraway objects and air. Close-up objects are bright and have darker colors. How did Renoir use atmospheric perspective to help him show distance?

Artists usually apply more than one technique for showing space. Think about how you might use various techniques to capture a feeling of space.

Creating Drawings That Suggest Deep Space

Create your own Technique Sheet by dividing a paper into eight equal spaces. Draw examples of objects in the foreground, background, middle ground. Draw some of these objects overlapping. Use the techniques you have learned to suggest space in a drawing.

Sketchbook/Journal

Show positive and negative space by drawing several containers with handles, such as a coffee cup, plastic milk jug, or laundry detergent bottle. Or create an imaginary drawing with a horizon line that demonstrates linear perspective, foreground, background, middle ground, and overlapping. Label each drawing with the techniques you have studied. Record any notes you might have about space and perspective.

Space 19

Lesson 7 — Creating a Perspective Drawing

What techniques did this artist use to show distance?

Furuyama Moromasa. *A Game of Hand Sumo in the New Yoshiwara*, ca. 1740. Woodblock print, 13 by 18 1/2 inches. The Metropolitan Museum of Art.

Get the Picture

Linear perspective, as a technique for showing the illusion of depth, was rediscovered during the 1400s by Italian architect Filippo Brunelleschi. He developed the technique, which had been pioneered some 1400 years before by artists in Rome. His explorations inspired other artists in Europe and later in other Western countries, such as the United States. The technique has never been as popular with Eastern artists, where emphasis is on shape and pattern in two-dimensional artworks. Linear perspective is sometimes found in Eastern art, however, as in the Japanese artwork in . Follow the diagonal lines of the floor, walls, and ceiling to their vanishing points on the horizon line. What other techniques did the artist use to show distance? You may wish to review the techniques for showing space on page 18.

Get Set

Materials you will need:
- white drawing paper
- pencil
- ruler
- drawing board
- colored pencils

 Sincy, Wilkinson Middle School. *Hallway of Education*. Colored pencils on paper, 9 by 12 inches.

20 Lesson 7

How to Draw with Perspective

1. Stand in a long hallway and observe the illusion of linear perspective.

2. Use perspective techniques as you draw the hallway on white paper with a pencil and ruler.

3. Use colored pencils to add to the illusion of depth by drawing a geometric form three times. Show a decrease in size and brightness as it nears the background.

Drawing a Long, Straight Road

Imagine that you are on a long, straight road. Make notes about everything you might see in the sky and on the ground. Use colored pencils to create a linear perspective drawing of your vision.

Sketchbook/Journal

Use your viewfinder to help you see the illusion of depth. Draw several thumbnail sketches as examples of perspective you see inside and outside of your home. Then write a description of the problems and solutions you encountered in experimenting with perspective techniques.

Be an Art Critic!

1. **Describe** Describe the directions of lines in your drawing.
2. **Analyze** Identify the horizon line and vanishing point. Explain how these points helped you arrange the lines.
3. **Interpret** How would you explain the meaning of illusion of depth to a viewer who has never seen your hallway?
4. **Judge** Do you like using perspective techniques? Tell why or why not.

Creating a Perspective Drawing

Lesson 8

Value

What Is Value?

When artist Georgia O'Keeffe was twenty-seven years old, she decided to put away her colored paints and brushes and start from scratch. She took out her black charcoal and stacks of blank paper and began to draw shapes, forms, and spaces with different **values,** or shades of light and dark, as in **A**. She used white as the lightest value, black as the darkest one, and many shades of gray in between. Night after night she sat on the floor drawing images with black, white, and gray values. Later she would return to color with a better understanding of value, an element of art.

Techniques for Achieving Value

Artist Diego Rivera lived and worked in Mexico during most of his life. As a painter of **murals**, large artworks applied directly to a wall or ceiling, color was an important element to him. In order to make two-dimensional shapes appear full and round, however, he often practiced drawing values of black, white, and gray. Look at **B** to find areas where he applied **shading**, a gradual change from light to dark values. His drawing shows values that blend softly with one another to achieve the illusion of a three-dimensional form. The sleeping woman appears round and full, even though she is flat in the drawing. How would a simple contour of the woman's shape with no shades of value change the drawing? Look again at **A** to find **contrast**, the effect showing the difference between light and dark values. Artists create contrast to make darker areas recede, while lighter areas project. How does contrast help achieve the illusion of three-dimensional form in this artwork?

 By working with only sticks of charcoal and paper, Georgia O'Keeffe got in touch with her innermost thoughts and feelings.

Georgia O'Keeffe. *Drawing XIII*, 1915. Charcoal on paper, 24 1/2 by 19 inches. The Metropolitan Museum of Art.

What thoughts and feelings do you think Diego Rivera was suggesting?

Diego Rivera. *Study of a Sleeping Woman,* 1921. Black crayon on off-white laid paper, 24½ by 18⅓ inches. Courtesy of the Fogg Art Museum, Harvard University.

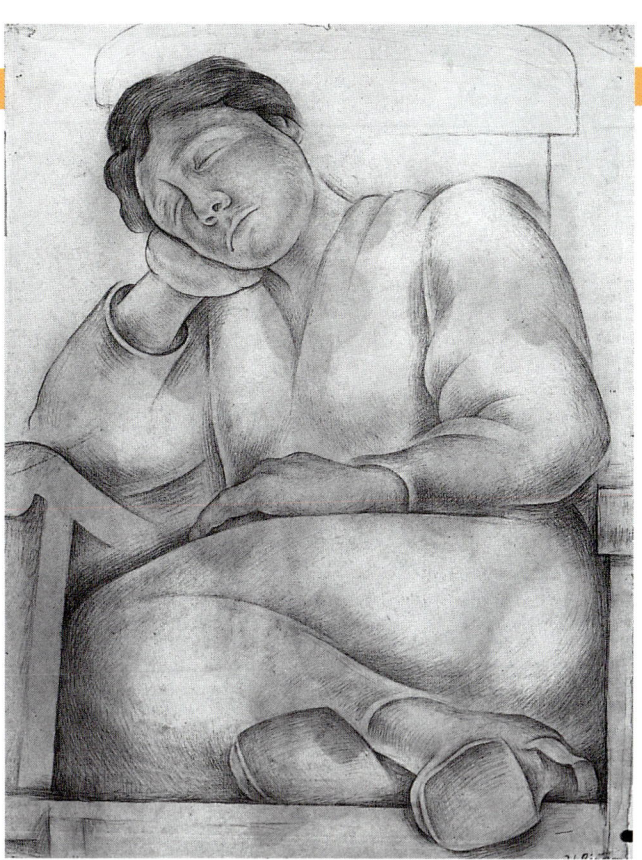

Value and Mood

Notice the importance of value in lines, shapes, and spaces in establishing the *mood,* or feeling, of **B**. Light values sometimes suggest a calm, gentle mood, while dark ones can seem angry, nervous, and forceful. What mood might the artist of **B** have intended? Why do you think so?

The Value Scale

Try matching the different values in **A** and **B** with the values in **C**. Where did each artist show dark values? light values? medium values?

Like Georgia O'Keeffe and Diego Rivera, you too will return to color and learn about how its values can affect your compositions. For now, allow yourself to explore the values of black, white, and gray. Think about how your explorations will help you grow as an artist.

Creating a Value Scale and a Drawing

On white paper, draw two 1" x 4" rectangles, and divide each into eight equal spaces. Create a Value Scale on this Technique Sheet that shows gradual shading. Leave the first space white and then show a gradual increase in shading. The last space will be black. Then create a drawing in which you show every example of shading from your Value Scale.

Sketchbook/Journal

Practice making sketches of values of the same object outside at different times of day. Record notes about how bright sunlight, shadows, clouds, and other effects change the way you see the object. Does a specific technique of showing value especially appeal to you? Explain why or why not.

Value Scale

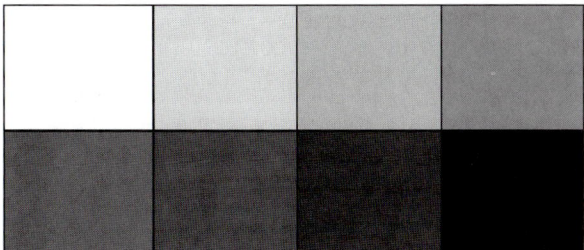

Artists use all eight values shown on this scale.

Lesson 9

Color

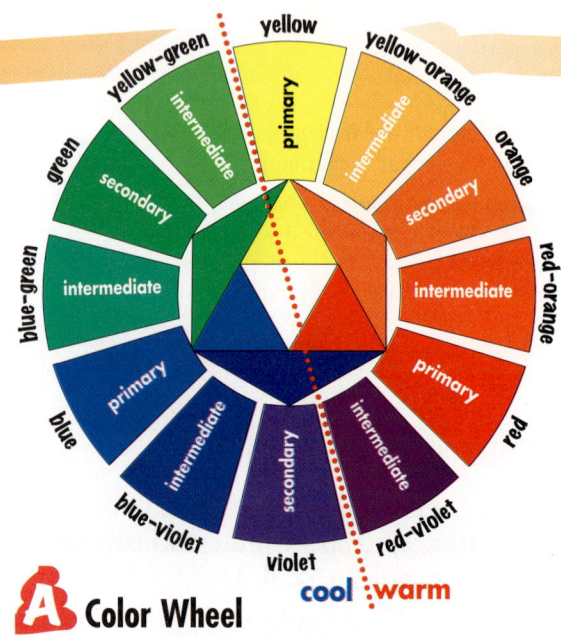

A Color Wheel

What Is Color?

In 1704, scientist Sir Isaac Newton published the results of his experiments in color and light under the title *Opticks*. By passing a beam of sunlight through an opening in a darkened room and into a prism, a clear wedge-shaped form, Newton showed that white light is a combination of the seven colors of the rainbow. The *color wheel* in **A** shows the same color spectrum arranged in a circle.

Newton's discovery helped artists better understand **color** as being the visual quality of objects caused by the amount of light reflected or absorbed by them. Until then, artists had understood color, an element of art, almost solely through its beauty. In this lesson and the next, you will learn more about the language of color and creative ways to use color in your compositions.

Kinds of Colors

Primary colors in pigments are yellow, red, and blue. Just as *primary* means "basic or first," these *hues* cannot be mixed from other colors. Primary colors, along with black and white, are the only ones needed to mix any color you might imagine. **Secondary colors** are orange, violet, and green. They are made by mixing two primary colors. Study the color wheel in **A**

Warm colors might remind you of a flickering fire and the summer sun. What mood do they convey?

Janet Fish. *Yellow Pad*, 1997. Oil on canvas, 36 by 50 inches. The Columbus Museum, Columbus, GA.
© Janet Fish/Licensed by VAGA, New York, NY.

24   Lesson 9

C

Cool colors might remind you of icy scenes, a rainy day, and a deep forest. How does the mood they convey differ from that of warm colors?

Sandy Skoglund. *The Green House,* 1990. Photo cibachrome, 52 1/4 by 64 inches.

to see how primary colors can be mixed to make secondary colors. **Intermediate colors** are mixed from a primary and a secondary color next to each other on the color wheel. Find examples of each of these key colors on the color wheel.

Colors and Feelings

The artist of **B**, Janet Fish, says, "To alter the color is to change the feeling." Artists know that colors can change the way a viewer feels. Some artists use **warm colors**—red, yellow, orange—to create a sunny mood. Others use **cool colors**—green, blue, violet—to remind the viewer of fear or loneliness. Discuss the mood in **C**, which artist Sandy Skoglund suggests by using the colors she applies to her **palette**, a flat board on which a painter holds and mixes colors.

Learning to mix colors effectively is a science that takes a lot of practice and patience. Artists typically begin by experimenting with primary colors. They often add a touch of black or a larger amount of white to a *hue*. As you explore color mixing, think about the colors you would like to use to suggest different moods in your compositions.

Creating Your Own Color Wheel

Use a sheet of white paper and tempera or acrylic paints to create a color wheel. Show primary colors; then mix paints to create secondary and intermediate colors. You may wish to use a small amount of white paint to create violet. Complete the background using warm and cool colors.

Sketchbook/Journal

As you mix new colors, write the approximate amounts of colors of paint you use to make them. Brush a dab of each color you made near your notes. Next time you paint, use your notes to remind you of how much paint to use.

Color

Lesson 10: Color and Colorists

This painting shows the artist's lifelong love of color.
Paul Klee. *Color Shapes,* 1914. Watercolor, 4 by 5 1/2 inches. Barnes Foundation.

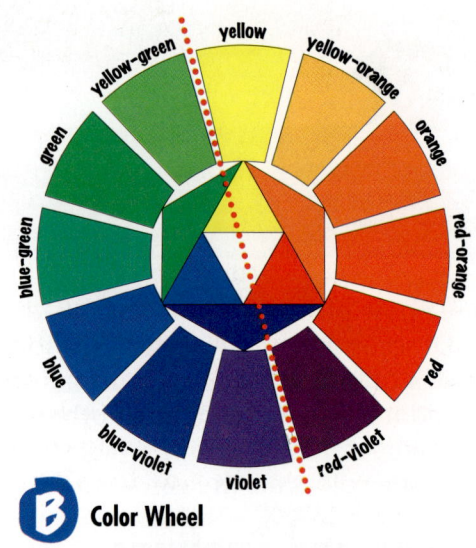

B Color Wheel

What Is a Colorist?

"Color possesses me. I don't have to pursue it. It will possess me always, I know it. That is the meaning of this happy hour: Color and I are one. I am a painter."

—from Paul Klee's diary, April 16, 1914

Paul Klee, who painted **A**, was a **colorist,** an artist who uses color with great skill. A colorist creates shape and form more by the positioning of colors than by the use of line.

Properties of Color

Just as you have certain attributes, such as the texture of your hair or the shape of your eyes, so also do colors have attributes, or **properties. Hue,** another word for color, is one of those properties. It is the visual quality of objects caused by the amount of light reflected by them. Hues are usually referred to by their common names, such as red, orange, yellow, green, blue, and violet.

During your exploration of **value** in black-and-white sketches, you were introduced to a second property of color. The value of a color is the lightness or darkness of it. Artists may mix a hue with white to create a **tint,** a lighter color value. Or they may mix a hue with black to create a **shade,** a darker color value.

Intensity, the third property of color, is the brightness or dullness of a hue. The color wheel in **B** shows bright, strong hues of high intensity. They are sometimes referred to as "pure" color. You can make a low-intensity hue by mixing colors directly across the color wheel. Artists adjust the intensity of their colors for purposes such as changing the mood of a composition, creating the hues of a specific season, or providing contrast between bright and dull objects.

Intensity Scale

Color Schemes

Do you ever struggle with decisions about which colors of clothing to wear together? How do you decide? Artists plan ways to combine colors to achieve special effects in their compositions. **Color schemes,** plans for combining colors in a work of art, affect the way the viewer feels about an artwork.

Monochromatic

Monochromatic derives its name from the prefix *mono,* which means "one," and the base word *chrome,* which means "color." A **monochromatic** color scheme uses different values of a single hue by showing tints and shades of the same hue. Such a plan can help unify an artwork, but be careful! This color scheme sometimes appears dull and uninteresting.

Analogous

The hues in an **analogous** color scheme are side by side on the color wheel, and they share a hue. What hue is common to blue, blue-green, and blue-violet? Notice on the color wheel that warm and cool color schemes can be analogous.

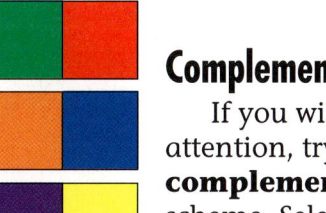

Complementary

If you wish to attract attention, try wearing a **complementary** color scheme. Select an outfit that features two colors directly across the color wheel. Artists often use complementary color schemes for a bold and jarring effect in their compositions.

Neutral

A **neutral** color scheme is made of black, white, and various tints and shades of gray. Many artists include brown, too. Neutral color schemes often reflect a calm, quiet mood.

As you practice mixing colors, think about how they relate to other colors in your compositions. Consider how you can change the look and feel of a color by altering its value and intensity. Then think about the effect such a change has on the mood of your artwork.

Experimenting with Many Colors

Create three **Color Mixing Sheets** by mixing colors of tempera or acrylic paint in small dots. Include examples of (1) tints and shades, (2) high and low intensity, and (3) a variety of color schemes. On another sheet of paper, make a contour drawing of an interesting object. Paint your drawing by repeating your favorite colors from your Color Mixing Sheets.

Sketchbook/Journal

Use colored pencils to show light and dark values by shading a contour drawing in your sketchbook.

Lesson 11

Texture

What Is Texture?

The horse's coat is as shiny as gold.

His hands are sandpaper.

Writers may use similes and metaphors like those above to describe **texture,** the way something feels to the touch or how it may look. Words like *rough, silky, shiny,* and *dull* help them describe the texture of an object. Visual artists *show* texture, an element of art, to accomplish the same goal.

Types of Texture

Artists know that texture may be sensed by touch and sight. They work one or both types of texture into their compositions to help viewers understand surfaces.

Tactile Texture

In the language of art, **tactile texture,** often called *actual texture,* is the way a surface would feel if you *could* touch it. The image in **A** shows many kinds of tactile texture. This buffalo is constructed of photographic film, videotape, metal shavings, nails, paintbrushes, and other recycled materials that lend a sense of

A Describe the tactile texture in this artwork.

Holly Hughes. *Buffalo,* 1992. Found object mixed media, 78 by 54 inches. Capitol Building, New Mexico.

tactile texture. Point out rough, smooth, bumpy, hard, and soft textures you might feel if you could touch the artwork.

Visual Texture

Visual texture, sometimes called *simulated texture,* is the way a surface appears through the sense of vision. The paint on a new car appears shiny, while the rubber on its tires appears dull. Point out the visual texture of **B**. What object did artist Holly Hughes place in the buffalo's

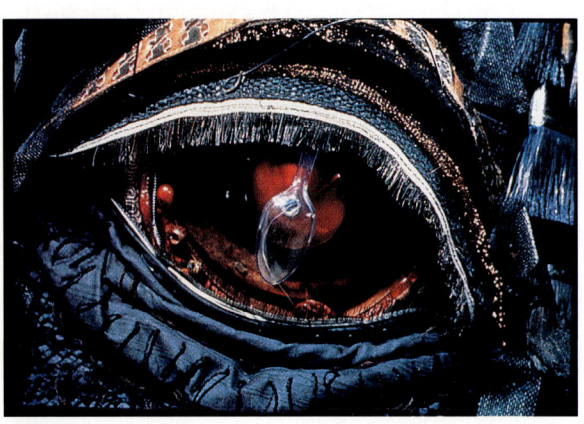

B Notice the visual texture in this detail of **A**.

Holly Hughes. (Eye Detail) *Buffalo,* 1992.

C

How would you describe the tactile and visual texture in this artwork?

Audrey Flack. *Energy Apples,* 1980. Oil over acrylic on canvas, 47 3/4 by 48 1/4 inches. Courtesy Louis K. Meisel Gallery, New York.

eye to capture the illusion of visual texture? Why do you think she felt the center of the eye should appear shiny? Now observe the visual texture in **C**. Point out areas where drops of water and the fruit juice appear shiny. Notice the contrast created by artist Audrey Flack's use of both shiny and dull textures on the paint tray.

The title of **C**, *Energy Apples,* supported by a shiny visual texture, suggests apples and other fruits are fresh and vibrant. "Some titles just appear; they seem to be woven into the structure of the composition," commented Flack. "Others are elusive and only emerge through struggle, battle, or debate. Some works never get a name; others get two."

Look around you to discover shiny, dull, rough, and smooth textures. What other textures can you find? How might you show these textures on paper?

Rubbing and Drawing to Show Tactile Texture

Make rubbings of a variety of tactile textures by placing paper over "raised" surfaces, such as the bottom of a tennis shoe or the veins of a leaf, and then rubbing the paper with the sides of oil pastels or crayons. On another sheet of paper, explore ways to show tactile texture with your pencil by drawing shapes that resemble those you rubbed and by varying the amount of pressure you apply to the lines. Then cut shapes from your texture rubbings, arrange them on your drawing, and glue them into a pleasing composition.

Sketchbook/Journal

Look again at the textures you rubbed. Describe some of them with similes and metaphors.

Texture

Lesson 12: Balance

"I like to work from things that I see—whether they're [hu]manmade or natural or a combination of the two," commented artist Ellsworth Kelly in 1963. Like many other artists, Kelly preferred *observation* as a source of inspiration to help him plan designs. Other sources of inspiration for artists come from *memory* and *imagination.*

Along with having an inspiration for a plan, artists follow basic guidelines in planning their designs. In the language of art, guidelines for planning are called *principles of design.* In all, seven principles guide artists to plan their designs. They are balance, emphasis, proportion, pattern, rhythm, unity, and variety. In this lesson, you will learn about one of these principles: balance.

What Is Balance?

A toddler learning to walk, a pendulum swinging back and forth, the sun setting as the moon rises: each of these images speaks of **balance.** To an artist, balance is about arranging elements of art according to their "visual weight"; that is, no one part of the work overpowers any other part. Artists arrange elements in three kinds of balance: symmetrical, radial, and asymmetrical.

Symmetrical Balance

In **symmetrical balance,** also known as *formal balance,* both sides of the artwork are arranged about the same. Sometimes they are a mirror image. The arrangement in **A** shows symmetrical balance. It is a symbol of strength and dignity.

A Why is this gold sculpture an example of symmetrical balance?

Artist unknown, Tolima culture. *Pectoral,* ca. A.D. 600–800. Gold, height 9 inches.

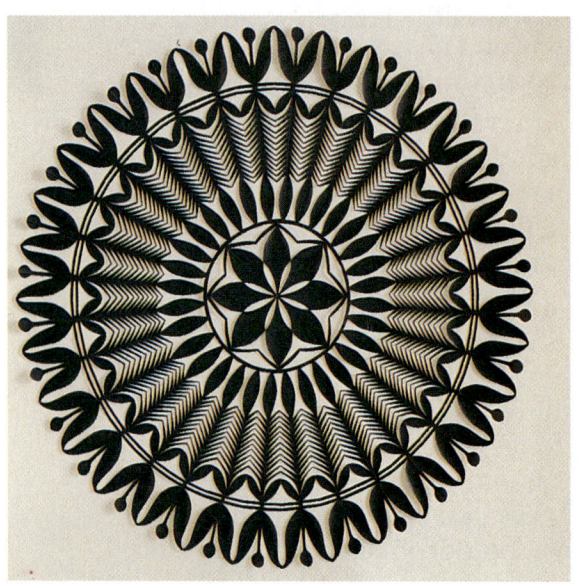

B How are symmetrical balance and radial balance, as shown in this paper-cut, similar?

Stanislawa Dawid. *Big Star,* ca. 1962. Cut paper, diameter 11 3/4 inches. The Museum of International Folk Art, Santa Fe, NM.

C

How might YOU feel riding in this boat? Winslow Homer. *Breezing Up,* 1873–1876. Oil on canvas, 24 1/8 by 38 1/8 inches. National Gallery of Art, Washington, D.C.

Radial Balance

Another type of balance, in which lines or shapes spread out from a center point, is called **radial balance.** A bicycle wheel is an example of radial balance. Some church windows, fireworks, and targets also show radial balance. Notice the way in which lines and shapes change together as they radiate from the center in **B**.

Asymmetrical Balance

Asymmetrical balance, also known as informal balance, is arranged like a seesaw that is set for a heavy player on one end and a light one on the other. One side of the artwork is larger, while its visual weight is offset with a smaller, yet significant, object. For example, an image of a huge tree might appear on one side of a drawing with three bright red apples on the other. How might those apples lend visual weight to such an image? How does the boat in the foreground of **C** help create asymmetrical balance? Notice a smaller ship in the background. How does it help offset the boat's visual weight?

You will know that your composition is balanced when the visual weight feels and appears right. As you explore the different types of balance, consider how each of them might help you express your ideas and feelings.

D

Michelle, Corbett Junior High School. *Crayons.* Pencil, colored pencil, and colored marker on paper, 12 by 18 inches.

Creating Drawings Showing Balance

Fold a sheet of 12" x 18" drawing paper into three equal sections. In each section draw sketches of pencils or other objects to show symmetrical, radial, and asymmetrical balance. Label each section accordingly and add color with your favorite medium.

Sketchbook/Journal

Draw several thumbnail sketches of objects you notice on your way to school that represent balance. Describe the way the elements are arranged according to their visual weight.

Balance 31

Lesson 13

Emphasis

A How do color and size help guide your eye to the focal point of this painting?
Leonora Carrington. *Red Cow*, 1989. Oil on canvas, 24 by 36 inches. Private collection.

What Is Emphasis?

Attorneys in a court of law often emphasize an important point by repeating it, raising their voices, or calling attention to it with hand gestures. Similarly, artists control what elements and objects they want to stand out in their artworks by using **emphasis,** a principle of design.

Ways to Show Emphasis

Just as an attorney calls attention to a point in more than one way, so too do artists have techniques for showing emphasis. They may use line, shape, color, texture, space, and size to help them show dominance, a focal point, or contrast.

Dominance

One way to show emphasis is through **dominance,** in which one element or object in the composition is the strongest or most important part of the work. The dominant element might be a special shape, a bright color, or an unusual brushstroke. What elements and object did the artist of **A** use to show dominance?

Focal Point

Another way to show emphasis is to plan a **focal point,** or center of interest. Artists often set apart one element from the others to set up a center of interest. They may manipulate size, as in showing one object to be larger. Or they may use space to create a focal point, for example, by

Lesson 13

B How does color guide your eye to the focal point?
Gabriele Münter. *Girl with Doll*, 1908–1909. Oil on cardboard, 27 1/2 by 19 inches. Milwaukee Art Museum, gift of Mrs. Harry Lynde Bradley.

C Maria, Wood Middle School. *3 in a Row*. Tempera and marker on paper, 12 by 18 inches.

placing the object in the center of the work. You can establish a focal point with lines pointing toward an object or with bright-colored shapes. How did the artists create focal points in **A** and **B**?

Contrast

A third technique for creating emphasis is through **contrast.** You have learned that light tints placed against dark shades produce contrast in value. Likewise, contrast can be achieved by using **intensity,** the brightness or dullness of a hue. Notice how the cow in **A** seems to stand out from the background. The artist placed light hues against dark ones. She also used a high-intensity red to contrast with the low-intensity hues.

As you experiment with emphasis, keep in mind its purpose—to call attention to an important part of the composition. Think about the message you are trying to convey as you plan for emphasis.

Creating a Drawing with Emphasis

Select an interesting drawing from your sketchbook or create a new design. Your drawing might show an animal or a person, as in **A** or **B**. Select an area for emphasis, and draw a circle around it. On another sheet of paper, draw the design showing dominance, by magnifying and adding detail to the encircled area. Using colored pencils or paint, show contrast by adding color and value to the emphasized area.

Sketchbook/Journal

Draw several thumbnail sketches of plants, and select parts of the plant, such as flowers, to enlarge and show emphasis. Record notes about emphasis as you draw. Use your notes to describe how you made the plant parts you selected stand out.

Emphasis 33

Lesson 14

Principles of Design

Proportion

The circumference of this monumental sculpture is more than 19 feet!

Artist unknown. *Olmec Head*, 1200–900 B.C. Volcanic stone, approximately 9 by 7 by 6 feet. Museum of Anthropology of Xalapa, Veracruz, Mexico.

What Is Proportion?

When you mix dough for a batch of cookies, you pay attention to the proportions of the ingredients. Too much flour makes the cookies hard and dry, whereas too much liquid causes them to be thin and runny. Similarly, artists know that **proportion** refers to how parts of an artwork relate to each other and to the whole. They often show proportion through the size or placement of something in the composition. This principle of design can lend interest to an otherwise ordinary composition.

Size Relationships and Proportion

Consider this: artists think of the human body as being of **normal proportion.** In comparison to, say, a mountain or an ant, a person's height, width, and depth appear normal in size. Therefore, you might say that everything else on Planet Earth relates in size and proportion to your own body! You will learn about how the parts of the human body relate to each other and the whole in Unit 4.

Artists sometimes manipulate **size relationships** to alter the proportions of their compositions to add interest. Look at the artworks **A** and **B** to find examples of unusual size relationships. Artists think of unusual size relationships in three categories: monumental, miniature, and exaggerated.

Monumental artworks are of larger-than-life proportions. They are big, bigger, biggest! Their size is enormous in comparison to what is normally expected, and they create a sense of awe in the viewer. Why do you suppose artists would create huge artworks? How does the size of this sculpture compare with the size of your own head? Now look at the mural in **B**, which fills a large part of an entire wall. It, too, is of monumental size.

Miniature artworks are of smaller-than-normal–size proportions. They often create a feeling of protectiveness in the viewer. Artists often make models of miniature proportions, many of which sit on tabletops. These small-scale models include buildings the size of toy blocks to represent a community, furnished dollhouses, and vintage ships. Why would an artist create a miniature artwork?

Notice the exaggerated size of the woman's head, shoulders, and hand.

B

Diego Rivera. *The Riches of California,* 1931. Fresco, approximately 22 by 13 feet. The City Club of San Francisco.

 James, Oak Crest Middle School. *Leopard Feathers.* Colored markers on paper, 9 by 12 inches.

Some artworks include **exaggerated**, or distorted, proportions of an object to show emphasis. In **B**, several parts of the mural are exaggerated in size. These parts do not relate to each other in normally expected proportions. Why might Rivera have exaggerated the size of the woman in this monumental painting? How is the title of the artwork a clue?

Placement of Objects and Proportion

You have learned about techniques artists use to show space in compositions. These include placing objects in the foreground, middle ground, or background, as well as overlapping objects to show depth and space. The placement of objects helps artists show proportion.

As you work with proportion in your compositions, keep in mind the size and placement of objects. Look again at **A** and **B** to review some techniques that can help you.

Drawing Proportion

Arrange at least three different objects or forms close to one another. On a sheet of paper, draw each object in the foreground once. Draw each object again in the middle ground and in the background. Use colored pencils, crayons, markers, or pastels to add color to your objects. Remember to overlap objects to show depth. For special effects, try showing some miniature and some monumental size relationships.

Sketchbook/Journal

Find several small magazine pictures of animals to glue into your Sketchbook/Journal. Showing proportion, draw some thumbnail sketches of them.

Proportion 35

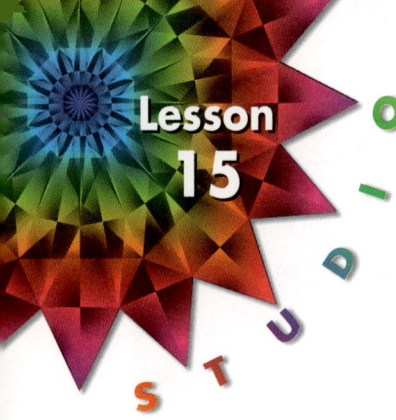

Lesson 15

Drawing Altered Proportions

What do you notice about the proportions of these figures?

Fernando Botero. *Dancing in Colombia*, 1980. Oil on canvas, 74 by 91 inches. The Metropolitan Museum of Art.

Get the Picture

Colombian artist Fernando Botero is known for creating altered proportions in his artworks. Once you have seen a Botero painting or sculpture, you will always recognize his **style,** or personal way of expressing his ideas. He gives everything in his artworks a serious roundness, which he calls *plasticity.* His figures of people appear round and full, creating a stylized—almost toylike— appearance for people of all walks of life. Notice, for example, the body and facial forms of each person in **A**. Can you tell who might be wealthier? older? a better musician or dancer? Why might Botero have wanted the figures to look similar in character?

Study the way Botero manipulated proportion in **A**. Even though the dancers appear miniature, and the musicians appear monumental, the viewer's eye is drawn to the rhythm of the dancers in the center. Why might the artist have wanted the dancers to be the focal point? Notice the musical instruments. Where are the strings? Why would the artist omit such details on stringed instruments?

Get Set

 **Materials you will need:**

- pencil
- 12" x 18" white drawing paper
- round, shiny, reflective ball
- felt-tip pen
- crayons or oil pastels

36 *Lesson 15*

How to Draw Altered Facial Proportions

1. Draw a large circle in the center of your paper. Draw around a cylinder or the base of a can to help you.

2. Look at your reflection in a shiny, reflective ball. In the circle on your paper, draw what you see with a felt-tip pen.

3. With crayons or oil pastels, fill the background with what you see around your reflection.

B

Nicholas, Applied Learning Academy. *Untitled*. Felt-tip pen and crayon on paper, 9 by 12 inches.

Making a Funny Collage of Body Proportions

Find photos of parts of the human body in magazines. Include a variety of sizes. Create a collage by assembling them in ways that show altered proportions. For example, one figure could have very long arms, tiny legs, and a large nose. Write a funny title for your collage.

Sketchbook/Journal

Write about how your drawing makes you feel about yourself. Draw some thumbnail sketches of your hand's reflection in the shiny ball.

Be an Art Critic!

1. **Describe** Point out exaggerated proportions in your drawing.
2. **Analyze** How did you arrange the lines and shapes in your composition to show altered proportions?
3. **Interpret** How does the relationship among sizes of shapes in your drawing affect its meaning?
4. **Judge** Do you like the results of altered proportions within your composition? Tell why or why not.

Drawing Altered Proportions 37

Lesson 16

Rhythm and Pattern

A How do lines and shapes in this artwork form pattern? rhythm?
M.C. Escher. *System Drawing E66*, 1945. Ink and watercolor. Private collection.

What Is Rhythm?

Rhythm, a sense of visual or actual motion in an artwork, is created by repeating visual elements. Just as rhythm in your favorite dance step creates movement, rhythm in an artwork causes your eye to move around the composition. Artists create several types of rhythm to make their works seem active.

Regular Rhythm

A **regular rhythm** has one beat and is made by repeating the *same* element, such as a shape, without variation. For example, if you draw a series of small triangles spaced evenly across your paper, you will create regular rhythm. ▲▲▲▲▲

Alternating Rhythm

An **alternating rhythm** is made by repeating two or more elements on a regular, *alternating* basis, such as a triangle-circle, triangle-circle, triangle-circle. ▲●▲●▲● Look at the alternating rhythm of the positive and negative spaces in **A**.

Progressive Rhythm

A third type of rhythm, **progressive rhythm,** is built on regular changes in a *repeated* element. These changes may progress from small to large, as in a series of circles that progressively increase in size. The changes may also progress from light to dark, or bottom to top. Study the lines of the dancer's skirt in **B**. Notice how they progress from bottom to top in a regular, yet somewhat jazzy and flowing, rhythm. ●●●●●

 Lesson 16

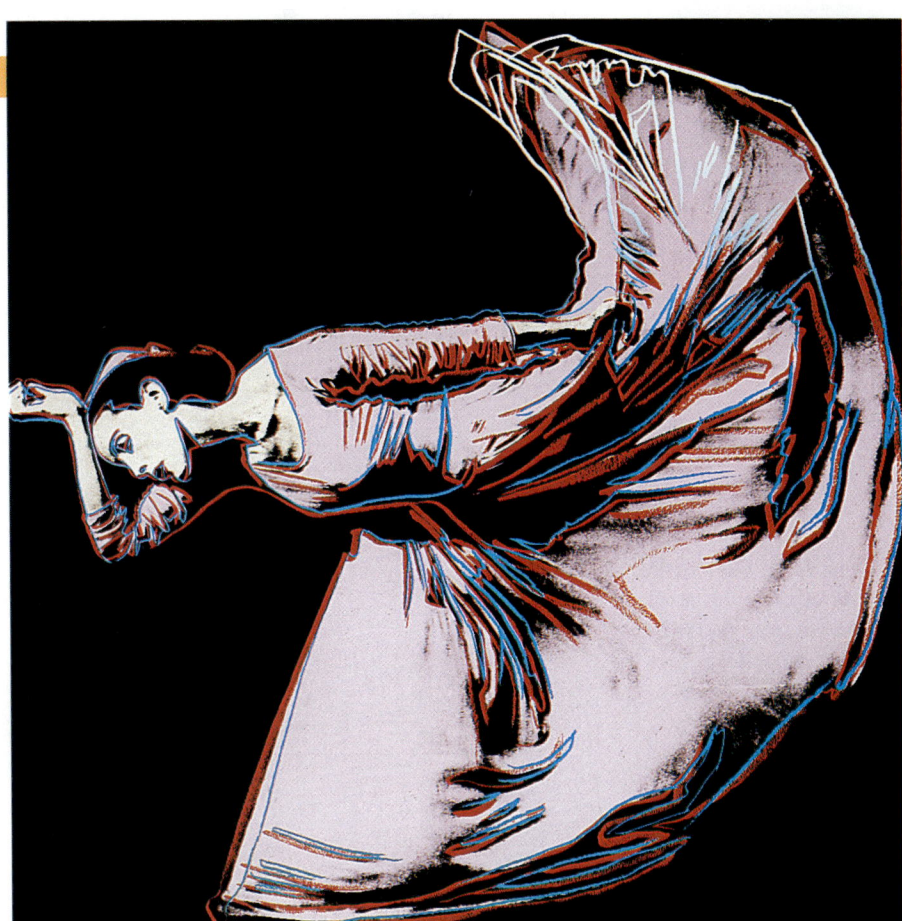

B The artist of this composition shows progressive rhythm.

Andy Warhol. *Letter to the World—The Kick,* 1986. Serigraph, 35 1/2 by 35 5/8 inches. Courtesy of SBC Communications Inc.

What Is Pattern?

Sometimes artists repeat not just elements, such as the lines in **B**, but the same exact objects again and again. In this way, a pattern is formed. **Pattern** is a repeated use of an element in a regular way. A rug, wallpaper, and the clothing you wear often show pattern. Even books on a shelf may form a pattern. Identify some lines, shapes, or colors around you that make patterns. Which artwork on these pages shows a pattern?

Rhythm and pattern are two principles of design that sometimes go hand-in-hand. As you observe your surroundings—a flower garden, waves on the water, friends moving to and from classes—you may notice that many patterns also show rhythm. Together or alone, pattern and rhythm work to help create interest in compositions. Think about how you might work pattern and rhythm into your own compositions.

Drawing Patterns

Begin a pattern Technique Sheet by drawing nine blank boxes to fill a paper. In each box, using pencil and a black marker, draw a pattern you have observed in your school or home environment or a pattern from your imagination. Include patterns with lines, geometric shapes, organic shapes, positive and negative space, texture, symmetrical balance, asymmetrical balance, and radial balance.

Sketchbook/Journal

Draw some thumbnail sketches of patterns you find during a 30-minute search outside. Label patterns according to those you observe in nature and in human-made objects.

Rhythm and Pattern   39

Lesson 17 STUDIO

Showing Emotions with Pattern and Rhythm

 How would you describe the technique this artist used to show rhythm? Point out patterns.

Bridget Riley. *Cataract III*, 1967. Emulsion PVA on linen, 86 1/2 by 86 15/16 inches. British Council Collection, London.

Get the Picture

Stare at **A** for about 15 seconds. Did you get dizzy? become uncomfortable? become uptight? Artist Bridget Riley intends for all of these sensations to happen to the viewer of her *Op Art* paintings, a term that originated during the 1960s to describe artworks that create optical illusions.

The stimulus for Riley's compositions comes from the world of nature and from feelings. Through her art, she conveys sensations, such as the movement or stillness of a summer day, forces and progressions of birds in flight, and breathing or touching.

In Riley's *Cataract III* in **A**, optical illusion is carried to a point where the two-dimensional plane seems to be warped. Using a bit of color, the artist achieves a pulsating "current" effect. When you look at it, you experience an immediate and intense optical response to her carefully planned rhythmic design.

Get Set

 **Materials you will need:**

- hand mirror
- Pattern Technique Sheet from Lesson 16
- fine-tip markers of warm and cool colors
- fine-tip black marker
- sheet of white drawing paper

How to Show Emotions with Pattern and Rhythm

1. Use a mirror to draw your facial features showing an emotion, such as happiness, sadness, anger, surprise, or fright.

2. Draw a variety of organic shapes onto the face to enhance each feature. Fill in the background with a cool color, showing one of the patterns from your Pattern Technique Sheet.

3. Select patterns from your Pattern Technique Sheet that convey movement. Fill in the organic face shapes with several of those patterns in warm colors.

B

Michelle, Lowell Middle School. *Untitled.* Tempera on paper, 12 by 18 inches.

Drawing Pattern and Rhythm with Computer Tools

Using a computer drawing program such as Super Paint, Pagemaker, or ClarisWorks, create a variety of sizes, types, and colors of shapes. Experiment with computer-generated fill patterns and textures in each shape.

Sketchbook/Journal

Look again at the patterns you created for your Pattern Technique Sheet. Write about the emotions they convey.

Be an Art Critic!

1. **Describe** Name the types of patterns you used on your face drawing. Identify warm and cool colors in your composition.

2. **Analyze** How would you describe the various rhythms shown in each organic shape? Tell how the rhythmic shapes, as seen together, create a larger rhythm for the whole face.

3. **Interpret** How does your drawing make you feel? What mood does it convey?

4. **Judge** Do you feel a sense of rhythm in your completed composition? How do you think your drawing will affect other viewers?

Showing Emotions with Pattern and Rhythm

Lesson 18

Unity and Variety

A How did this artist show both unity and variety?

Henri Matisse. *Pianist and Checker Players*, 1924. Oil on canvas, 29 by 36 3/8 inches. National Gallery of Art, Washington, D.C.

Most people like to be with others, and they like to be alone. They enjoy being a part of a group, but they enjoy standing out as individuals. Artists feel the same tension about the way they arrange the elements of art. They plan for all the parts to look as if they belong together. At the same time, they may use varied elements to add interest to their composition.

What Is Unity?

In the language of art, **unity** is a principle of design that occurs when the elements of art and principles of design in the composition belong together. Almost all artists strive for unity in their compositions.

As an artist, you can achieve unity through more than one technique. As a painter, for example, you might:

- Repeat a color, a shape, or another element.
- Use one major color or shape.
- Combine related colors, such as in an analogous color scheme.
- Arrange one shape, such as a triangle, with parts of that shape.

Notice how artist Henri Matisse arranged color to show unity in **A**. Which color unifies spaces in the artwork to create a pleasing composition? Now study how the photographer of **B** unified this composition. Tell why the objects appear unified.

 Lesson 18

 Each fork has a different design, yet they are unified. How are they harmonious?

Composition Checklist

PRINCIPLES OF DESIGN

ELEMENTS OF ART	Balance	Emphasis	Proportion	Pattern	Rhythm	Unity	Variety
Line							
Shape							
Form							
Space							
Value							
Color							
Texture							

 A checklist like the one above can help you measure your progress as you create compositions for your Portfolio.

What Is Variety?

Variety, another principle of design, involves combining one or more elements of art to provide interest. Variety can be the ingredient you need to make your artwork pop! It often goes hand-in-hand with harmony, combining the elements of art to accent their similarities. If your composition seems to have too many red lines and shapes, for example, you may need to add some splashes of blue and orange for variety. Notice how Matisse created interest through variety among patterns, shapes, and colors in **A**. How does each fork in **B** differ from the other? Explain how both unity and variety work together in **A** and **B**.

As you progress through your studio projects, you will find that unity and variety occur almost effortlessly. You might wish to make a checklist like the one in **C** to keep track of all the elements and principles you use in compositions from studios in this book. For each element used, make a check mark in the box under the principle or principles you have used to arrange the element.

Creating a Design with Unity and Variety

Use oil pastels or crayons to create a drawing of you and your family involved in a favorite activity at home. Show how color and shape can work together to make interesting patterns. Focus especially on unity and variety in your composition.

Sketchbook/Journal

Draw several thumbnail sketches of examples of variety and unity you find in objects at home or in photographs. Make notes describing the variety and unity you find in them. Include in your notes the different ways that variety and unity contribute to a pleasing, yet interesting, composition.

Unity and Variety

Talk About Art

> "... There are certain pictures I have painted that will be liked one day."
> —Vincent van Gogh
> 1853–1890

Vincent van Gogh hoped to be a famous artist during his lifetime. Sadly, he died a poor man and a not so well-known artist. One of his friends, Dr. Gachet, commented, "He was an honest man and a great artist. . . . There were only two things for him: humanity and art. Art mattered more to him than anything else, and he will live on in it."

In 1990, Van Gogh's *Portrait of Dr. Gachet* sold for $82.5 million—setting a world record for an artwork! Today you can view his paintings in many major art museums across the globe. His images have been reproduced on T-shirts, bags, caps, scarves, and posters, and Van Gogh himself is the subject of a popular song entitled "Vincent."

Van Gogh painted many **self-portraits**, or images of himself, one of which is shown in **A**. In studying Van Gogh's paintings, you may be struck by his passion for line, color, space, and texture. You may marvel at his use of unity, variety, emphasis, pattern, and rhythm. Through his brushstrokes, this artist exhibited an appreciation and understanding of the elements of art and principles of design. As you explore Van Gogh's artworks, you may also discover a technique he especially liked to use. It is called **impasto**, meaning a thick textured layer of paint. Look for the strokes of his brush in **A**.

 How did the artist use line, color, shape, and rhythm to convey mood in this self-portrait?

Vincent van Gogh. *Self-Portrait with Straw Hat.* Paris. Summer 1887. Oil on canvas, 15 3/4 by 12 2/3 inches. F469, JH 1310. Amsterdam, Rijksmuseum Vincent van Gogh, Vincent van Gogh Foundation.

B
Vincent van Gogh. *Enclosed Field with Rising Sun,* 1889. Oil on canvas, 27 2/3 by 35 1/3 inches. Private collection.

Notice the same impasto technique Van Gogh used in **B**. This **landscape**, an artwork of mountains, trees, fields, and other natural scenery, conveys the artist's sense of emotions. What might he have been saying about the beginning of a new day?

As an art critic examining **B**, consider the skills you have learned about elements of art and principles of design. You may find that your understanding and appreciation of Van Gogh's landscape has grown since your "At a Glance" introduction at the beginning of this unit.

Experimenting with Impasto Brushstrokes

Select a contour drawing from your Sketchbook/Journal or create a new one. Add gel medium to acrylic paint as you mix the hues for your palette. With an impasto brushstroke, make your contour drawing come alive!

Be an Art Critic!

Look at B to answer these questions:

1. **Describe** Name the directions of the lines throughout the painting. Where do you see organic shapes? Find the horizon line and vanishing point.

2. **Analyze** How did Van Gogh use warm and cool colors? Where do you see rhythm? What shapes show movement?

3. **Interpret** How would you explain the mood of this painting? What might the artist have been saying about the weather? about his feelings?

4. **Judge** Do you think Van Gogh had a favorite element of art or principle of design? Explain. Would you expect this painting to command a high price? Tell why or why not. Do you think it should? Explain.

Portfolio Project

 **Materials you will need:**
- acrylic paint with gel medium
- 12" x 18" white paper
- crayons or markers
- pencil
- black marker

Painting an Impasto Landscape

Will you create a landscape from memory, observation, or imagination? How will you establish the mood of your landscape?

1. With a black marker, draw a 1-inch outline inside the edges of a 12" x 18" sheet of white drawing paper.

2. With crayons or markers, draw a texture or pattern inside the "frame."

3. Create a contour drawing of a landscape. Include animals or signs of weather to establish the mood of your landscape.

4. Paint your landscape with impasto brushstrokes.

Gallery

A Soraya, Dover Elementary School. *Setting Sun.* Colored markers, tempera, and acrylic on paper, 12 by 18 inches.

B Laurie, Spring Branch Middle School. *African Horizon.* Colored markers, tempera, and acrylic on paper, 12 by 18 inches.

Art Links

MUSIC

Creating Melodies

Just as artists draw lines through physical space, musicians create "lines" of notes through musical space. The pattern of such a line is called **melody**. The pattern is made by varying two elements: **rhythm** and **pitch**. Try repeating these sets of "words" out loud, and you'll hear two different rhythms:

1. **pat pat pat pat**
2. **patta pat pat patta pat pat**

Now fill three glasses with different amounts of water. Thin glasses with stems are best. Tap each glass lightly with a metal spoon. You will hear different *notes*—a difference in *pitch*. Tap the glasses in any order, playing with rhythms, until you find a pleasing pattern. You have just created a *melody*.

Painters look for colors that go together: they call it harmony. However, that word actually comes from music: it refers to notes that go together. Tap your three glasses at the same time. Do they sound good together? Play with the water level until they do—that's harmony. Listen for both elements—harmony and melody—the next time you play a CD.

DANCE

Exploring Basic Elements of Dance

Have you ever watched people dancing? What makes one dancer look different from another? Both, after all, are **bodies** in **motion** to a **rhythm.** But look closer. Dancers make different **lines** with their bodies—for example, when they stretch or point. They make different **shapes.** They move at different **speeds** and **heights**—they bound, walk, crouch, even crawl. They express various **moods** by the way they move.

Explore the elements of dance by playing "freeze" with a group of friends. Let one person act as leader. He or she plays a tape of dance music. The rest of you move freely. Suddenly, the leader stops the tape and the dancers freeze. The leader comes to each one and says one of five words: *line, shape, speed, height,* or *mood.* Each dancer then starts moving as before, but changes the element—line, shape, speed, height, or mood—spoken to him or her by the leader. Watch yourselves on videotape later and try to guess what element each dancer was changing.

48 Unit 1

THEATRE

Comparing Elements of Drama in Movies and Plays

A movie is different from a book even if the two tell the same story: they are different art forms with different elements. However, a movie is also different from a play, even though it has many of the same elements—story, actors, sets, lights, and so on. Here's one difference. In a movie, you see what the movie camera points at—and the movie camera can point at anything and at any angle or distance. In live theatre, you have only the stage to look at, and you see it from only one angle and distance.

Explore this difference. Get together with some friends and watch any movie you want on video. Then discuss how to make a stage play from that movie. First chart how the play will have to be different. Next list the scenes you will have in your play. A scene is all the action that takes place in one episode. As soon as you say, "Meanwhile, somewhere else" or "Two hours later," you're into a new scene. Can you turn the movie into a play with no more than 20 scenes? How?

LITERATURE

Matching Literary Style to Texture

Many words used to describe texture in art are also used to describe style in writing. You may hear a writer's language described as smooth, harsh, slick, or gentle, for example. What texture do you feel in these words by Emily Dickinson and Richard Kennedy?

> There's a certain slant of light
> on winter afternoons
> that oppresses
>
> —Dickinson
>
> Now maybe it's sad and maybe it's spooky, but there was a man who lived just out of town on a scrubby farm and no one had seen his face for years.
>
> —Kennedy

Get together with a group of friends. Each of you bring a typical paragraph from one of your favorite stories or poems. Exchange these excerpts randomly. Read the writing that has come to you. Then create a picture or clip a photograph that reflects the texture of the language. As a group, post your artworks and photographs on a wall. See if you can match each artwork to the writing that inspired it.

ArtLinks

Unit 1

What Have You Learned?
Explore the Language of Art

Horace Pippin. *Domino Players*, 1943. Oil on composition board, 12 3/4 by 22 inches. © The Phillips Collection, Washington, D.C.

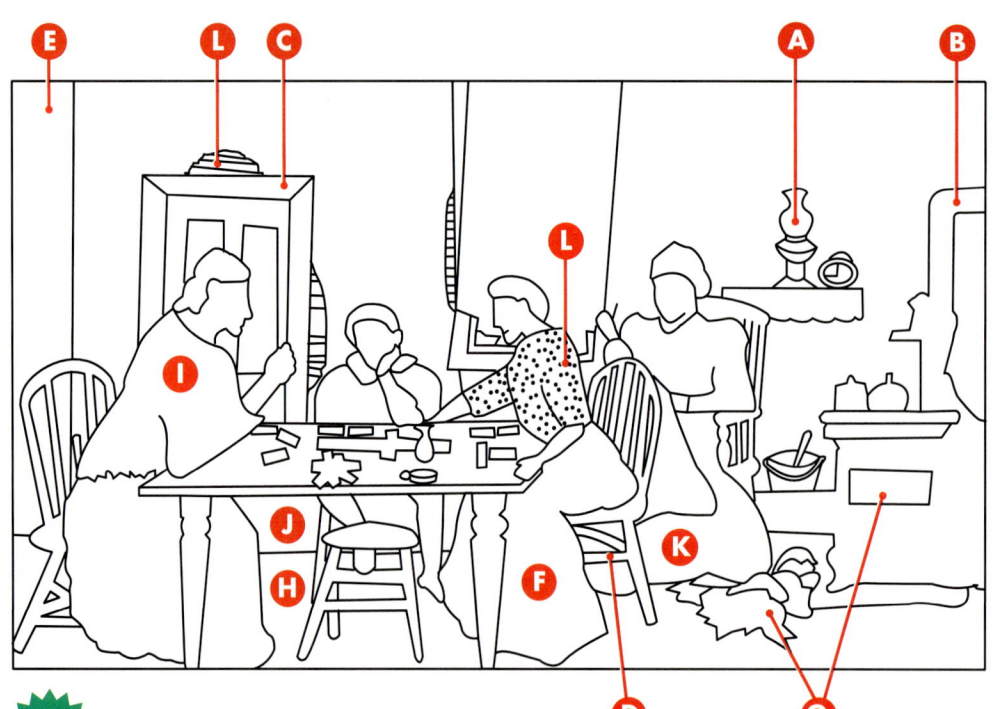

B Line drawing of Horace Pippin's *Domino Players*.

WRITE Can You Find . . . ?

Where Am I?

Match each art term at the right with the definition below and the letter in the illustration of Horace Pippin's painting on page 50.

I relate to an **element of art** that is:

A a two-dimensional area with height and width
B a path of movement
C a shape such as a circle, a triangle, and a square
D a slanted edge or line
E a line that runs up and down
F the lightness or darkness of a color
G the brightness or dullness of a hue
H a color scheme that uses different values of a single hue
I a shape often found in nature that is irregular and uneven
J the empty space around an object
K the space between the foreground and the background
L a reference to how things feel or appear

line
diagonal
vertical line
geometric shape
organic shape
shape
value
intensity
monochromatic
texture
negative space
middle ground

- *How do the elements of art relate to one another in the painting?*

Who Am I?

Match each art term at the right with the correct definition below.

I am a **principle of design** that:

1. repeatedly uses an art element in a regular way
2. describes the feeling that everything belongs together
3. shows what artists want to stand out in their artworks
4. repeats elements to create a sense of motion
5. is about arranging elements according to their visual "weight"
6. refers to the relationships of the parts to the whole
7. involves combining one or more elements of art to provide interest

rhythm
balance
unity
variety
proportion
pattern
emphasis

- *How do the principles of design contribute to the mood of the painting?*

What Have You Learned?

Write About Art

 Sofonisba Anguissola. *The Chess Game*, 1555. Oil on canvas, 28 3/4 by 38 3/4 inches. Museum Narodowe W. Poznaniu, Poznan, Poland.

 Henri Matisse. *Pianist and Checker Players*, 1924. Oil on canvas, 29 by 36 3/8 inches. National Gallery of Art, Washington, D.C.

TALK OR WRITE — In Your Own Words

Compare and contrast A and B.

1. What is similar?
2. What is different?
3. What is special about each painting?
4. Compare **A** and **B** to Horace Pippin's painting on page 50.

Re-View

WRITE — Do You Know the Artist?

Match the artwork and artist at the left with the theme and medium at the right.

1. Vincent van Gogh, *Self-Portrait with Straw Hat*	Fantasy interior/Photography
2. Holly Hughes, *Buffalo*	Animal sculpture/Mixed media
3. Leonora Carrington, *Red Cow*	Solitary figure/Painting
4. Sandy Skoglund, *The Green House*	Self-portrait/Painting
5. Janet Fish, *Yellow Pad*	Still-life/Watercolor painting
6. Winslow Homer, *Breezing Up*	Abstract composition
7. Gabriele Münter, *Girl with Doll*	Abstract sculpture/Alabaster
8. M.C. Escher, *System Drawing E66*	Animal/Painting
9. Barbara Hepworth, *Merryn*	Glass sculpture
10. Isabel De Obaldía, *Sebastian's Beast*	Seascape/Painting

 Unit 1

Put It All Together

"Art is a harmony parallel to nature."
—Paul Cézanne

TALK AND WRITE ## How Does a Work of Art Speak?

A Paul Cézanne. *The Artist's Father*, 1866. Oil on canvas, 78 1/8 by 47 inches. National Gallery of Art, Washington, D.C.

1. **Describe** What has the artist shown? Look carefully. Describe the subject or theme of this artwork. Identify as many objects and symbols as you can.

2. **Analyze** How is the theme reflected in the elements of art and principles of design? Analyze the visual qualities of the artwork by writing three or more words that describe each element or principle listed below.

> **Example:**
> line— *curved, horizontal, implied,* and so on

color   shape   texture   value
space   pattern   emphasis

Follow how your eye moves around the composition. How do the elements work together? How is variety achieved? What provides unity?

3. **Interpret** What is the meaning of this artwork? Describe the mood. How does the work show Cézanne's feelings about his father? Explain. What does this painting remind you of? How does it make you feel?

4. **Judge** French artist Paul Cézanne (1839–1906) painted several oil portraits of his father between 1865–1871. This portrait, *The Artist's Father*, was painted in 1866, early in Cézanne's career as an artist. What else would you like to know about this artwork? Why? What makes this painting special? Explain.

 In Your Journal

Reflect on your art-making process.

- What skills did you learn and use? Explain.
- What elements and principles did you enjoy using? Why?
- How did you put your ideas into your final artwork?
- What new ideas do you have for making art?

What Have You Learned?

Unit 2

M.C. Escher. *Triangle System I A3 Type I,* 1938. Pencil, ink, and watercolor, 13 by 9 1/2 inches. Private collection.

The Creative Art Process

A central goal of most artists is to have others appreciate their artworks. However, artists often gain even more satisfaction from the **creative process** they experience while making their artworks. After all, what painter, sculptor, or weaver has not become deeply engaged with the **art media** they use to create their artworks? Can you imagine how carefully artist M.C. Escher worked to achieve the design on the preceding page? He was driven by the creative process.

Just how does creativity come about? No one can be certain. However, scholars have many theories about this wondrous aspect of human nature. Many scholars describe the creative art process as having four stages:

- *Saturation* is the stage in which an individual is caught up with an idea or a problem.
- *Incubation* is the stage in which a person allows an idea to develop.
- *Illumination* is the stage at which the idea "gels."
- *Verification* is the stage in which the individual puts the idea into concrete form while checking and modifying it for its usefulness or purpose.

Current research tells us that the stages of the creative process are recursive and fluid rather than sequential. That is, they are interwoven, repeated, and altered in progress. Some scholars go so far as to say the creative process is unique to each person. Yet many educators agree that the creative art process involves the following general experiences:

- *Getting your idea.* Find insights for your artworks as you review your Sketchbook/Journal, work on another project, use your imagination, make observations in your environment, or dabble in a medium.
- *Developing your idea.* Create some sketches of your initial idea. You may modify or slightly change it to bring it into a visual form or you may rethink your idea completely.
- *Trying out your idea with a medium.* You may have a medium in mind, or you may want to experiment with a variety of media. At this point you are ready to express yourself in a meaningful way.

As you engage in these experiences, you will find that you go back and forth through the stages of the creative process. The Studio activities in this unit offer you many opportunities to revisit and build upon your own wondrous creative nature. You will experiment with a variety of art media that may open new doors to the creative art process.

 **At a Glance**

What is happening in this artwork?

What do you notice about the way the artist arranged the shapes?

What mood does this artwork seem to convey?

Lesson 1: Drawing

 Attributed to Rogier van der Weyden. *Men Shoveling Chairs,* date unknown. Pen and ink on paper, 11 3/4 by 16 3/4 inches. The Metropolitan Museum of Art.

Why Do Artists Draw?

Drawing is a visual language that most artists use to help them communicate and solve problems. It is a visual record of how well your mind, feelings, and senses work together. Drawing is one process used to make artworks. A drawing can be a work of art unto itself, or it can be a plan for a composition, such as a painting, a sculpture, or a collage. To create a drawing, you use a type of art medium, such as pencil or charcoal.

Just as many writers jot down daily thoughts in journals, artists practice drawing each day in their sketchbooks. They find that when they draw, they develop their ability to see differently. They improve their **perception;** that is, they become more aware of the elements in their environment by using their senses. The drawing process enhances their powers of creative thought.

Art Media for Drawing

Pencil, colored pencils, crayons, oil pastels, charcoal, and chalk pastels are only a few of the many art media that artists use to create drawings. As you read the credit lines for images in this book, you may notice even more kinds of art media for drawing. For example, some drawings are done with an ancient fluid medium known as pen and ink, as in **A**. Today, ink pens for drawing vary from disposable ballpoint and felt-tip pens to high-quality fountain pens with various sizes of tips. Other art media for drawing include watercolor and water-based markers, along with found objects, such as twigs and toothpicks.

Techniques for Shading

Artists enhance their drawings by applying **shading techniques**, ways of showing light and shadow to give a feeling of depth and texture. They choose among four main types of shading techniques:

Blending — changing the value little by little

Stippling — creating dark values by applying a dot pattern

Hatching — creating thin parallel lines

Cross-hatching — creating lines that cross each other

Eugène Delacroix. (Detail) *Une Femme d'Alger*, 19th century. Pen lithograph. The Metropolitan Museum of Art.

Drawing in Ink

Collect examples of line drawings from newspapers and magazines that illustrate drawing techniques. Using a black felt-tip pen and other drawing media, create a Technique Sheet of basic forms. Shade them with drawing techniques you observe in the magazine and newspaper drawings.

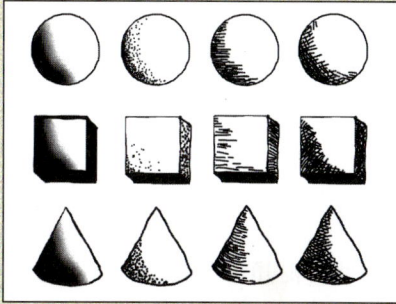

What shading techniques did the artists of **A** and **B** use in their drawings? Notice in the credit lines the art media these artists selected. Why do you think each artist chose such a medium? In what ways do you think each medium affected the shading techniques used?

As you practice drawing in your Sketchbook/Journal, keep in mind the many drawing media, techniques, and approaches available to you. They will help you grow in the creative process.

Sketchbook/Journal

Draw several objects, and practice using shading techniques. Make notes about each technique.

Drawing

Lesson 2
STUDIO
Gesture Drawing

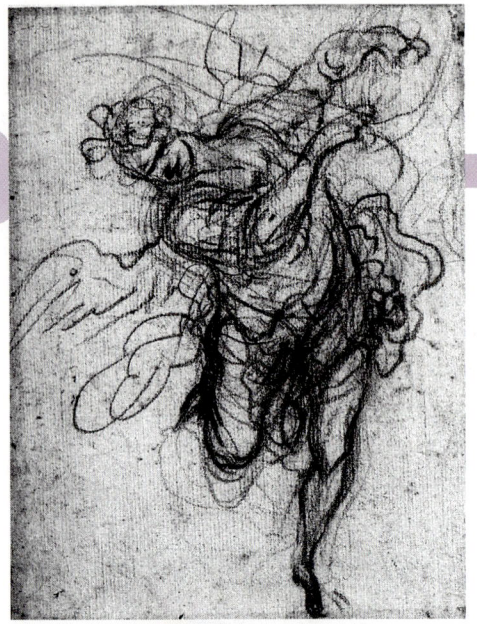

What basic human movement does this gesture drawing show?

Artist unknown, Italian. *Dancing Figure,* 16th century. Red chalk, 6 1/4 by 5 1/4 inches. The Metropolitan Museum of Art.

Get the Picture

Just as writers sometimes get writers' block, a state of mind in which their flow of words temporarily shuts down, so too do artists sometimes become stuck in trying to express themselves visually. A common remedy for such a condition is **gesture drawing.** Using this technique, artists move a drawing medium, such as a pencil, quickly and freely over a surface to capture the form and actions of a subject. Some gesture drawings may be quick scribbles, while others are done with more precision. This type of drawing helps to loosen the mind and free the imagination.

As in **A** and **B**, most gesture drawings are not meant to represent a specific individual. Instead, they show impressions of the human form in motion.

Get Set

 **Materials you will need:**

- 12" x 18" white drawing paper
- #2 pencil
- black felt-tip pen
- colored pencils, crayons, colored markers, pastels or oil pastels

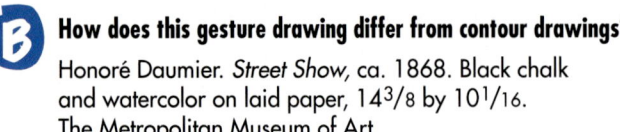

How does this gesture drawing differ from contour drawings?

Honoré Daumier. *Street Show,* ca. 1868. Black chalk and watercolor on laid paper, 14 3/8 by 10 1/16. The Metropolitan Museum of Art.

How to Create a Gesture Drawing

1. Use a pencil or a black felt-tip pen to create gesture drawings on a sheet of white paper. Show a classmate in at least four different stop-action poses, such as running, dancing, throwing, and walking.

2. Create a background of different kinds of colored lines by drawing contour lines around each gesture drawing.

Simone, Kealing Junior High School. *In Action*. Oil pastel on paper, 9 by 12 inches.

Making a Gesture Flipbook

Cut a sheet of 9" x 12" drawing paper into twelve 3" x 3" squares. Staple the paper in the top center. Create a gesture drawing of an action figure in the center of the first square. The figure can be animal or human. On the remaining squares, redraw the same figure in different stop-motion poses. Develop an unusual background for your figures with a contrasting color scheme. Thumb quickly through your drawings to see your figure in motion!

Sketchbook/Journal

Practice gesture drawing each day for a week by finding something in motion to draw in your Sketchbook/Journal. Observe a person engaged in a sport, an animal playing, or a person bending and stretching. Draw fifteen scribbled gesture drawings in fifteen minutes or less.

Be an Art Critic!

1. **Describe** What is happening in your drawing? Describe each figure and its action.
2. **Analyze** What principles of design do the contour lines in the background bring to your composition?
3. **Interpret** Do you think the meaning of your artwork was influenced by the technique of gesture drawing? Explain.
4. **Judge** What are your impressions of your gesture drawing? Would you like to frame it? Explain.

Lesson 3: Painting

A Artist unknown. *Hall of Bulls and Horses*, date unknown. Montignac, France.

Why Do Artists Paint?

Some of the oldest paintings in the world are preserved on walls of caves, as in **A**, where artists painted them thousands of years ago. We can only wonder what inspired these cave dwellers to brush or rub ground-up rocks mixed with animal fat onto cave walls. Perhaps they simply wanted to express themselves visually.

Today many artists such as Helen Frankenthaler, who created **B**, express their thoughts and feelings through painting. During the 1960s, Frankenthaler and a group of other painters invented a style of painting known as *Color Field*, in which the artist brushes or pours thin paints onto large canvases. The wet blending of colors creates soft edges. Notice the soft edges in **B**. Color-field paintings usually have no recognizable **subject**, such as a person or an animal. This type of painting is called *Nonobjective Art*. Artists who create Nonobjective paintings often express their feelings through the artform.

Read the credit line for **B**. Notice the dimensions of the painting. One art critic wrote: "[Frankenthaler] sees what is big in feeling, what is spacious and vital in relationships. Her paintings…convey this message of space, light, and energy.…"

Art Media for Painting

Most painting media contain a powdered **pigment,** a coloring material made from crushed minerals and plants or chemicals. The coloring grains and powder in a pigment are bound together by a **binder,** such as wax, egg, glue, resin, or oil. Whereas cave painters probably used animal fat as a binder to hold together pigments from crushed minerals and plants, Frankenthaler used oil to hold together the pigments in **B**. Sometimes artists use a **solvent,** a liquid such as turpentine or water, to control the thickness or thinness of the paint. Solvents are also good for cleaning paint from brushes or other applicators.

Art media for painting are typically two types: oil-based paint and water-based paint.

B Where do you see primary, secondary, and intermediate colors in this composition?

Helen Frankenthaler. *Moveable Blue*, 1973. Acrylic on canvas, 70 by 243 1/4 inches. Courtesy of SBC Communications Inc.

Oil-Based Paint

For more than five hundred years, artists have used **oil-based paints** as their media. The binder for pigments in oil-based paints is linseed oil, with turpentine as the solvent. An advantage to using oil-based paints is that they dry slowly. Artists using thick oil paints have time to experiment with the paint as they create their compositions. However, thinned oil paints dry quickly.

Water-Based Paint

You have probably painted with tempera, watercolor, or acrylic—all **water-based paints.** Their solvent is water, and they dry quickly. Water-based paints have different qualities. For example, tempera paints are thick and **opaque**—that is, you cannot see through them to the paper, as in **C**. Watercolor paints have gum arabic as their binder. They have a **transparent** quality, in which light passes through them to reveal the paper. Also, notice the transparent quality in **B**, an acrylic painting.

Techniques for Painting

Many painters use a paintbrush and **palette,** a tray or board on which colors of paint are mixed. However, Frankenthaler sometimes pours her paint directly onto the canvas, which lies on the floor. If you did not have a paintbrush, what other objects could you use for painting? Artists have used toothpicks, sticks, wires, sponges, cottonballs, pipecleaners, rollers, marbles, their hands, and other tools. They have also mixed their paints with many substances, such as sand or sawdust, to give them texture.

As you prepare to use watercolor, let your mind and fingers relax. A successful watercolorist uses imagination during the process of composing.

Experimenting with Watercolor

To help you with this Studio, refer to page 257.

Prepare your paints by dropping several drops of water onto each paint color on your palette. Review pages 26–27 to help you mix colors to create secondary, intermediate, complementary, warm, and cool colors. Prepare your *wet wash* sky by sweeping a clean, water-charged brush across the paper, covering the entire area. Charge your brush with a color, and paint broad brushstrokes across the top. By using less color, lighten the *wash* as you paint to the bottom of the page. Tilt your paper to soften any rough edges of paint.

When your first wash has dried, create a wash for the ground. Paint broad brushstrokes of another color over the bottom half of your paper, leaving some areas of the foreground and middle ground untouched. Let your paper dry completely.

Use your imagination to discover the shapes and figures that were untouched during the second wash. Remoisten your palette with drops of water. With a slightly damp brush, apply darker shades of paint around the edges of the shapes and figures you found.

C

Merissa, Ed White Middle School. *Untitled.* Watercolor on paper, 18 by 24 inches.

Sketchbook/Journal

Draw several thumbnail sketches of interesting designs you wish to paint with watercolors. Practice painting washes. Make notes about the techniques you discover.

Painting 61

Lesson 4 — STUDIO: Painting a Landmark

 Paul Cézanne. *Mont Sainte-Victoire Seen from the Bibemus Quarry*, ca. 1897. Oil on canvas, 25 1/3 by 31 1/4 inches. The Baltimore Museum of Art.

Get the Picture

Every city, state, and country has its *landmarks*—telltale stones or trees, historic buildings, significant hills, or other geographic features associated with legend or fact. Landmarks are symbols of regional lore that help define the culture of an area.

Artists have forever made a visual record of landmarks, as in **A**. It is one of many paintings of Mont Sainte-Victoire in France by artist Paul Cézanne. He created this visual record of a popular landmark near his home. When you first view the painting, where does your eye go? How did the artist use shape and color to emphasize the mountain? As he painted this image, Cézanne studied various forms in nature. Identify the natural forms in **A**. How did Cézanne's approach to painting shapes make them appear three-dimensional?

Get Set

 **Materials you will need:**

- 12" x 18" watercolor paper
- #2 pencil
- white crayon and/or white oil pastel
- watercolors, watercolor pencils, brushes, water container
- paper towels
- palette
- oil pastels, crayons, chalk pastels

How to Create a Relief Print

1. Arrange and glue strands of string on cardboard to create a contour drawing of you doing your favorite activity.

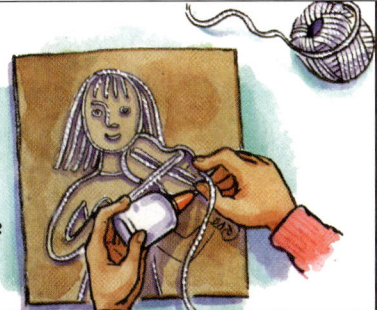

2. When the plate is dry, roll a light color of printing ink over it with a brayer.

3. Carefully place a clean sheet of paper on top of the inked plate. Press lightly, pull the print, and examine it. Now is the time to change your plate in any way you wish.

4. When the glue and ink are dry, repeat the printing process. Use the same print, but apply a darker color of ink. Be careful to register the print—that is position it as you did for the first inking.

5. Continue changing your plate and printing with darker colors until you are satisfied. Then start again with clean paper to make more prints!

Making a Foam-Block Relief Print

Re-create a favorite design from your Sketchbook/Journal by drawing it onto paper the size of a clean foam-tray. Transfer the design to the surface of the foam-tray printing plate by pressing with a ballpoint pen or pencil. Ink the surface of the plate and make prints.

Sketchbook/Journal

Draw several thumbnail sketches of interesting ideas for relief prints that you discover in your home, classroom, and outdoors.

Be an Art Critic!

1. **Describe** Name the types of lines and shapes you used in your composition.
2. **Analyze** How did the addition of colors change your print? Describe the changes you made to your plate, and explain why you made the changes.
3. **Interpret** How would you describe the meaning of this print of yourself?
4. **Judge** Which part of the printing process did you enjoy most? least? Would you like to be a printmaker? Explain.

Making a Relief Print

Lesson 7: Collage

 How did the collagist use exaggeration of proportion to show emphasis?

Romare Bearden. *Sunset and Moonrise with Maudell Sleet*, 1978. Collage on board, 41 by 29 inches. Estate of Romare Bearden. © Romare Bearden Foundation/Licensed by VAGA, New York, NY.

What Is Collage?

You have learned about art processes such as drawing, painting, and printmaking. Now consider that some artists like to arrange materials and glue them to a flat surface. **Collage** is a process in which the artist glues bits of cut or torn paper, photographs, fabric, or other materials to a flat surface. An artist who creates a collage is called a **collagist.**

Why Do Artists Create Collage?

Artists are always considering creative ways to express their ideas. Collage can be used for creative expression. Artists choose this artform for a variety of reasons. Some like the way the colors and shapes complement each other, overlapping and in unusual proportions, as in **A**. Others have a special personal or commercial message to convey, such as a political or comical theme.

Romare Bearden, the artist of **A**, had a social message to convey about a strong woman he recalled from his childhood in Charlotte, North Carolina. "She was a woman with a green thumb," he commented about the gardener to whom he pays tribute in this collage. In what ways does she appear as a figure of strength?

Art Media and Techniques for Collage

Materials for making collages are as varied as are the kinds of lines, shapes, and textures in the world. Some common materials are magazine and newspaper pictures, brightly colored paper, pieces of fabric, and hand-drawn images. These collage parts are typically glued onto a paper or cardboard background and enhanced with paint or markers. Notice the shapes of painted paper and photographs from magazines that Bearden used in **A**. Why do you think he chose those materials? How does the soft texture of watercolor affect the mood of the collage? What figures and objects do you see in the foreground? middleground? background? How does this arrangement help you understand the meaning of the composition?

 Romare Bearden was a young artist during the Harlem Renaissance.

C Matthew, Alamo Heights Junior High School. *Untitled.* Collaged tissue paper and marker on paper, 12 by 18 inches.

Career Link

Romare Bearden

Collagist Romare Bearden, in B, adopted collage as his medium long after he had received a degree in mathematics, became a writer, and mastered the medium of painting. Born in Charlotte, North Carolina, he grew up in Harlem, a part of New York City. As a young man in Harlem, he was influenced by other African American artists and intellectuals during an artistic movement in the 1920s known as the *Harlem Renaissance.* Bearden later reminisced about those years: "Everything you did was geared to groove," he recalled. In 1935 he studied collage at the Art Students League in New York City under the well-known collagist George Grosz.

The mid-1960s marked Bearden's preference for collage. By painting shapes and cutting them out, he incorporated bold color into his compositions. "I paint on collage. I consider them paintings," he explained.

Making a Collage

On a sheet of 12" x 18" white drawing paper, create a collage of an elderly person you know who has an interesting hobby or job. With a black felt-tip pen and using your memory, draw a contour of the person from the waist up, filling most of the paper. Inside the figure, glue magazine and newspaper photographs that reflect the person's activities. Use markers to create the background by drawing in other reminders of the hobby or job.

Sketchbook/Journal

Draw several thumbnail sketches of you involved in your favorite hobbies. Make notes about materials to use for making a collage of your sketches.

Collage 69

Lesson 8: Textiles and Fiber Art

 This textile, an example of Kente cloth, was created by hand in Africa.

Artist unknown, Asante people, Ghana. *Kente Cloth,* 20th century. Silk, 120 by 71 1/3 inches. The British Museum.

What Are Textiles and Fiber Art?

Perhaps you have seen a handmade quilt or a knitted sweater at home or in a museum. Each of these is an example of a **textile,** an artwork made from cloth or fibers, such as yarn. **Fibers** are slender, threadlike materials that come from animals (silk, wool), plants (linen, flax, cotton), and chemicals (nylon, rayon). **Fiber artists** create **fiber art** from these long, thin threadlike materials.

Textiles and other fiber arts, such as embroidery, crochet, and lace-making, belong to a type of art known as **craft. Craftspeople** who create handmade quilts, for example, are artists who have become highly skilled at making artworks by hand. Most craftspeople have received training in a certain art form, and their craft is often their career. Their artworks are either useful or decorative objects, which are often displayed in museums. Baskets, ceramics, jewelry, and furniture are other types of crafts created by artists around the world. What kinds of crafts have you seen in your community or in other places?

The Kente cloth textile in **A** is a craft that was made by hand in Africa. Read the credit line to discover the artist's country and the medium used to make this textile.

Art Media and Techniques for Textiles

Textile artists have many ways of creating plans for their artworks. Some of them prefer to imagine a design or to make a sketch with a pencil. Others create more elaborate plans by painting colored designs on paper. Still others, as in **D**, plan their textiles on a computer. By taking advantage of special software tools, a student artist created a simple pattern using broad bands of color similar to patterns in Kente cloth textiles. How might this computer-drawn design be used to create a textile?

Most textile and fiber art involves weaving or stitchery. These techniques are ancient artforms, yet they continue to be popular among today's craftspeople.

Weaving

When artists **weave**, they interlock threads or fiberlike materials to create a fabric. The fabrics of the clothes you are wearing were probably woven in a factory on a machine-driven loom. A **loom** is a frame that holds fibers for weaving, usually at right angles to one another. Textiles that are considered fine artworks are woven by hand on looms and are called "handwoven fabrics." Because of the time and skill involved to make them, these textiles often command a high price. All textile weavings have **warp**, lengthwise fibers, and **weft**, fibers that cross over and under the warp. Notice the warp and the weft in the clothes you are wearing. Is the fabric made of a loose or a tight weave? Was it woven by hand or by a machine?

Stitchery

Stitchery is a term for artwork created with a needle, thread or yarn, and cloth. Some textiles are examples of **appliqué**, as in **B**, in which fabrics are stitched to a background. **Quilting** is a type of stitchery, in which the artist stitches together two layers of cloth with padding between the layers, as in **C**.

D Brendan, Conackamack Middle School. *Kente Cloth Design.* Computer-drawn image, 3 by 6½ inches.

As you examine textiles, notice their subtle variations in texture. Perhaps you have some examples of weaving or stitchery at home to study. As you explore the world of textiles and fibers, inquire about the plans and techniques the artists use.

Making a Textile Design

With colored markers, design on paper a ceremonial Kente cloth showing special line patterns. If you have access to a computer, use a draw program to develop your design. Then print out your textile design for your Portfolio.

Sketchbook/Journal

Compare your hand-drawn composition with your computer-generated composition. What qualities does each one have to offer? Which one would you like to use as a model for a textile? Write about your decision.

Textiles and Fiber Art

Lesson 9: Sculpture

What Is Sculpture?

You have learned that shapes are two-dimensional, whereas forms have three dimensions. Many artists who work with forms create **sculpture.** These artists are called **sculptors.** They create artworks by **sculpting**—the process of taking away from a form or adding to it.

Art Media and Types of Sculpture

The media that sculptors use vary from hard to soft (as marble and cloth), old to new (as rusted iron and shiny copper), and stiff to pliable (as wood and modeling clay). Each medium has its own appeal to sculptors and viewers alike. Regardless of the media used, artists think of sculpture as being of two forms:

Sculpture in the Round

The Chinese artwork shown in **A** is an example of *sculpture in the round,* or free-standing sculpture. This artwork is surrounded on *all* sides by space. What might you see from the back?

Relief Sculpture

The wooden sculpture in **B** is an example of *relief sculpture,* a type in which forms project from a background. These forms are meant to be seen from *one* side. What do you think you would see if you went around to the back of this sculpture?

 The sculptor who modeled this figure used glazes to add color.

Artist unknown, Chinese. *Lokapala, the Guardian King*, ca. A.D. 700–755. Earthenware with three-color lead glaze, height $32^{1}/_{2}$ inches. The Nelson-Atkins Museum of Art.

 This wooden sculpture from South America is a relief sculpture.

Francisco Matto. (Detail) *Red Relief with Mask and Animals*, 1960. Carved and assembled wood, painted with oil, $77^{2}/_{3}$ by $29^{1}/_{2}$ by 2 inches. Museo de Arte Americano de Maldonado, Uruguay.

Techniques for Sculpture

Sculpture is created through four basic processes. Sculptors use one or a combination of these processes.

Modeling

All types of clay are good media to use for building up and shaping, or **modeling**, a sculpture. Ceramic clay, which is taken from the earth, is ideal for modeling. The ceramic sculpture in **A** shows a *lokapala*, a figure placed on the side of a king's tomb to guard against evil spirits. In the Buddhist tradition, the guardian stands on a smaller figure as a symbol of victory over its enemies. What mood does this sculpture convey?

Assembling

Artists assemble, or construct, new or used objects to make **assemblages**, as in **C**. These sculptures are often made of recycled objects that assume new meaning.

Casting

Another way of building up a sculpture is through **casting**. Some sculptors begin casting by modeling an object of wax, covering it with a heat-resistant mold, and then melting the wax. In the hollow space, they pour molten metal. When it cools, the mold is removed to reveal, for example, a cast bronze sculpture. Many sculptures in public places, as in **D**, are made by casting. Name some examples of cast sculpture in your community.

Carving

The technique called **carving** requires the sculptor to cut or chip away pieces from a block of material. As in **B**, the block may be wood. Stone, clay, paraffin wax, and plaster blocks can also be carved. Five hundred years ago, artist Michelangelo said his job as a sculptor was merely to chip away the stone around the idea, or image, locked inside the stone. "Taking away ... brings out a living figure in ... hard stone," he claimed about the technique of carving.

Making a Paper Sculpture

Use construction paper to create different examples of ways to sculpt paper. You might try cutting and tearing, folding, scoring and shaping, making forms (cylinder, cone, cube), curling, and pleating. Glue your examples onto a Technique Sheet of white drawing paper, and label each example. Using a small paper bag and paper sculpting techniques, create a hand puppet that celebrates a major event or holiday. Be sure to add paper sculptures to the front, back, and sides.

Sketchbook/Journal

Study the lines, shapes, and forms of your paper sculpture. On your Technique Sheet, draw and label other examples of ways to sculpt paper.

Lesson 10 STUDIO: Making a Relief Sculpture

What is the difference between this full view and a detail of Matto's relief sculpture?

Francisco Matto. *Red Relief with Mask and Animals,* 1960. Carved and assembled wood, painted with oil, 77 2/3 by 29 1/2 by 2 inches. Museo de Arte Americano de Maldonado, Uruguay.

Get the Picture

The sculpture in **A** is the full view of the *relief sculpture* you saw on page 72. On the front side, figures and objects project outward from a wooden background. Sculptor Francisco Matto carved some of the wood away from this surface to show the figures and objects through the subtractive method of sculpting.

At age 15, having been inspired by the artworks of Henri Matisse, Matto began to teach himself to paint designs on pieces of wood. Later he incorporated styles of *Pre-Columbian artists,* those who lived in the Americas before Columbus arrived. Matto used **symbols**—letters, figures, or signs that represent real objects or ideas—to express his thoughts and feelings. Read the title of **A** to help you identify some symbols in the sculpture. What are your impressions of Matto's style? Does it remind you of another style you have seen from another part of the world?

Jonathan, Math Science & Technology Magnet School. *An Artist's Pyramid.* Relief sculpture: cardboard, foam core, and acrylic paint, 9 by 11 inches.

Get Set

Materials you will need:
- large piece of cardboard
- cardboard scraps, matteboard scraps, or foam core
- glue or gluestick
- white latex paint
- paintbrush
- water container
- tempera paint

 Lesson 10

How to Create a Relief Sculpture

1. Make a sketch of a design for the facade, or front, of a house you would like to live in. Include symbols that show your favorite objects and animals.

2. Arrange scraps of cardboard, matte board or foam core on a larger piece of cardboard. Work from large to small in several layers.

3. Show the shapes of symbols on the top layer. Glue the scrap pieces in place.

4. When the glue is dry, paint your relief sculpture with white latex paint. Add a few drops of glue to the paint.

5. When the white paint is dry, paint only the top layer with the colors of your choice.

Creating a Metal Relief Sculpture

Create a relief sculpture with cardboard scraps to show a symbol of transportation. Cover your sculpture with aluminum foil, pressing gently with a pencil eraser to show the relief.

Sketchbook/Journal

Draw a sketch of the front of your school as you would like to see it. Shade parts of your drawing that you would carve away in a relief sculpture. If you include symbols, label them with descriptive terms.

Be an Art Critic!

1. **Describe** Name some shapes and forms in your composition. Are they geometric? organic?
2. **Analyze** Which principle of design stands out most clearly to you?
3. **Interpret** Tell about meanings the symbols hold for you.
4. **Judge** If you could build a house with a front that resembles your relief sculpture, would you keep the plan you created or change it? Explain.

Making a Relief Sculpture

Lesson 11: Architecture

 Filippo Brunelleschi. *Dome of the Florence Cathedral*, 1420–1436. Florence, Italy.

What Is Architecture?

Artists who plan buildings and other structures are referred to as **architects.** The art and science of planning buildings is called **architecture.** Architects design many structures, most of which are parts or combinations of traditional geometric and organic forms. An example of such a form is a **dome,** which is like half of a hollow ball or sphere.

The dome in Florence Cathedral in **A** was planned by architect Filippo Brunelleschi more than 500 years ago. It still towers over the city today. In designing the dome, the architect had to overcome some major obstacles concerning what the weight and balance of the dome would be during construction. The weight of the dome is estimated to be more than 25,000 tons! Can you guess how long it took to construct such a dome? The credit line may help you answer this question.

Art Media and Techniques for Architecture

In planning designs for structures, architects are concerned about both the **interior,** or inside, and the **exterior,** or outside, of the structure. Windows, doors, roofs, floors—all parts of the structure must be carefully planned.

An architect begins planning a structure by asking questions and gathering answers. Who will use the building? Where will it be? What purpose will it serve? How much space is needed? Next the architect makes sketches of the **floorplan,** the arrangement of rooms inside the building. Discussions with the client help the architect make adjustments to prepare the **blueprint,** a photographic print used to copy the final drawing. The architect renders an **elevation,** a drawing that shows one side of the structure. Typically, the architect asks a **landscape architect** to create a pleasing outdoor design by using plants, rocks, trees, and other materials. What kinds of landscape designs might you envision for **A** and **C**?

Both Brunelleschi and Pei created public spaces that embrace their environmental settings, each taking advantage of the views offered by their respective cities. Brunelleschi created a prominent structure that towers above the city of Florence, while Pei used windows to frame the Dallas cityscape. How might you design a similar structure for your city?

Career Link

I.M. Pei

American architect I.M. Pei was born in China and came to the United States to study architecture in 1935. Today he is known throughout the world for his designs of public buildings and urban complexes.

Many of Pei's creations are buildings he designed especially for the arts. One such example is the Meyerson Symphony Center in Dallas. Pei's design of the center incorporates many forms, such as cubes, cones, and cylinders.

The sweeping curves of the structure's exterior in **C** reach out to invite visitors into the building. How do these curves affect the design of the center's interior in **D**? Imagine where Pei incorporated the 2,100-seat concert hall in **E** into the center's design.

I.M. Pei. *West Facade of The Morton H. Meyerson Symphony Center*, 1989. Dallas, Texas.

I.M. Pei, architect, and Russell Johnson, acoustician. *Eugene McDermott Concert Hall*, of *The Morton H. Meyerson Symphony Center*, Dallas, Texas.

I.M. Pei. *Lobby of The Morton H. Meyerson Symphony Center*, 1989. Dallas, Texas.

Designing an Architectural Plan

Brainstorm ideas for an architectural plan of an art, science, or other museum. Draw a floorplan and a blueprint, to include such areas as galleries, meeting rooms, a restaurant, restrooms, a gift shop, and offices. On the grounds, include gardens, trees, sidewalks, benches, and so forth. On another sheet of paper, design and sketch the front elevation of the museum.

Sketchbook/Journal

Write a description of your architectural plans. Tell about where the structure will stand in your community and the materials needed to build it.

Architecture

Lesson 12
STUDIO
Making an Architectural Model

Get the Picture

The temple in **A** was planned and constructed in Athens, Greece almost 2,500 years ago. It stood largely untouched on a high hill until about A.D. 1687, when the Turks used its stones to build a fort.

The temple was restored in 1835, and again in 1940. Notice in **B** the type of **columns** used—the vertical postlike structures that carry weight. They are constructed in three parts: the **capital, shaft,** and **base.**

Can you find the Athena Nike temple in **C**? This **model,** a small copy that represents the larger version, shows all the buildings of the Acropolis. The name for this structure is derived from the Greek *akros,* meaning "highest," and *polis,* meaning "city." The early Greeks chose this high hill as an easy place to defend, and their chief lived there for protection. Later on, as cities built up around the bottom of the hill and protected the Acropolis, Greek architects built temples on the hill.

A Notice the Greek columns near the top of this temple.
Callicrates. *Temple of Athena Nike,* 427–424 B.C. Acropolis, Athens, Greece.

C Artist unknown. *Restoration Model of the Acropolis,* 5th century B.C. The Royal Ontario Museum, Toronto.

capital — shaft — base

 B

Get Set

Materials you will need:
- cardboard, matteboard, foam core
- paper, scissors
- glue or glue stick
- toothpicks, found objects
- tempera paint with an added dab of glue

78 **Lesson 12**

How to Create an Architectural Model

1. Create a model from the plan for a museum that you designed in Lesson 11. Begin by arranging cardboard, matte board, and foam core to resemble your plan.

2. Glue the forms together.

3. Glue on found objects as details for your model.

4. When your model is dry, paint it in an appealing color scheme.

Designing the Interior of Your Dream School

Redesign the interior of your school to become your "dream school." Use a shoebox and other recyclable containers as rooms. Include areas such as closets, bathrooms, a library, a computer area, an office, and a cafeteria.

Sketchbook/Journal

Draw several thumbnail sketches of interesting architectural designs in your community. Make notes about the different designs, focusing on features you like and dislike.

Be an Art Critic!

1. **Describe** Make a two-part list of the forms in your model—organic and geometric.
2. **Analyze** How closely does your model resemble the architectural plan for it? Describe the similarities and differences.
3. **Interpret** What is the purpose of your museum? Tell how the community might use such a building.
4. **Judge** What is the best feature of your design?

Making an Architectural Model

Lesson 13: Computer Art

Artists and Computers

First came the prehistoric discovery that animal fat mixed with ground-up rocks would make paint. Thirty-two thousand years later, the invention of the digital **computer** has provided an exciting modern art medium for creative expression. Unlike traditional art media, computers help artists save time through the touch of a key or the click of a mouse. Zip! A rectangle appears on the screen. Click! The shape is instantly filled with a chosen pattern of lines. Click, click! The pattern becomes pink and green. All this in thirty seconds and with no clean up. Is it any wonder that so many artists today rely on computers to help them plan and design works of art?

A Computer artist Barbara Nessim set aside traditional media to use computer art programs instead.

Barbara Nessim. *Modem: Close Encounter of the Computer Kind,* 1983. Computer-generated image, $10^{3/4}$ by $10^{3/8}$ inches. Copyright 1998 Barbara Nessim.

Computers as an Art Medium

Computers have made as big an impact in the area of fine art as it has in other aspects of our lives. With a growing variety of **software applications,** artists are drawing and painting right on the computer screen. Graphic designers can use the mouse as a pencil or paintbrush. From the **tool box** an artist can select colors and widths of lines, draw a background, or have the computer create different patterns. Some artists prefer a **stylus** and a **graphics tablet** to use as an electronic pencil and paper. The stylus is moved across a pressure-sensitive surface, and a line appears on the computer screen. Using a **scanner,** an artist can import one of their flat artworks into the computer and then make changes, add details, or paste onto an existing electronic composition. A computer **printer** prints the new artwork for display. What if you make a mistake or would like to see your artwork in different colors? With a "click" of the mouse you can change colors, add patterns, and even erase!

Lines created on the computer are thousands of points of data called **pixels** used to create bit-mapped images. In **A**, Barbara Nessim created straight lines by positioning pixels side by side in a row, and she created shapes by putting pixels side by side in several directions. The pixels in **A** are very large, compared to other electronic artworks that have smooth lines and edges. Nessim enlarged her design to make the pixels visible. Notice how the pixels create a gridlike pattern with tiny patches of black, white, or color.

"For me art is the same in any chosen media. It is the soul of the creator transformed into a tangible or sometimes not so tangible art object."

—Barbara Nessim

Career Link

Barbara Nessim

In 1981 artist Barbara Nessim taught herself to draw and paint using a new art medium, the computer. Her experience with machinery began in the 1960s when she created monoprint etchings and used the printing press as her medium. Soon she realized that her creative process would change drastically with the advent of the "Electronic Age."

Working as an Artist-in-Residence for a large magazine in New York City, Nessim experienced the potential power of the computer as an art tool. She began to think about how her lifelong passion of creating sketchbooks could be improved with this new medium. Her vision was to have the drawings displayed simultaneously. In conceiving her "visual novel," which could be read in different ways, she drew on her understanding of how the written language is read. For example, Hebrew is read right to left and Japanese is read both horizontally and vertically. The artforms tell stories of people moving from one country to another, engaging in daily activities and exchanging cultural ideas, beliefs, and values.

Nessim's computer drawings and paintings are parts of many public and private collections; they appear in museums and galleries worldwide. You may also have seen them in magazines and newspapers or on her website (http://www.nessim.com).

Kim, Teague Middle School. *Self-Portrait.* Computer-generated design, 8 1/2 by 11 inches.

Tools		Functions
▸	Selection tool	Selects objects.
▭	Selection tool	Defines a rectangular space around an object.
◯	Lasso Selection tool	Selects only the object.
✎	Pencil tool	Draws straight lines and curves.
╲	Line tool	Draws lines.
🖌 or 🖌	Brush tool	Paints lines of different thicknesses.
▭	Rectangle tool	Draws rectangles and squares.
◯	Oval or round tool	Draws ovals and circles.
🪣	Fill tool	Adds color, values, or patterns to closed objects or shapes.
▭	Eraser tool	Changes one color to another.
🔍	Zoom tool	Enlarges or reduces images

Making Computer Art

Create a drawing of a figure using a drawing program on your computer or scanning a contour drawing you created in your Sketchbook. Using a software application with drawing and painting tools, add form, color, texture, and value to your drawing on the screen. Use this drawing three times to create a design. Create a background for your composition. Scan a design from your Sketchbook or use the drawing tools to add texture and color.

Sketchbook/Journal

Print out your computer-generated sketches and place them in your Sketchbook/Journal. Take notes about the techniques you learned creating art on the computer.

Lesson 14: Still Photography

What Is Still Photography?

Just as writers describe images through words from their own point of view, so do photographers create images from their own particular angles. The art and science of making a picture with a camera and film is called **still photography.** The artistic part of making a photograph involves the creative eye of the **photographer,** or camera artist.

A How would you describe the photographer's angle as she composed this image?

Judy Walgren. *Portrait of a Kenyan Elder,* 1997. Black and white photograph.

Media and Techniques for Still Photography

Photographers have many techniques for creating artistic photographs. Some techniques help the photographer as the image is being taken with the camera. For example, the photographer must know how to arrange a composition or identify an existing one. Other techniques are applied in the darkroom during the printing process. Some examples include exposing the film to light, processing it with chemicals, and printing it on light-sensitive paper.

A still photograph is created as a single frame on a roll of film. Many artists prefer black-and-white photography, as in **A**, because it showcases the value scale and contrast in their compositions. The photographer of **B** created a portrait as a **photographic collage,** a picture made by combining parts of different photographs. He used photographs he had taken with a still camera.

B What qualities does this photographic collage reveal about the subject that might not have been apparent in a single image?

David Hockney. *Stephen Spender, Mas St. Jerome II,* 1985. Photographic collage, 20 1/2 by 20 1/4 inches. © David Hockney, 1990.

Career Link

Judy Walgren

The photographer in C, Judy Walgren, is an artist of still photographs. Many of her photographs address the "four W's and H" of journalism—*who, what, when, where,* and *how.* In this way, she is a *visual reporter* who records images of people, places, and events. In 1994, Walgren was a member of a team of visual reporters who received the Pulitzer Prize for International Reporting for their outstanding achievement in photojournalism.

Walgren's photographs show people in Islamic countries, in the United States, and in African countries, as in A. Notice that she chose to blur the background of A, while she focused on her subject. How does this technique contribute to the composition? As a still photographer, Walgren creates visual reports from interesting angles. For example, she composed A from below, looking upward. In what way does this technique suggest a message of strength about the subject?

"There's nothing I'd rather be doing than shooting pictures," Walgren said. "I have wanderlust and an affinity towards the Third World. They have a joy for life that we'll never understand in the West."

D Stephanie, Honey Grove Middle School. *In the Eye of the Tiger.* Collaged photographs on paper, 22 by 15 inches.

Creating a Photographic Collage

Decide on a subject to show in a photographic collage. Collect magazine and newspaper pictures about your subject. Arrange them in a composition on a sheet of white paper. Glue them to the paper and give your photographic collage a title.

Sketchbook/Journal

Take photographs of interesting designs you see around you and place them in your Sketchbook/Journal. Label the contents of your photographs.

Still Photography 83

Lesson 15 STUDIO: Creating a Storyboard

Get the Picture

Many visual artists use motion picture film or video as their medium. You may view their artworks as motion picture films at movie theaters or as videotaped programs on television. Some videotaped programs, such as , appear as artworks in museums.

Video art is a popular and relatively inexpensive medium for creating motion pictures. An artist who operates a video camera is called a **videographer**.

With a **camcorder**, a small hand-held video camera, and a blank videotape, you can practice being a videographer creating a video program. In preparation to use a camcorder, you need to create a visual plan of the video production, known as a **storyboard.** This series of drawings on small cards shows instructions for the videographer. They may be tacked onto a larger posterboard. The storyboard will help you visualize and arrange your ideas about the **scenarios,** all the action that takes place before the camera changes **angles** or positions. As you plan your storyboard, keep in mind the characters, setting, problem, and solution of your program. What will your program be about? Do you want to create a fantasy or a realistic program? These questions need to be answered before you begin creating your storyboard.

 Motion pictures of these children are projected on a large screen.

Bill Viola. *Passage*, 1987. Video/sound installation, 12 by 16 by 54 feet. San Francisco Museum of Modern Art.

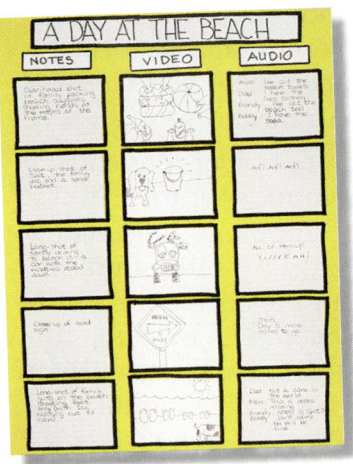

 Richard, Ed White Middle School. *A Day at the Beach.* Posterboard, file cards, and markers, 28 by 22 inches.

Get Set

Materials you will need:
- sheet of notebook paper
- pencils
- 24 unruled 3" x 5" white file cards
- thin-tipped colored markers
- medium-tipped black marker
- 24 thumbtacks
- sheet of white posterboard

How to Create a Storyboard

1. In a group, make a list of video scenarios showing people, places, and events for a five-minute video program.

2. Have each group member choose one or two scenarios to sketch on individual file cards. Work together to arrange the scenario cards in a sequence, placing them vertically in the center of a sheet of posterboard.

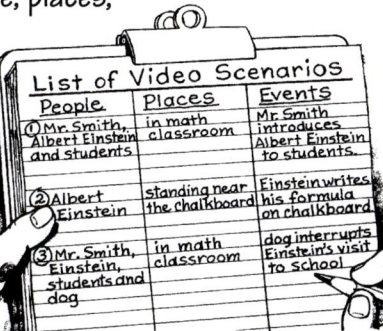

3. Give your storyboard a title and headings for notes. Under *Video*, write special instructions for the videographer. Under *Audio*, write words for the characters to say.

Drawing a Storyboard as a Comic Strip

Draw a storyboard in the format of a comic strip. Include words the characters say in bubbles. Write notes for the videographer above each frame.

Sketchbook/Journal

Make notes about sound effects and where they might go on your storyboard.

Be an Art Critic!

1. **Describe** How would you describe the purpose of your storyboard to someone who has never seen one?

2. **Analyze** How will the videographer understand where to stand in each scenario?

3. **Interpret** What message was your group trying to convey through the storyboard?

4. **Judge** What responses did your storyboard receive from other groups? How would you evaluate your storyboard?

Creating a Storyboard

Talk About Art

"Every closed contour, no matter what its shape, whether a perfect circle or an irregular random form, evokes in addition the notions of 'inside' and 'outside' and the suggestion of 'near' and 'far away', of 'object' and 'background'."

—M.C. Escher
1898–1972

The words of Maurits Cornelis Escher reflect his fanciful and sophisticated perception of space. Today he is well known for his precision-crafted woodblock prints. Each one is a **tessellation**—a pattern of shapes that fit together in a way that leaves no space in between. Each tessellation is a puzzle for the eye to unravel and is admired for the interplay of positive and negative space, as in **B**.

Escher learned the basic techniques of printmaking as a youth in the Netherlands. For many years afterward, he polished his skills, gained a thorough understanding of the properties of his materials, and learned to control the use of printmaking tools.

One day Escher discovered that technical mastery was no longer his only goal. As he explained, "Ideas came into my mind quite unrelated to graphic art, notions which so fascinated me that I longed to communicate them to other people." Suddenly the method by which he presented his images became less important, and the message they conveyed became his focus. He began to experiment with a wide range of subject matter for his prints. Many of his subjects were inspired by his observations of people, places, and objects during his travels. Escher later departed from mathematical compositions, as in **B**, and turned instead to creating prints of imaginative and dreamy landscapes with strange creatures and unusual perspectives. You may wish to explore these and other images by Escher on the Internet. As you view them, consider how the creative process played a key role in their origins.

 M.C. Escher. *Self-Portrait*, 1943. Lithographic ink, 9 3/4 by 10 inches. Private collection.

M.C. Escher. *Triangle System I A3 Type I,* 1938. Pencil, ink, and watercolor, 13 by 9 1/2 inches. Private collection.

Escher chose a subject from among his many sketches. As you review your sketches, think of a subject that may begin your printmaking career!

Making Sketches for a Print

In your Sketchbook/Journal make some sketches of people, places, and objects that you think might provide ideas for the subject of a print later on. Jot down notes about how each sketch might be used in a storyboard. Consider scanning a contour sketch into a computer. Create a tessellation by cutting and pasting the sketch into a puzzle-like design.

Be an Art Critic!

Look at B to answer these questions:

1. **Describe** Point out organic and geometric lines, as well as tints and shades. How would you describe the subject of this composition?
2. **Analyze** Discuss the positive and negative spaces. How did the artist show contrast between them?
3. **Interpret** How would you describe the mood of this composition? What message does it seem to convey?
4. **Judge** Would you decorate a wall or a small gift with this design? Explain.

Talk About Art

Portfolio Project

 **Materials you will need:**
- 2 sheets of white drawing paper
- #2 pencil
- scissors, tape
- dark marker, colored pencils, markers, or watercolors

Making a Tessellation

1. Draw a rectangular shape that is 2" wide and 3" long.

2. Cut out a shape on the left side of the rectangle and tape it to the right side of the rectangle.

3. Cut another shape out of the top of the rectangle and tape it to the bottom of the rectangle.

4. On white paper, draw around the edges of the shape the rectangle has become. Repeat at least six times, fitting the shapes as in a puzzle.

5. Outline each "puzzle piece" with a dark-colored marker and add color to your design with colored pencils, markers, or watercolors.

Gallery

 Sherell, Drew Middle School. *Tessellation.* Tempera and marker on paper, 8 1/2 by 11 inches.

B Susan, Drew Middle School. *Untitled.* Tempera and marker on paper, 8 1/2 by 11 inches.

Portfolio Project

Art Links

MUSIC

Interpreting a Song

A painting of something in the real world is never just a copy: it is an interpretation of the artist's feelings toward the subject. The artist's choices—everything from the medium to the colors—builds this interpretation. The same is true when musicians perform a song: they make it their own with a series of choices.

You can prove this to yourself. Just compare the same song as recorded by two different artists. Listen to both versions and jot down the differences.

Then try working out your own interpretation of a song. Even something as simple as "Mary Had a Little Lamb" can be interpreted. You can stretch the notes, play with tempo, and add drum beats. You can get some friends to sing with you and create harmonies. The choices are endless. Record your song several times as you work. Later listen to the recording. Notice how your interpretation develops as you go along.

DANCE

Exploring Expression Through Movement

Visual artists create patterns of shape and color to express moods and feelings. Dancers do the same when they paint the air with their moving bodies. If you were going to create a dance, how would you find movements that express certain feelings? You might start by borrowing movements from real-life situations.

Read the situations below; then close your eyes and see if distinct movements come to mind:

- A girl hits her thumb with a hammer.
- A lonely boy tries to coax a shy cat out of the bushes.
- A girl opens a test she thought she flunked—she has gotten an A!
- A boy opens a test he thought he aced—he has flunked!

Choose a situation that makes images of movement spring strongly to your mind. Use those movements as the basis for a dance. You can exaggerate the movements, repeat them, slow them down, stretch them out, set them to music...congratulations! You have begun the process of creating a dance.

THEATRE

Performing a Monologue

A sculptor molds a lump of clay into a shape. An actor's clay is the written text. But how does an actor shape what the writer has created? What can the actor possibly add?

Explore an actor's creative process by performing a monologue, a long speech by one character. Find a monologue in a play or a novel that takes about 20 seconds to read aloud. As you study it, consider:

- What is the character *doing* while he or she is talking?
- When does the character *pause* and why?
- What is the character's underlying *feeling*? Where does it break through, and how can you show it?

Perform your monologue with movement and pauses. Build up to the moments when strong feelings break through. Have a friend tell you when to slow down or speed up. When you are comfortable with the monologue, time yourself as you perform it. You will find that it takes much longer to perform than just to read. The extra time reflects what you have added as an actor.

LITERATURE

Choosing a Story Form

Visual artists work in many different media—stone, ink, or yarn, for example. The medium affects how they create their artworks and what their works express. Writers make similar choices. The seed of a story may be a first line, a premise, a character, or a plot idea. But how that seed grows depends on the form the writer chooses: the same seed will grow differently in a novel than in a poem.

Check this out for yourself. Take the first sentence of any novel or short story you like. Make it the first line of a poem. Break it into lines that look like poetry. Then add more lines that go with the first one. Keep going until the poem feels finished. Where did that first sentence take you when you saw it as a poem?

You can go the other way too. Take the first line of any poem. Use it as the beginning of a short story, and see where the story goes.

ArtLinks

Unit 2

What Have You Learned?
Explore the Language of Art

Miriam Schapiro. *Master of Ceremonies*, 1985. Acrylic and fabric on canvas, 90 by 144 inches. Collection of Elaine and Stephen Wynn. Courtesy Steinbaum Krauss Gallery, New York. © Miriam Schapiro.

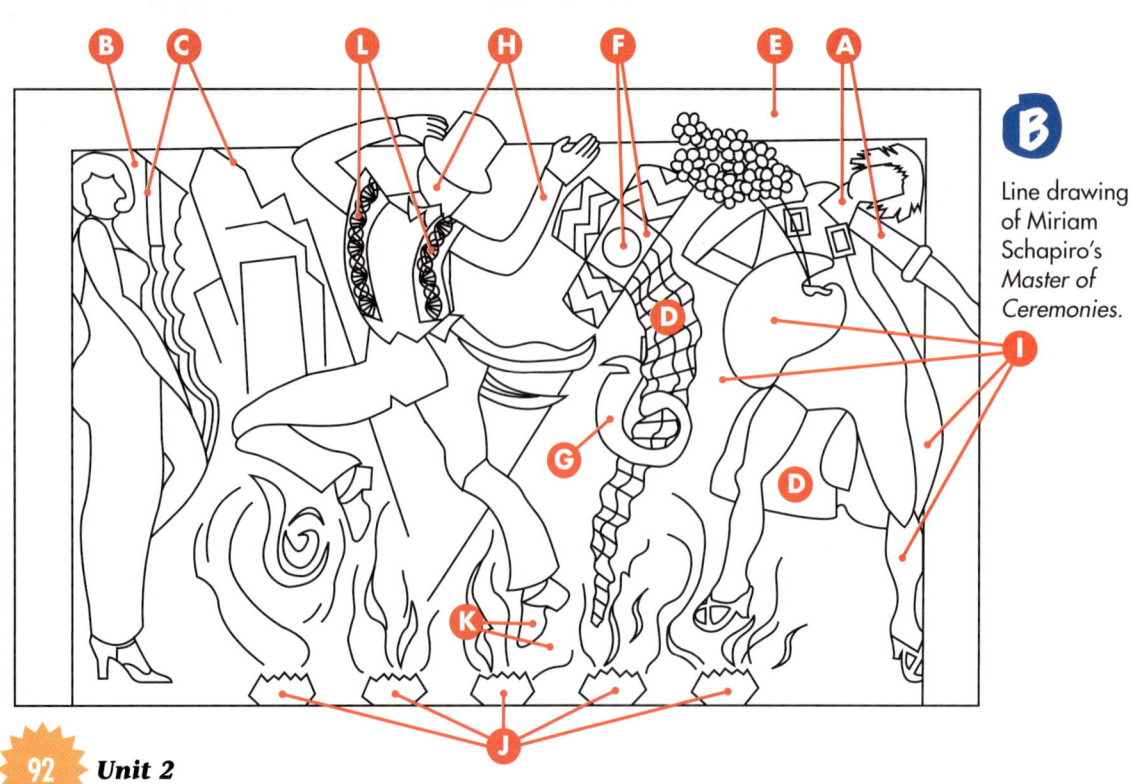

Line drawing of Miriam Schapiro's *Master of Ceremonies*.

Can You Find...?

Where Am I?

Match each art term below with the letter in the illustration of Miriam Schapiro's artwork on page 92.

1. line
2. fabric border
3. pattern
4. geometric shape
5. overlapping
6. organic shape
7. repetition
8. color
9. intensity
10. proportion
11. texture
12. negative space

Do I Belong?

Find the term that *does not belong* in each art process. Indicate where it belongs and tell why.

1. **Drawing:** blending, sketching, cross-hatching, contour, weft, eraser, pencil, pen and ink, shading
2. **Painting:** opaque, pigment, transparent, oil-based paint, in the round, water-based paint, binder, intensity, complementary colors, hue, neutrals, shades, tints, painter
3. **Collage:** photomontage, overlapping, texture, shapes, papers, fabric, repetition, collagist, distortion, palette, dominance, negative space, assemblage, mixed media
4. **Printmaking:** monoprint, transfer, impression, editions, brayer, keyboard, relief print, printing plate, ink, printing press, printmaker
5. **Sculpture:** ceramic clay, relief, carving, modeling, assembling, armature, wire, additive method, intaglio, subtractive method, sculptor, casting
6. **Textiles and Fibers:** fabric, needle, appliqué, weaving, darkroom, quilting, spokes, loom, tapestry, warp, weaver
7. **Architecture:** dome, organic, blueprint, gesture, elevation, interior, geometric, architect, building
8. **Computer Art:** art software, hardware, printer, pixels, scanner, tool icons, glue, paint programs, stylus and graphics tablet, monitor
9. **Photography and Video:** still photography, floorplan, camera, viewfinder, photomontage, photojournalism, storyboard, video art, videographer, motion picture, exposure, lens

What Have You Learned?

Write About Art

 Elizabeth Catlett. *Baile (Dance)*, 1970. Lino-cut, 16 by 30 inches. © 1996 Elizabeth Catlett/Licensed by VAGA, New York.

B Rufino Tamayo. *Danza de la Alegria (Dance of Joy)*, 1950. Oil on canvas, 41 7/8 by 28 inches. Photograph ©1996 Sotheby's, Inc., New York. Reproduction authorized by the Olga and Rufino Tamayo Foundation, A.C.

 Miriam Schapiro. *Anna and David*, 1987. Painted steel and aluminum, 35 by 31 by 9 feet. Commissioned for J.W. Kaempfer Building, Rosslyn, Virginia. Courtesy of Steinbaum Krauss Gallery, New York. © Miriam Schapiro.

TALK OR WRITE — In Your Own Words

Compare and contrast A, B, and C.

1. What is similar?
2. What is different?
3. Imagine the sound and movement in each artwork. What makes each artwork special?
4. Compare and contrast **A**, **B**, and **C** to Miriam Schapiro's *Master of Ceremonies* on page 92. How does *Master of Ceremonies* relate to *Anna and David*? What is special about each of Miriam Schapiro's creations?

Re-View

WRITE — Do You Know the Artist?

Match the artwork and artist at the left with the theme and medium at the right

1. Filippo Brunelleschi, *Dome of Florence Cathedral*
2. Honoré Daumier, *Street Show*
3. Helen Frankenthaler, *Moveable Blue*
4. M.C. Escher, *Triangle System I A3 Type 1*
5. Antonio Frasconi, *Weighing Fish*
6. Paul Cézanne, *Mont-Sainte Victoir*
7. Romare Bearden, *Sunset-Moonrise with Maudell Sleet*
8. Barbara Nessim, *Modem: Close Encounter of the Computer Kind*
9. David Hockney, *Stephen Spender*
10. Bill Viola, *Passage*

Performing figures/Gesture drawing
Nonobjective painting/Acrylic
Video/Sound installation
Church/Architecture
Landmark/Oil painting
Tesselation/Pencil, ink, and watercolor
Abstract portrait/Photographic collage
Portrait in landscape/Collage
Illustration/Computer generated
Market scene/Colored woodblock print

 Unit 2

Put It All Together

"What matters is the complex relationship of color and form from one area of the painting to another. Eventually everything is intertwined."
—Janet Fish

TALK AND WRITE   How Does a Work of Art Speak?

 Janet Fish. *Kara,* 1983. Oil on canvas, 70 1/4 by 60 1/2 inches. The Museum of Fine Arts, Houston, Texas.

 Janet Fish. *August and the Red Glass,* 1976. Oil on canvas, 72 by 60 inches. Virginia Museum of Fine Arts.

1. **Describe** What has the artist shown in **A**? Look carefully and identify as many objects and symbols as you can. Describe the subject or theme of this artwork.

2. **Analyze** How did artist Janet Fish use the elements of art and principles of design to reflect the theme of **A**? Describe and analyze the visual qualities of *Kara* by writing several words that describe each art term listed below.

   Example:
   line— *curved, horizontal, bold, implied,* and so on

   pattern   shape   value
   complementary colors   contrast   space
   neutrals   shadow   emphasis
   tints   texture

   Follow how your eye moves around the composition. How do these elements work together to achieve variety? What elements provide unity?

3. **Interpret** What is the meaning of *Kara*? Describe the mood. What is Kara thinking about? How would the mood of this painting change if Kara were smiling?

4. **Judge** Look closely at **B**. How does this oil painting resemble a watercolor painting? Compare the visual qualities of **A** and **B**. How do the opaque colors in **A** "speak" differently from the transparent hues in the glasses and their reflections in **B**? How does each artwork make you feel? Why?

 **In Your Journal**

Reflect on your art-making process.

- How did you generate ideas for your theme as well as ways of working with the medium?
- How did you develop your ideas by elaborating and refining them?
- How did you put your final ideas into a meaningful form?
- Describe the creative process it took to get to your final product.

What Have You Learned?

Unit 3

Artist unknown, Nkanu culture. *Figure (drummer)*, date unknown. Carved wood with pigments, height $27^{3}/_{4}$ inches. © The Tervuren Museum, Royal Museum for Central Africa, Belgium.

A World of Art and Artists

Have you ever stumbled onto a *relic*—an object that reflects a custom or belief from the past? Perhaps you found an arrowhead, a brass doorknob, or a child's metal toy. Or maybe you have seen relics preserved in museums. Most museum relics are artworks designed and made by artisans of the past. They tell us something about our own history. In fact, artworks are sometimes the only things that have survived from ancient cultures. Most art was made to be saved—to preserve visual stories of people who walked this earth in earlier times. These visual stories may help you understand rituals performed in earlier societies, such as the African drummer figure on page 96. They may take you to a time 30,000 years ago, when people lived in caves. Or they may show you the ideas, beliefs, and values of artists who lived recently. Such an examination of **art history,** the study of art of different ages and cultures, may answer questions you have about your life today.

People who study art history are called **art historians.** Like art critics, art historians analyze and examine art. Yet, they also record turning points, discoveries, and changes in the world of art. They learn about the artists who created the artworks, and the *context,* or setting in which they lived and worked. This information helps them understand the meaning of each artwork. Art historians also study *cultural* and *artistic traditions,* such as forms of government, religious beliefs, and social activities.

The *Western tradition* began in Egypt, Greece, and Rome. It later spread to all of Europe and then to North America. Traditions from earlier times or in other parts of the world especially include art that is *functional,* or used for a purpose. Ceremonial masks and costumes, cooking utensils, and tools are examples of such artistic traditions.

As you read this unit, imagine that you are an art historian researching a brief history of Western and non-Western art. What will you look for? How will you classify the information you get? What resource materials might tell you more about the artists and artworks that especially interest you? How do each artist and artwork relate to the rest of art history? You may find yourself making connections between the history of art and other areas of history you have studied.

 **At a Glance**

What do you notice first about this sculpture?
What is the figure doing?
How does this sculpture differ from others you have seen? How is it similar?

Lesson 1: Mysteries of Long Ago

Artists have developed many techniques and tools over the years, but the beauty and spiritual power of art have been present since the beginning of the human race. This is why great art is often called "timeless." Art historians consider art created before the origins of our annual calendar as being in two groups: Prehistoric and Ancient. Often this art was created as a form of communication. Is it any wonder that many aspects of it remain a mystery?

 This cave painting is the oldest known example of Prehistoric art in the world.
Artist unknown. *Pictograph*, ca. 30,000 B.C. Chauvet Grotto, France.

Prehistoric Art

In 1995, tests on paintings of a rhinoceros and a bison in a cave in southeastern France, in **A**, proved that the artworks are more than 30,000 years old! This exciting find, according to the Culture Ministry in Paris, indicated that humans "acquired early on the mastery of drawing, [and] making paintings that were veritable works of art." This example of **Prehistoric Art** (30,000–3500 B.C.) was created at a time in which people were nomadic and lived mainly by hunting and gathering food. The cave painting in **B** shows another example of Prehistoric Art. Read the credit line to find out where it is located. What assumptions might you make about art and artists on different continents in prehistoric times?

 How does the location of this image compare with that of **A**?
Artist unknown, South African. *Rock Painting*, date unknown.

Ancient Art

If someone should ask you to describe the objects in **C**, you might say they appear to be gigantic, rough-cut stones. But how would you respond to these questions: *What was the purpose of the stones? How did they get there? How old is this architectural wonder?* Answers to these and other questions about Stonehenge remain a mystery. That is why it is sometimes referred to as "the Riddle of Salisbury Plain."

C Stonehenge is sometimes referred to as "the riddle of Salisbury Plain."

Artist unknown. *Stonehenge,* ca. 1800-1700 B.C. Stone, height approximately 13 feet. Salisbury Plain, Wiltshire, England.

Scientists have determined that Stonehenge, as an architectural form, belongs to a period of art called **Ancient Art** (3500 B.C.–A.D. 400). This ancient monument on Salisbury Plain in England still stands as a shrine to ancient spiritual traditions. Early architects used stone for religious purposes. Notice the mighty upright stones, called *menhirs,* in which ancient people believed that departed spirits lived. The "table" slabs, called *dolmens,* resting on the upright stones were used as altars or open tombs. The circular arrangement of menhirs around a dolmen, known as a *cromlech,* probably served religious and astrological purposes. The cromlech may also have been the architectural ancestor of today's temples, churches, and mosques.

Through time, some of the menhirs fell or were carried away to make bridges and milldams. From the positions of many of the stones still remaining in place, scholars have guessed that the monument probably looked like the diagram in **D**. The entire monument was surrounded by an earth wall about 300 feet around. The menhirs formed a circle 105 feet in circumference. Near the center curve of the inner horseshoe-shape was a flat block of blue marble, 15 feet long, which was probably an altar. This stone, and two others in line with it, were arranged to point toward the rising sun on the longest day of the year, or the summer solstice. How might this information help you, as an art historian, resolve a part of the mystery of Stonehenge?

In exploring art history, keep in mind that you can bring back the mood of prehistoric artworks in your own studios. Create some tools that resemble those of prehistoric artists, and let your imagination soar!

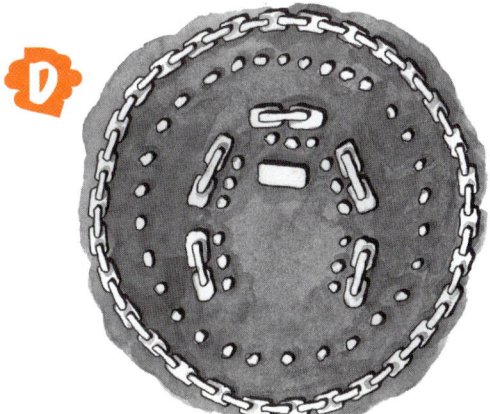

D

Creating a Cave Painting

Collect pictures of animals that may have roamed the earth during prehistoric times, such as buffalo, bison, horses, and deer. Gather materials to use as prehistoric art tools—charcoal, colors made from berries, and sticks frayed on the ends. Crumple a large brown paper bag to resemble a cave wall. Paint gesture drawings of the animals on your "cave wall" using your prehistoric art tools.

Sketchbook/Journal

Make several gesture drawings of animals. Make notes about Prehistoric Art.

Mysteries of Long Ago

Art of Ancient Egypt

Lesson 2

 Artist unknown, Egyptian. (Detail) *Egyptian Rulers and Their Crowns*, date unknown.

A Story About Egyptian Crowns

Ancient Egyptian civilization grew up 5,000 years ago (3000–500 B.C.) along the Nile River in Africa. Farmers grew crops, and craftsworkers used new technology to create tools, pottery, and jewelry. Boats delivering goods from village to village filled the river. Paintings of bloody battle scenes during this time suggest there were wars between the villages. Towns in Upper Egypt banded together to support a king who wore a white crown, while those in Lower Egypt had a king with a red crown.

Notice the three crowns in **A**, a stone relief carving from ancient Egypt. The middle crown is a *symbol* for, or represents, a victory that occurred about 3100 B.C., when King Menes' army of Upper Egypt overthrew the army of Lower Egypt. Menes' new and double crown symbolized the unification of Egypt.

This king became the first pharaoh, which would become the title of all the rulers of Egypt. Egypt's artists and craftspeople worked for the pharaohs. These artisans kept the temples supplied with beautiful objects, such as decorative furniture, golden dishes, jewelry made with gems, and handwoven textiles. In exchange, the artists and craftspeople received food and clothing.

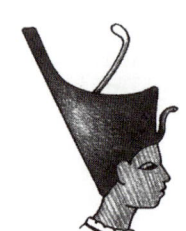  

Egyptian Tomb Paintings

Along with the stone relief carving in **A**, the wall painting in **B** tells a story about Egyptian people. Much of the information we have about ancient Egypt comes from such paintings, which decorate the walls and coffins in the tombs of wealthy Egyptians. These *tomb paintings* show scenes from the previous daily life of the buried Egyptian. How might you interpret the scene in **B**?

Notice the positions of the figures in both **A** and **B**. How would you describe the main difference in these artworks and those from other cultures? The Egyptian culture's artistic rules for showing people were to show the head, arms, and lower body in *profile*—in a side view—while showing the eye and upper torso in a front view. Observe how the figures in **A** and **B** demonstrate those rules.

King Tut's Tomb

In the Egyptian desert lies the final resting place of 30 pharaohs, known as the Valley of the Kings. One of those pharaohs ruled Egypt from the time he was about nine years old until he died at about age 18 (around 1358–1346 B.C.).

 Artist unknown, Egyptian. *Fishing Scene: Attendants with harpoons and string of fish*, 1436–1411 B.C. Copy of the original wall painting from the Tomb of Kenamun, 17 by 20 2/3 inches. Egyptian Expedition of The Metropolitan Museum of Art.

C Artist unknown, Egyptian. *Tutankhamen*, mask from mummy case, ca. 1340 B.C. Gold, lapis lazuli, and cornelian, height 21 1/4 inches. Egyptian Museum, Cairo.

Today Tutankhamen (Tut), the young pharaoh, is best known for his magnificent tomb, which was filled with art objects. This discovery was made in 1922, during a time when scholars had begun to open the tombs of ancient Egypt. Contents of these tombs were examined and later displayed in museums all over the world. Tut's tomb is the only known royal tomb to have escaped grave robbers. The value and beauty of the artworks in his small tomb give a clear idea about why thieves have been attracted to the graves of many pharaohs.

You may be familiar with King Tut's golden mask in **C**, which shows what he looked like when he was alive. His sarcophagus, or coffin, is made of carved red granite. Inside it are three coffins, one inside another, carved in human form. The innermost coffin is made of 242 pounds of solid gold. Inside the final coffin, the mask in **C** covered the head and shoulders of the mummified king. Read the credit line to discover all the materials artists used to create the mask. You will learn more about King Tut's tomb in the next lesson.

Imagine the excitement of experiencing a discovery of ancient art! How do these "stories" of art history help you envision that excitement?

Designing a Mummy Case

Use pencil and white drawing paper to create a design for a mummy case. On brown or white craft paper, redraw your design to be at least four feet tall. Cut out your design, and use gold or silver foil, markers, colored construction paper, and other media to add color to your design.

Sketchbook/Journal

Create some sketches of other mummy case designs. Make notes about Egyptian art.

Art of Ancient Egypt 101

Lesson 3: Designing Your Own Throne

Get the Picture

As you read in Lesson 2, King Tut's tomb was found in 1922. It had remained untouched for more than 3,000 years! Egyptians believed in a kind of eternal life after death, with things being more or less as they were while they were alive. The wealthy had tombs filled with tomb paintings, beautiful ornaments, and many kinds of furniture created by the best artists and artisans.

The royal throne in **A** is an example of the furniture found in King Tut's tomb. Notice that the throne is protected by lions. They do not appear ferocious, probably because the artist intended to emphasize the symbolic nature of their power. The carving on the throne is covered in gold with inlays of gems. Why do you think the artist portrayed the queen as attentive to the king with the sun god shining down on him? Would you like to sit in this chair at school? Explain why or why not.

A Artist unknown, Egyptian. *Throne of Tutankhamen*, ca. 1340 B.C. Gold-sheathed wood, carved and inlaid with precious stones. Egyptian Museum, Cairo.

Get Set

Materials you will need:
- cardboard or an old chair
- tape, glue, or glue gun
- 9" x 12" white drawing paper
- #2 pencil
- colored pencils or markers
- water-soluble paint
- brushes
- scissors
- discarded plastic jewelry, gold or silver foil, and other found objects

B Laurie, Spring Branch Middle School. *The Beaded Throne*. Foam core, mixed media, 12 by 14 by 26 inches.

How to Create Your Own Throne

1. With several classmates, plan the design for a throne. Use cardboard or an old chair as your base.

2. Make several thumbnail sketches of your framework, and sketch designs for decorating your throne. Use pencil, colored pencils, or markers on white drawing paper.

3. Work with your group to create the best parts of each person's design. Then decorate your base with those parts to create a throne.

Designing a Crown

Use pencil and white drawing paper to create a design for a crown.

On poster board, redraw your design to fit your head. Cut out your crown from the poster board. Use gold or silver foil, markers, colored construction paper, and other media to add color and detail to your design.

Sketchbook/Journal

Conduct research about Egyptian hieroglyphics and make sketches and notes of your findings.

Be an Art Critic!

1. **Describe** Tell about the special features of your group's throne.

2. **Analyze** Compare your throne with those of other groups. How are they alike? different? What special features do you notice about each one?

3. **Interpret** Describe the Egyptian king or queen who might sit on your throne. Include personality traits and physical appearance.

4. **Judge** Would you like to sit on your throne? Why? What setting would you give your throne? Explain.

Designing Your Own Throne

Lesson 4: Art of Ancient Greece

A What does this sculpture convey about the lifestyle of Spartan women?

Artist unknown, Greek. *Spartan Woman*, 6th century B.C. Bronze, height 4 1/2 inches. The British Museum, London.

The Civilization of Ancient Greece

While the Egyptians focused on the afterlife, the ancient Greeks (650–150 B.C.) concentrated on life in their time. They held in high esteem the physical form of humans, as well as their ability to reason.

A Story About the Art of Sparta and Athens

Many artifacts have been preserved from Sparta and Athens, two of Greece's city-states. These simple handmade tools or objects made by ancient artisans offer clues about the differences between life in the two cities. The sculpture in **A** shows an athletic Spartan woman running. Children in Sparta began their athletic training at age seven. Boys learned to read and write and trained to be soldiers. Girls trained to become strong mothers of strong children. Both girls and boys practiced playing ball games, throwing spears called javelins, and running.

Had you grown up in Athens, your life would have been different from that of children in Sparta. Boys worked with their fathers as farmers, or in stoneworking or pottery shops. Some wrestled or boxed at a gymnasium after work. Athenian girls did not practice sports, and they were not encouraged to ask questions or enter into discussions. Some worked in the fields to harvest crops. Most helped their mothers with duties such as weaving cloth from sheep's wool. How does the painting of Athenian women on the vase in **B** help you understand the context of their lifestyle? How do the two artworks help you understand the differences between life in Sparta and life in Athens?

 What clues about ancient Athens does the painting on this vase offer?

Artist unknown, Greek. *Women Gathering Fruit,* ca. 5th century B.C. Red-figured cup. Musée Vivenel, Compiègne, France.

C

Etruscan vase painting was inspired by Greek art.

Painter of Micali. *Hydria with Running Figures,* date unknown. Museo Gregoriano Etrusco, Rome.

Greek Style of Painting

Writings from ancient Greece tell us that Greek painters were often better known than Greek sculptors. Unfortunately, no known paintings on panels or walls survive. However, we can get a glimpse at styles of Greek painting by studying Etruscan vase painting, which imitated Greek-imported artworks. The Etruscan vase in **C** is a fine example of the Greek "black-figured" style. In addition to the beauty of such vases, they also served the practical purpose of holding olive oil. How would you describe the subject painted on this *twin-handled vase?* If you assume that the vase is indeed fashioned after the Greek style, which culture—Spartan or Athenian—do you think it represents? What technique did the artist use to show a sense of movement?

A popular athletic celebration today was first held nearly 3,000 years ago in ancient Greece. You know the celebration as the Olympic Games! Think about how you might show movement on a poster to advertise an Olympic event.

Making a Poster for the Olympics

Collect magazine and newspaper photographs of athletes competing in events that are also part of the Olympics. Ask a friend to role-play the movements while you create a gesture drawing of your favorite event. Include your gesture drawing on a poster to advertise the next summer or winter Olympics. Remember to work the title, date, place, and other information into your design. Add color using markers, construction paper, or other color media.

Sketchbook/Journal

Draw several thumbnail sketches of poster designs for an athletic event at your school. Make notes about the art of ancient Greece.

Art of Ancient Greece

Lesson 5: Art of Ancient Rome

The Civilization of Ancient Rome

Not far from Greece, ancient Romans (753 B.C.–A.D. 476) were building their empire in Italy. The Romans eventually conquered the Greeks. By 100 B.C. the Roman republic extended around the Mediterranean Sea and included millions of people. Romans admired Greek civilization so much that they collected and copied many Greek artworks. In this way, the art of both Greece and Rome spread throughout the area.

Style of Roman Portraiture

Not all Roman art was imitative. While Greeks emphasized ideal beauty and proportions in art, Romans were more concerned with functional and realistic aspects of art. Roman artists often painted or sculpted **portraits**, artworks showing a person or a group of people. Many Roman portraits, as in **A**, focus on how the subject actually looked, rather than the Greek approach of how an ideal subject might look. Notice that the sculptor worked carefully to show imperfections and other individual traits, which bring character to the person's face. This representational style possibly originated with the custom of making wax death masks of ancestors for the family shrine. Perhaps in a museum you have seen a marble portrait that was re-created from such masks.

 What distinguishing features do you see in this Roman sculpture that you most likely would not see in a Greek sculpture of the same model?

Artist unknown, Roman. *Portrait Bust*, ca. A.D. 54–117. Marble, lifesize. Museo Lateranense, Vatican Museums.

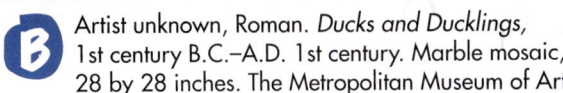 Artist unknown, Roman. *Ducks and Ducklings*, 1st century B.C.–A.D. 1st century. Marble mosaic, 28 by 28 inches. The Metropolitan Museum of Art.

 Laine, Dobie Middle School. *Clear, Blue Waters*. Mosaic of torn construction paper and magazine photographs, 12 by 16 inches.

Roman Mosaics

As a way of expressing their ideas and feelings, Romans created many **mosaics** on walls, furniture, sidewalks, and other surfaces. Some mosaics showed colorful patterns of geometric and organic shapes. Others conveyed realistic stories about people, events, places, and animals, as in **B**. Like most modern mosaics, those from ancient Rome were made of **tesserae**. These small bits of materials such as glass, colored tiles, or pieces of marble, as in **B**, were glued onto a flat surface such as wood or cement. The spaces around the tesserae were filled with *grout*, a plasterlike substance. Many Roman mosaics were so finely constructed that the various shades of tesserae showed shadows of objects.

The kinds of art that Romans created continues to be popular today. Where have you seen a mosaic? You can make your own mosaic by gathering found objects such as glass, broken tiles, and shells.

Making an Animal Mosaic

Cut and tear into small pieces, or tesserae, a variety of colors of construction paper and colored pages from magazines. Using white chalk on black construction paper, draw a large animal shape. Arrange the tesserae on the black paper, using contrasting tints and shades to make your subject stand out. Glue the tesserae in place.

Sketchbook/Journal

Draw several thumbnail sketches of ideas for mosaics. Make notes about ancient Rome.

Art of Ancient Rome

Lesson 6
Designing a Model with Arches

Get the Picture

Roman engineers, sculptors, and architects often worked together to build beautiful and useful structures. These monuments, such as aqueducts, temples, and bridges, reflected the empire's great power and wealth. For places of entertainment, they built huge stadiums. Notice the *Colosseum* in **A**, which held 50,000 spectators! People came to see gladiators fight wild animals—lions and bears—or each other. Sadly, the gladiators were enslaved people, condemned criminals, or prisoners of war, who were forced to fight for their lives in the bloody contests.

Some people say the most outstanding feature of Roman architecture, which is still popular today, is the classic *arch*, a semicircular form. The diagram in **B** shows various types of Roman arches. Notice their long-lasting strength. Roman architects mixed sand, lime, and bits of brick and stone to make the first cement. This cement became the binder, holding together the larger stones and bricks in structures. Almost two thousand years later, during the nineteenth century, a stronger form of concrete gained popularity and is widely used today.

 Architect unknown, Roman. *Colosseum*, ca. A.D. 72–80. Rome, Italy.

 Julia, Hill Country Middle School. *My Town.* Tempera on paper, 12 by 18 inches.

Get Set

Materials you will need:
- photographs of arches
- 9" x 12" white drawing paper
- #2 pencil
- 12" x 18" white drawing paper
- colored pencils

Lesson 6

How to Design a Model with Arches

1. Collect photographs of different types of arches from magazines and newspapers.

2. Practice drawing all the arches you see in B. Draw sketches of the arches in the photographs you found.

3. Design an arch of your own. You might combine some features of many arches you have learned about.

4. Use colored pencils on a clean sheet of paper to create an imaginary design of a space station that showcases your arch and others.

Designing Your Own Restaurant

Draw several designs of the front of a restaurant of the future that will serve your favorite kind of food. Create your restaurant using your favorite media.

Sketchbook/Journal

Sketch your own designs for arches. Make notes about their features.

Be an Art Critic!

1. **Describe** Tell a friend about each feature of your model space station. Include line, shape, color, and texture.

2. **Analyze** Find examples of symmetrical and asymmetrical balance in your composition.

3. **Interpret** What kind of music would be appropriate to play in your space station? Explain why.

4. **Judge** Would you like to live in the space station you designed? Explain.

Designing a Model with Arches

Lesson 7: Art of the Middle Ages

What Are the Middle Ages?

The *Medieval Period* (A.D. 400–about 1400) represents the one thousand years that followed the fall of the Western Roman Empire. In the past, historians have also referred to this period as the **Middle Ages**—as though these years filled a gap between two, more important periods. The Middle Ages indeed occurred between the time of the ancient Greek and Roman civilizations and the "rebirth" of the ideas of those civilizations during the fifteenth century. A wealth of creative energy and beautiful artworks emerged from the Middle Ages.

Medieval Animal-Style

Medieval artists were especially productive in northern Europe and England—and extended through Asia to the borders of China. Animals became a popular subject for jewelry and other ornamentation. These artworks represented the **animal style**, especially popular in Germany and Scandinavia. Sculptors in Norway created splendid ship carvings that included animal-style ornaments for Vikings to place on the front of their ships. Vikings believed these wood carvings, as in **A**, had symbolic power. By their own laws, they removed these figures from their ships before they landed at a port. They were afraid they might frighten spirits of the land.

The animal style was popular among Scandinavian artists.

Artist unknown, Scandinavian. *Dragon's Head,* ca. A.D. 850. Carved wood. Viking Ship Museum, Bygdoy, Norway.

Reinhard, St. Luke's Episcopal School. *The Sword of Freedom.* Tempera and marker on paper, 12 by 18 inches.

Look closely at the detailed subtractive carving in **A**. If you have a magnifying glass, study the variations in texture and pattern. What mood would you give this dragon? Is it laughing? crying? seething? Does it appear friendly? angry? attentive? asleep? Where would you display such a sculpture? Why?

 Architects of castles designed structures to last many centuries.
Architect unknown. *Caerlaverock Castle*, ca. A.D. 1270. Dumfries, Scotland.

D Christopher, Kirby Middle School. *Charging.* Tempera on paper, 12 by 18 inches.

Medieval Castles

During the Middle Ages, wars broke out among kings and other wealthy landholders. These landowners fought each other to hold onto their lands. As protection from invaders, wealthy English and European rulers and landowners had architects design *castles*. These fortlike dwellings had high stone walls and strong towers. Notice the *crenations,* or curved and scalloped edges, in **C**, which appear around the top of each tower. Why do you think the windows are small and narrow?

Situated in Scotland, Caerlaverock Castle was often attacked during neighboring English battles. Typical of castles, Caerlaverock is surrounded by a moat and a drawbridge for added protection. This castle is about 700 years old. How many new buildings in your community may last that long?

Creating a Medieval Design

Draw a sketch of a family crest that you might like to hang on your wall. In the design, show a dragon, a lion, or another animal, along with your initials. Enlarge the sketch on poster board, cardboard, or matte board, and cut it out. Color your crest with a variety of media. Make a part of the design in relief by placing cardboard or foam core behind it.

Sketchbook/Journal

Draw a sketch of other objects that might be symbols on a family crest. Make notes about what each object might symbolize.

Art of the Middle Ages

Lesson 8

Creating an Illuminated Storybook

Get the Picture

You have learned about animal-style Viking sculptures and Medieval castles. Yet, art in Europe during the Middle Ages was devoted almost entirely to serving the Christian church. This period in history is known for its soaring cathedrals, sculptures of religious figures, paintings of Christian scenes, stained glass for churches, needleworks, and illuminated books about religion. These **illuminations,** as they were called, were handpainted illustrations for books. They often showed scenes from Bible stories. The story in **A** is about King David, a figure from the Old Testament. Notice how each frame tells a part of a story. These illustrations helped the masses of people who could not read to understand the history of Christianity.

Stained-glass windows, such as the sparkling rose window in **B**, served a similar purpose. They were designed to portray the history of Christianity to illiterate churchgoers through images and symbols from the Bible. Many of these elegant windows still illuminate interior spaces of Medieval cathedrals throughout England and Europe. Notice that the pieces of brightly colored glass are held together by thin strips of lead. Is the tradition of Medieval stained-glass windows present in your community today? Give examples.

A Artist unknown, French. *Wenceslaus Psalter,* ca. 1250–1260. Ink, tempera colors, and gold leaf on vellum, bound between pasteboard covered with deep violet morocco, $7^{9}/_{16}$ by $5^{1}/_{4}$ inches. The J. Paul Getty Museum, Los Angeles.

Get Set

Materials you will need:
- 3 sheets of 9" x 12" white drawing paper
- #2 pencil
- colored pencils, markers, and other media
- gold or silver nontoxic markers or paint and brush
- stapler

B Artist unknown, French. *Rose de France,* ca. A.D.1200. Stained-glass window, Chartres Cathedral, Chartres, France.

How to Make an Illuminated Storybook

1. Fold three sheets of paper in half and staple them together on the center fold.

2. Write one or two sentences on each page that builds into an adventure you and your friends have in a Medieval castle. Use an interesting lettering style, and leave white spaces for illustrations.

3. Illustrate each sentence of your story with colored markers. Add gold or silver with marker or paint to each page.

4. Give your book a title, and decorate the front of your illuminated storybook.

Making a Stained-Glass Window

Fold a sheet of 9" x 9" black construction paper into fourths and then into a triangle. Cut small shapes from the completely folded edge. Unfold the paper until you find the first fold. Cut more shapes from that fold. Unfold the paper completely. Glue a variety of colors of tissue paper to the back of your design.

 **Sketchbook/Journal**

Draw sketches of Medieval castles. Make notes about architectural features of castles.

 **Be an Art Critic!**

1. **Describe** What is happening in your illuminated storybook?
2. **Analyze** Compare the illustrations from page to page. How are they similar? different?
3. **Interpret** How does the setting of your story affect the mood of the illustrations?
4. **Judge** Which page of your storybook would you select to showcase in an advertisement of your work? Explain.

Creating an Illuminated Storybook 113

Lesson 9
Architecture in the Early Americas

American Culture Before Columbus

You have probably learned about Columbus and other European explorers. During the fifteenth and sixteenth centuries, they happened onto two large continents due west of their homelands. They were surprised to find the Americas inhabited by a variety of well-developed cultures. In fact, North and South America were inhabited by Native American civilizations that were probably as old as civilizations in Europe and Asia. These American cultures had developed their own languages, writing, art objects, such as ceramics and jewelry, and architecture. Among cultures belonging to that *Pre-Columbian era*—the centuries before the arrival of Columbus in the Americas—were the Mayan and the Anasazi civilizations. Each of these cultures created its own style of architecture.

Mayan Architecture

The Mayan civilization (ca. A.D. 300–900) was a powerful culture in what is now Mexico, Guatemala, and Honduras. The Maya were masters of higher-level thinking skills. They developed an elaborate calendar and a written language. They also developed large temple constructions of stone. An agricultural society, the Maya farmed the land around these stone temples. At the top of the 200-foot–high pyramid in **A** is a temple with three rooms. This *Temple I* still stands today in Tikal, Guatemala. It is only one among hundreds of nearby temples. The priests who lived in the temples held great power. The farmers followed the priests' predictions about agricultural cycles, based on the refined Mayan calendar. Walls and roofs of Mayan temples were painted by artists, and some contained a burial chamber. What similarities might you draw between Mayan and Egyptian civilizations?

Scholars believe that Tikal, the Mayan city that surrounded this temple, may have had a population of 75,000–100,000 during the Late Classic period (A.D. 550–900).

Architect unknown, Mayan culture. *Temple I,* ca. A.D. 300–900. Tikal, Guatemala.

 **How does the architectural design of this housing structure compare with some modern apartment complexes?**

Architect unknown, Anasazi culture. *Cliff Palace*, ca. A.D. 600. Mesa Verde National Park, Colorado.

 Lindsey, Collins Intermediate. *Performing and Visual Arts Museum*. Mixed media, approximately 18 by 16 by 12 inches.

Anasazi Architecture

The *Anasazi*, a Navajo word meaning the "Ancient Ones," have lived in North America from about 5500 B.C. to the present. Their name refers to prehistoric Basket Makers and Pueblo Indians of North America. About 1,400 years ago, the Anasazi began building their homes into cliffsides in what is now southwestern Colorado. The village is now called Mesa Verde, or Green Tabletop. The Anasazi lived in their cliffside village from about A.D. 600 to 1300. A major center of Anasazi trade and religion took place in the Cliff Palace, shown in **B**. Notice that this architectural design is similar to that of a modern apartment complex. Each of the rooms is joined by a connecting wall, and everyone shared outdoor common space. Today tourists of Mesa Verde often wonder: How did the Anasazi safely manage their children while living on the side of a steep cliff? The question remains unresolved.

What kinds of artworks from Native American cultures have you seen? Explore ways in which their architecture has influenced modern buildings and structures in your community.

Combining Old and New Designs

Use a pencil and white drawing paper to create a plan for modernizing one or more structures of early American architecture. Include people in modern dress in the foreground, middle ground, and background. Use a variety of media to add color.

Sketchbook/Journal

Describe the people who might use the structure you designed. Draw some sketches of them at work and at play.

Architecture in the Early Americas

Lesson 10: Art of the Renaissance in Europe

Leonardo da Vinci kept many detailed sketchbook/journals, in which he recorded ideas and observations as they came to him.

Leonardo da Vinci. *Mona Lisa*, 1503–1506. Oil on wood, 30 1/4 by 21 inches. Musée de Louvre, Paris.

What Was the Renaissance?

During the last years of the Anasazi civilization at Mesa Verde, an exciting change was emerging in the ideas and artworks of Europe. This cultural shift began in Italy. During the next 300 years, it spread throughout Europe. The **Renaissance,** as it is called, means "rebirth or reawakening." Many Europeans decided to "awake" from the Middle Ages to rediscover Classical Greek and Roman ideas and art. In addition, an enthusiasm for learning about humanity arose. Europeans took part in the rise of cities, voyages of discovery, the beginning of free thinking, and the origins of modern science. They reaped the benefits of new inventions, such as the printing press. In essence, the Renaissance was a period of new and renewed understanding that departed from Medieval times and laid the foundation for modern art and society.

A New Age for Artists

During the Renaissance, new ideas and technological advances inspired an outpouring of artistic expression. People began to think of artists as individuals of creative genius, rather than as craftspeople. Both men and women became recognized for the beautiful artworks they created.

Leonardo da Vinci

The *Mona Lisa* is a world-famous painting and a favorite of its Renaissance creator—Leonardo da Vinci. Leonardo, as he was called, was born in Italy and began his artistic career as an apprentice at the age of fifteen. By the time he died, at age 67, he had explored the fields of art, science, mathematics, and philosophy. Is it any wonder that he is called a "Renaissance person"?

If you study Leonardo's portrait of the *Mona Lisa,* you may see another of his inventions. It is called **sfumato**—a technique of painting soft, blurry, smokelike edges in the background. This otherworldly landscape, along with the subject's faint smile, create a mysterious mood. What message do you think the artist intended to convey through this painting?

 Sofonisba Anguissola realized success as an artist during the Renaissance.

Sofonisba Anguissola. *Portrait of Amilcare, Minerva, and Astrubale Anguissola*, ca.1559. Oil on canvas, 61 13/16 by 48 1/32 inches. Nivaagards Malerisammling, Niva, Denmark.

Students of Brentwood directed by Frederick Graber and Sammie Gray. *Celebrate Austin*, mural for magazine cover design. Acrylic paint on canvas, 48 by 60 inches. Photograph © Andrew Yates, courtesy of Celebrate Publications, Austin, Texas.

Sofonisba Anguissola

Study the portrait in **B**, by the first woman artist of the Renaissance to gain an international reputation. Sofonisba Anguissola portrayed her family—her father, sister, brother, and family dog—in this painting. Notice the implied—in fact, invisible—diagonal line created by the gaze of the children's eyes. The background is painted with the sfumato technique. Why would a Renaissance artist include what appear to be Roman ruins?

Murals were also a popular form of painting during the Renaissance. To create murals, painters enlarged and transferred their designs onto the ceilings and walls of buildings. They worked with others to paint the colorful murals. Think of a story you could create as a mural that might inspire your community to celebrate the arts.

Creating a Renaissance Mural

Work with a partner to create a horizontal design for a mural to celebrate a "rebirth," or renaissance, of the arts in your community. Transfer your design to 36" x 54" white craft paper, using a three-inch square grid. Add color to the mural using tempera paint.

Sketchbook/Journal

Write a journal entry about whether you like to work alone or with other people. Include your experience in making a mural. Draw sketches of you alone and working with others.

Art of the Renaissance in Europe 117

Lesson 11: Eastern Art of Long Ago

 How does the subject of this painting from India resemble those of cave paintings you have studied?

Attributed to Miskin. *Buffaloes in Combat,* late 16th century. Brush and ink with color on paper, 6 7/8 by 9 1/2 inches. The Metropolitan Museum of Art.

What Is Eastern Art?

You have probably seen examples of Western art in your community. But what about Eastern art—the art of Asia? This includes the artworks of China, Japan, Tibet, India, Vietnam, and other countries in the Eastern Hemisphere. In this lesson you will explore the art of two Eastern cultures: India and China.

The Art of India

The earliest Indian artworks were sculptures created by artists of the Indus civilization (2500–1700 B.C.). Along with the coming of Eastern religions, from about 550 B.C.–A.D. 700, came a host of new artforms. Architects designed temples and mosques with sandstone pillars and columns. Sculptors formed mythical images of people and animals from clay, stone, and bronze. Painters created murals in caves and decorated reliefs carved to show stories from traditional Hindu, Buddhist, or Islamic religions. Semi-precious stones and beautiful tiles became tesserae for mosaics on walls and sidewalks.

The painting in **A** was created in India at about the same time the Renaissance in Europe was at its peak. Its subject—bulls fighting, with men dancing in the background—was common among Indian paintings. How does this subject matter compare to that of early cave paintings in France and South Africa, you may recall from Lesson 1? What conclusions might you draw about art around the world?

B

Can you find embroidered stitchery on this banner?

Artist unknown, Chinese. *Winged Tiger*, 19th century. One of a pair of banners, silk embroidery on silk, 46 1/2 by 46 inches. The Metropolitan Museum of Art.

C

Dolores, Hill Country Middle School. *Untitled*. Construction paper, tempera, and markers on paper, 36 by 54 inches.

The Art of China

Art in China was flourishing at the same time that the Renaissance took place in Europe. During the Ming dynasty (A.D. 1368–1644), Chinese artists developed fine *porcelain*. Dishes and vases made of this translucent ceramic are among the most treasured of Chinese artworks. Silk was another type of medium special to China at that time. The Chinese perfected and exported textiles made of these materials to other countries.

Study the lively design of the silk banner in **B**, a nineteenth-century silk textile from China. Notice the tiny stitches, which were *embroidered*, or sewn onto the silk background, to show the flying tiger and other designs. The textile artist planned slits around the borders to allow the wind to pass through the banner without tearing it.

Identify modern dishes, banners, and other objects that were popular long ago in Eastern art. What is similar about the old and the new designs? How have they changed?

Creating a Banner

On drawing paper, create a vertical design for a school spirit or an event banner. Transfer the drawing to a 36" x 54" sheet of white butcher or kraft paper with a three-inch square grid. Use construction paper, tempera paint, and other media to add color.

Sketchbook/Journal

Describe the meaning of any symbols you might have used in your banner. Draw sketches to help explain the meaning of your symbols.

Eastern Art of Long Ago

Lesson 12: Western Art of the Nineteenth and Twentieth Centuries

 This realistic painting is one of Rosa Bonheur's best-known artworks.
Rosa Bonheur. *The Horse Fair,* 1853. Oil on canvas, approximately 8 by 16 feet. The Metropolitan Museum of Art.

Art of the Modern Era

Art of the past two hundred years (1800 to the present) is known for its many artistic styles and movements. During this time, artists were free to experiment in expressing their ideas and feelings. No sooner had one art movement begun than another followed closely behind. Artists worked alone and together as individuals and as group explorers of paint, sculpture, collage, and other media.

Realistic Art

Toward the middle of the nineteenth century, a group of artists began to see the canvas as an opportunity to express what their senses really perceived. They began to place a strong emphasis on **Realism,** a style of art that seeks to represent objects as they are perceived by the senses rather than to idealize or interpret them. This style of art, often called **Realistic Art,** became the dominant artistic style of the second half of the nineteenth century.

During that time, Rosa Bonheur was taking painting lessons from her father. In 1841, when she was only nineteen, she had her first exhibition at the Salon, an annual art show in Paris. By then she knew that animals were her favorite subject. In 1850 she began an eighteen-month study of horses for her most spectacular painting, *The Horse Fair,* in **A**. The restless subjects on the huge canvas seem to charge toward the foreground of the composition and then turn to disappear into the background. This realistic painting was the hit of the Salon of 1853, and two years later it sold for forty thousand francs (approximately $7,121 U.S. currency).

German Expressionism

By the time the twentieth century had arrived, artists had developed many more styles of art. In Germany a group of artists called *The Blue Rider* worked together to express their thoughts and feelings using color, shape, and rhythm. Their style of

 Can you find an identifiable subject in this painting?
Wassily Kandinsky. *Improvisation 19a*, 1911. Oil on canvas, 38 1/4 by 41 3/4 inches. Städtische Galerie im Lenbachhaus, Munich. GMS 84.

using simple designs and brilliant colors to express their feelings became known as **German Expressionism.** The style of **B** is an example of German Expressionism.

Nonobjective Art

The style in **B** is also considered an example of **Nonobjective Art**; the painting shows color, form, and texture—but not recognizable subject matter—as its content. The artist of **B**, Wassily Kandinsky, painted most often in this nonobjective style. However, he may have created some hidden imagery in this composition. Some say they can define mountains, hills, stooping figures, hands, and other shapes. What do you see in this painting? What mood does it convey?

Many differences separate Realistic Art and Nonobjective Art. Realistic Art portrays a specific subject, while Nonobjective Art does not represent real objects. Think about how you might use colors differently in both styles. Which style better represents the imagination?

Creating a Comparison of Art Styles

Fold a sheet of 9" x 18" white drawing paper in half. On one side, create a realistic drawing or painting of an object. On the other side, create an imaginative and colorful composition in a nonobjective style.

 ### Sketchbook/Journal

Make a list of styles from the Modern Art period. Beside each style, draw an example. Note the differences in your realistic and nonobjective styles of the same object.

Western Art of the Nineteenth and Twentieth Centuries

Lesson 13: Creating an Abstract Collage

Can you find the artist's abstract shapes of ivy leaves and flowers?

Henri Matisse. *Ivy in Flower,* 1953. Colored paper and pencil, 112 by 112 inches. Dallas Museum of Art, Foundation for the Arts Collection, gift of the Albert and Mary Lasker Foundation.

Get the Picture

In Unit 1 you read that Henri Matisse liked to draw and paint. Did you know that he was also a *collagist?* Look at his *Ivy in Flower* in **A**. It is a **maquette,** or a trial model for a larger artwork. In this case, the maquette is a collage for a stained-glass window. Notice the intended lack of depth and perspective as well as the simplified shapes in this **abstract** composition. In this way, Matisse challenged styles generally accepted in the art world since the Renaissance. He did not realistically portray a subject, but instead focused on simplified color and pattern with flat shapes. This mastery of two-dimensional representation led Matisse to the use of collage exclusively toward the end of his life. He was by then physically unable to work at his easel. With failing eyesight and sitting in his wheelchair, he cut large, bold shapes with scissors. Then he instructed his assistant where to place them on the wall across the room. In this way, he continued his career as an artist through the medium of collage.

Get Set

 **Materials you will need:**
- small sheet of paper
- scissors
- composition from your Portfolio
- 12" x 18" white drawing paper
- #2 pencil
- colored tissue paper
- glue and water mixture
- paintbrush
- oil pastels and/or black felt-tip pen

How to Create an Abstract Collage

1. Cut a hole in a sheet of paper. Look through it to find an interesting nonobjective design in a composition from your Portfolio.

2. Draw the design lightly with pencil on white drawing paper.

3. Glue colored tissue paper to your design to show color and shape.

4. When the tissue paper is dry, add more color using oil pastels. Outline some shapes with a black felt-tip pen.

Working from a Thumbnail Sketch

Choose a favorite abstract, thumbnail sketch from your Sketchbook/Journal. Lightly enlarge the design on drawing paper. Add color to your design with drawing or painting media.

Sketchbook/Journal

Describe emotions your abstract collage expresses. Create a sketch about any feelings it may help you express.

Be an Art Critic!

1. **Describe** Discuss the texture and color in your collage.
2. **Analyze** How does your abstract design differ from realistic designs you have created?
3. **Interpret** How would you describe the mood of this abstract collage?
4. **Judge** In what ways might you use or display your abstract artwork? How would a color change make your design different?

Creating an Abstract Collage

Talk About Art

 This Nigerian artist displays her pottery at the marketplace.

The term *African art* usually refers to the traditional art created by *African artists* living south of the Sahara Desert. Nearly all African peoples have produced artists such as dancers, musicians, storytellers, rock painters, architects, and masters at decoration. However, only those groups dwelling in the vast areas by the Niger and Congo rivers have produced the well-known wood sculptures, such as the one in **B**. Unfortunately, the names of many African artists, such as the one in **A**, do not appear on their artworks. For this reason, the credit line, as in **B**, reads "Artist unknown."

Before contemporary changes in governments, professional artists in Africa were often employed by the king or chief of a cultural group. They were assigned to create artworks that celebrated his interests and concerns. Many African artists, then and now are wood sculptors. After they carve a sculpture, such as the drummer in **B**, they smoke the wood and rub it with oil or clay to create the desired finish. Because wood does not last long, most African wood sculptures from more than 150 years ago have not survived. However, many stone and bronze sculptures from earlier African cultures are still in existence.

Ceremonial events are important sources of identity for members of many cultural groups. Artworks used in these ceremonial events represent the values and beliefs of these groups. Many African sculptures are made to help tribe members worship ancestors and spirits, ask the deities for a good harvest, and seek protection from evil. African artists seldom portray actual persons or animals in their ceremonial sculptures. Instead, they prefer to create human or animal images that represent the spiritual or humanistic ideas of their group.

Drummer figures, such as the one in **B**, are often used during rituals of initiation to male adulthood by family and friends in the cultural group. Their purpose is to frighten away evil. Notice the importance of color in this figure. Artists of the Nkanu people are noted for their emphasis on color and the natural facial expressions of their subjects. They sometimes choose organic shapes to draw attention to facial expressions. For example, like in other carvings of the Nkanu people, this drummer's head is shaped as an oval. The upper face is enclosed within a large egg-shaped relief line, and the encircled features are distinctly rounded. What other examples of organic shapes and forms do you see in **B**? What kinds of drumbeats might you imagine the sculptor had in mind for this ceremonial figure?

 **Many African sculptures, such as this one, are used during ceremonial events.**

Artist unknown, Nkanu culture. *Figure (drummer)*, date unknown. Carved wood with pigments, height 27 3/4 inches. © The Tervuren Museum, Royal Museum for Central Africa, Belgium.

Designing a Symbol of Celebration

Think of a family celebration or a special anniversary. Draw a sketch of a wood sculpture you might carve in honor of the celebration. Write about the intended meaning of your artwork.

Be an Art Critic!

Look at B to answer these questions:

1. **Describe** Tell about the forms you see in the drummer figure. How would you describe his facial expression? What do you notice about his feet?
2. **Analyze** How did the sculptor show emphasis? What special effect unifies this sculpture?
3. **Interpret** Based on what you have read about the drummer, how would you interpret the artist's intention? What message might the sculptor have intended the drummer to convey?
4. **Judge** If you were arranging an African exhibition in a museum gallery, where would you place this sculpture? Explain why.

Talk About Art 125

Portfolio Project

 **Materials you will need:**
- sketch paper
- #2 pencil
- clay and clay tools
- water color, tempera, or glaze
- brush

Creating a Clay Object About History

To help you with this Studio, refer to pages, 260–263. Imagine that you could go back in time to any period and place in the history of art. How might you portray your favorite object of that time period?

1. Create several thumbnail sketches of your favorite objects made by artists any time during the history of art.

2. Use ceramic clay to re-create a larger version of your favorite thumbnail sketch in three dimensions.

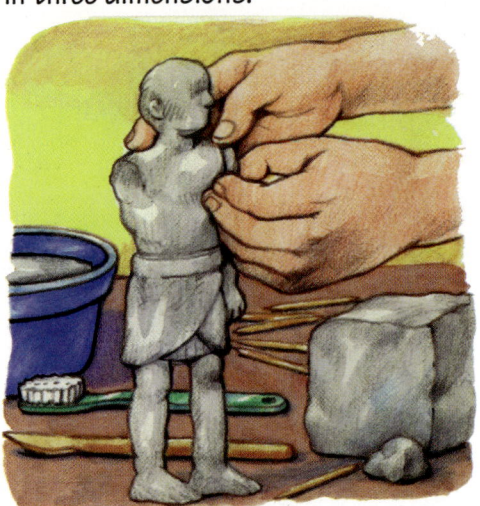

3. Remember to score any parts that fit together, and use slip to adhere them.

4. After your clay figure has been dried and fired, paint it with watercolor, tempera, or glaze.

Gallery

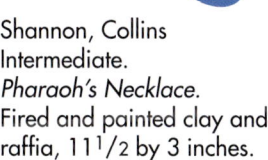
Kim, Collins Intermediate. *Bird of Prey.* Fired and painted clay, $7^{1}/_{2}$ by 3 by $3^{3}/_{4}$ inches.

Shannon, Collins Intermediate. *Pharaoh's Necklace.* Fired and painted clay and raffia, $11^{1}/_{2}$ by 3 inches.

Jenny, Collins Intermediate. *Ancient Vase.* Fired and painted clay, 4 by $6^{1}/_{4}$ inches.

Portfolio Project

Art Links

MUSIC

Exploring Instruments Across Time and Cultures

Visual art keeps changing as technology develops and artists invent new tools. So does music change: new instruments are invented, old ones are modified, and some fall out of fashion. The early keyboard, called the clavichord, gave way to the harpsichord. This instrument developed into the pianoforte, then the piano, the electric piano, and finally the synthesizer.

Collect and compare music played on various forms of keyboards in different centuries: for example, your collection may include music by Bach (harpsichord), Chopin (piano), Herbie Hancock (electric piano), and Jan Hammer (synthesizer). Listen to the works in chronological order. What impression do you get of the historical change from Bach's time to now? You may also compare music played on variations of the same kinds of instruments around the world: for example, the Spanish guitar, the Russian balalaika, the Indian sitar, and the Appalachian bluegrass banjo. How would you describe the various cultural "flavors"? Match each sound to a painting from that culture.

DANCE

Describing Familiar Dances Through New Eyes

When you see the art of another culture, you tend to notice how it differs from your own. The same is true of dance styles. In Irish line dancing, what may strike you is a certain stillness: the dancers' upper bodies hardly change position. Their legs do all the dancing. In Indian temple dancing, by contrast, you may notice only motion at first: in this dance style every part of the dancer's body–down to the eyeballs and fingertips–moves.

See if you can find a video or TV show of dancing from a culture that is not your own. You might look at African, Caribbean, Brazilian, Indian, Chinese, English, or any other style of dancing. Imagine a person from this culture watching the type of dance you are most used to seeing. What do you think he or she would notice? Describe what you consider "ordinary" dancing from this person's point of view.

THEATRE

Performing as a Chorus

The roots of painting go back to magic: for example, cave paintings created some 30,000 years ago in France were probably part of some ritual meant to help hunters find game. The roots of theatre also go back to rituals and magic. Greek drama, for example, grew out of ceremonies in which groups of people chanted certain verses together. This group was called the Chorus. It remained a "character" in Greek plays long after these plays had taken the form of dramatic stories.

You can get some sense of the emotional impact of a Chorus by working with a group of ten or more friends. Browse through plays for a solemn speech or select a speech such as the Gettysburg Address that takes at least a minute or so to read. Memorize and practice the lines until all ten of you can recite the words together—dramatically. Then perform your speech or monologue for an audience of friends or family. Notice how having many voices speaking as one adds power and mystery to the words.

LITERATURE

Debating "Experimental" Literature

In the twentieth century, visual artists broke down the connection between art and objective reality. They created abstract and non-objective art. Writers tried similar experiments, even though abstract literature may seem impossible. In the 1930s, Gertrude Stein wrote whole books full of "sentences" like these:

> *If it and as if it, if it or as if it, if it is as if it, and it is as if it and as if it. Or as if it. More as if it. As more. As more as if it. And if it. And for and as if it.*
>
> —from *Van or Twenty Years After*

Does this passage tend to show that "abstract" literature is possible? Or does it tend to show the opposite? Debate the question with a group of classmates.

ArtLinks 129

Unit 3

What Have You Learned?
Explore the Language of Art

Artist unknown. *The Court of Empress Theodora*, A.D. 547. Early Christian mosaic. S. Vitale, Ravenna, Italy. Photograph by Scala/Art Resource, New York.

Illustration of *The Court of Empress Theodora*.

TALK AND WRITE — Can You Find . . . ?

Where Am I?

Match each art term below with the letter in the illustration of *The Court of Empress Theodora* on page 130.

1. pattern
2. tesserae
3. overlapping
4. circular shapes
5. arch with vaulted dome
6. headdress/crown
7. warm color
8. geometric motif
9. decorative medallions
10. repetition
11. shadowy folds
12. negative space

How Am I?

Using the language of art, respond to the following questions.

1. Describe the three figures—their expressions and actions. What is the setting?

2. How were the figures and background created? Examine the facial features, noting the stylized proportions.
   What type of balance was used in the composition?

3. Follow how your eye moves around the mosaic.
   In addition to the barely visible tesserae, what provides unity?

4. How can you tell that the woman is a member of a royal family? What is the mood of *The Court of Empress Theodora?* What is happening here?

5. A group of craftspeople created this wall mosaic to decorate San Vitale Church in Ravenna, Italy in A.D. 547. Speculate how this mosaic "tells" a story to worshippers and visitors, then and now. Where do we see mosaics in our world today?
   How do they enhance architecture and public spaces?

What Have You Learned?

Write About Art

A Artist unknown. (Detail) *Queen Tiy from the Tomb of Userhat,* 18th dynasty. Limestone relief, 16¾ by 15½ inches. Courtesy of Musées Royaux d'Art et d'Histoire, Brussels, Belgium.

B Artist unknown. *Nataraja: Siva as King of Dance.* South India, Chola Period, 11th century. Bronze, height 44½ inches. © The Cleveland Museum of Art, 1996, purchase from the J. H. Wade Fund, 1930.331.

C Georges Rouault. *The Old King,* 1916–1936. Oil on canvas, 30¼ by 21¼ inches. Carnegie Museum of Art, Pittsburgh, Patrons Art Fund. 40.1. © 1997 Artists Rights Society (ARS), New York/ADAGP, Paris.

 In Your Own Words

Compare and contrast A, B and C.

1. What is similar?
2. What is different?
3. How does each artwork reflect the ruler's wealth and power?
4. What does each artwork "say" about its culture and history?
5. Compare A, B, and C to *The Court of Empress Theodora* on page 130.

Re-View

 Do You Know the Order?

For each *artform* below, number the *artworks* to indicate the correct chronological order.

Architecture
Colosseum, ca. A.D. 72–80
Caerlaverock Castle, ca. A.D. 1270
Cliff Palace, ca. A.D. 600
Stonehenge, ca. 2000 B.C.

Sculpture
Dragon's Head, ca. A.D. 820
Portrait Bust, Roman, A.D. 54–117
Tutankhamen (mask), ca. 1340 B.C.
Spartan Woman, 6th century B.C.

Painting
The Horse Fair, 1853
Fishing Scene, 1436–1411 B.C.
Improvisation 19a, 1911
Mona Lisa, 1503–1506

Other Artforms
Wenceslaus Psalter, ca. A.D. 1250–1260
Rose de France, ca. A.D. 1200
Winged Tiger, 19th century
Women Gathering Fruit, ca. 5th century B.C.

Put It All Together

"Art does not evolve by itself, the ideas of people change and with them their mode of expression." — Pablo Picasso

TALK AND WRITE ## How Does a Work of Art Speak?

Pablo Picasso. *Guernica*, 1937. Oil on canvas, 136¾ by 305 inches. Centro de Arte Reina Sofia, Madrid, Spain. © 1997 Estate of Pablo Picasso/Artists Rights Society (ARS), New York. Photograph by Giraudon/Art Resource, New York.

1. **Describe** What has the artist shown? Look carefully and identify as many objects and symbols as you can. Describe the subject or theme of this artwork. Describe the visual qualities of the artwork by writing several words that describe each art term below.

   Example: line— *curved, horizontal, implied,* and so on

color	values	shapes	distortion
movement	emphasis	contrast	juxtaposition

2. **Analyze** How is the theme of war reflected in the elements of art and principles of design? How do the elements work together to move your eye around the composition? How is variety achieved? What provides unity?

3. **Interpret** Explore the figures' gestures. What do you think they symbolize? Why do you think Picasso combined symbols such as the broken sword and flower? Describe the mood. How does the painting make you feel?

4. **Judge** Pablo Picasso painted this large mural in 1937 to express his horror and pain in response to Franco's bombing of the Spanish town of Guernica. Do you think Picasso achieved his intent? Explain. What impact does this artwork have on you?

In Your Journal

Reflect on art through history.

- How does art reflect history based on your exploration into a world of art and artists?
- What have you learned about how the art of different cultures reflects the events, ideas, and values in each historical period?
- Which artworks and periods are your favorites? Why?

What Have You Learned?

Unit 4

Frida Kahlo. *Frida and Diego Rivera*, 1931. Oil on canvas, 39 3/8 by 31 inches. San Francisco Museum of Modern Art.

A World of Subjects and Styles

Have you ever heard someone say, "I like her style," or "He has a style of his own"? An artist's **style** is her or his unique way of creating art through the use of various media, techniques, and subjects. An artist develops individual style by studying the works of other artists, exploring her or his own ideas, and trying new ways of expression. The style of artist Georges Seurat was a technique called *Pointillism*. Frida Kahlo, who painted the portrait across the page, often incorporated her heritage into her *Surrealist* painting style.

Style in art often goes beyond individual expression. Style can be the art of a region, such as the Italian Renaissance. Style can also be the art of a historical time period, such as *Abstract Expressionism* in the United States. In this unit, you will learn about the meanings of style.

If you could view every work of art in the entire world, you would see thousands of styles. However, you might be surprised at the similarities among subjects. Artists often include a **subject**, such as a person, animal, object, or scene in their artwork. Paintings from Asia may show dragons and butterflies, whereas those from Mexico may show dogs or snakes. Yet, both kinds of artworks show animal subjects. Frida Kahlo preferred to show people as subjects and would sometimes include animals.

As you study this unit, look for artworks that show styles and subjects that interest you. Take notes and make sketches of special ways that artists express themselves. As you work in your Sketchbook, try imitating artists' subjects and various styles. As you practice, use your own style of expression to give your composition a special quality.

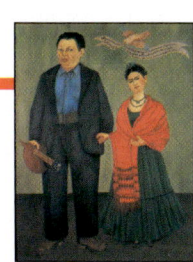

At a Glance

What do you notice most about the people in the portrait?

What objects suggest that the man is an artist?

How do you suppose the subjects feel about each other? about themselves? Explain.

Lesson 1: People as Subjects

Have you ever spent time sitting on a park bench, watching people go by? If so, you probably saw a variety of faces, sizes, ages, and types of human beings. Perhaps you asked yourself questions about their individual characters, beliefs, and lifestyles. People are generally fascinated by other human beings. This is why many artists throughout the history of humankind have traditionally chosen to portray people as their subjects.

Drawings and Paintings of People

John Biggers, artist of **A**, has selected people of Africa and African Americans as *subjects* of his drawings for more than fifty years. Well-known writer and poet Maya Angelou commented that, "John Biggers…leads us through his expressions into the discovery of ourselves at our most intimate level. His pen and pencil and brush take us without faltering into the individual personal world where each of us lives privately."

As an art student in college, Biggers began his exploration of the meaning of family and community. He examined the roles of elders and young people, and of men and women. His drawings reflect the passion for life that he found in these subjects. How would you characterize the women in **A**? Notice the kinship they show through body language and facial

A John Biggers. *Three Quilters (Quilting Party)*, 1952. Conté crayon, 30 by 40 inches. Dallas Museum of Art.

expression. Suppose one of the subjects had been shown looking toward the viewer or off the side of the canvas. How might such a change have affected the mood of this intimate composition? Examine the proportions of the women's hands. What was the artist trying to say? Notice examples of cross-hatching and other kinds of shading that help to provide intimate details.

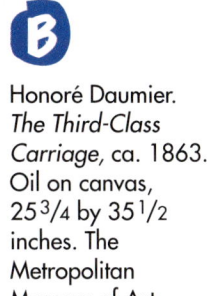 Honoré Daumier. *The Third-Class Carriage,* ca. 1863. Oil on canvas, 25 3/4 by 35 1/2 inches. The Metropolitan Museum of Art.

Now examine the painting in **B** by artist Honoré Daumier. He gives us a glimpse into a railway compartment of the 1860s. The passengers are poor and can afford only third-class tickets. Their clothing, body language, and facial expressions reflect Daumier's concern about unemployment and poverty in France. The credit line reveals that this artwork was created almost a century before Biggers's *Three Quilters.* Yet Daumier's *The Third-Class Carriage* is also a composition about the essence of what it means to be human. Read Angelou's comment once again. Do you think her statement might also apply to Daumier's painting? Explain.

Light Sources and Subjects

In many drawings and paintings, the artist has chosen a **light source,** or a point of illumination for emphasis, contrast, unity, or dramatic effect. In many cases, the viewer is required to imagine the light source as being somewhere outside the canvas. Look again at **A** to determine the light source the artist envisioned as he drew. Judging from shading and shadows, as well as bright areas, you could say the light source is from above, as in **C**. Notice how Daumier used light in his unfinished painting to create contrast for dramatic effect. The light source, as shown in **D**, seems to shine from an unseen window. How might the subjects' appearance help you imagine the location of other windows?

Drawing with Light Sources

Create a Technique Sheet of basic forms, such as spheres, cubes, cylinders, and cones. Draw each form one inch high three times at least. Using pencil and colored pencils, add shading and shadows that result from light sources shining from at least three different directions. Your light sources can be from the left, right, above, in front of, or in back of the form. Draw arrows next to each form to show the direction of the light source.

Sketchbook/Journal

Arrange several white objects on a flat surface and practice drawing the forms using several different light sources. Write notes about the different effects of the light sources.

People as Subjects

Lesson 2: Proportion and Full Figures

B How would you describe the character and mood of this figure?

Viola Frey. *Grandmother Series: July Cone Hat*, 1982. Glazed earthenware, four parts, overall 86 1/2 by 21 by 18 inches. The Nelson-Atkins Museum of Art, Kansas City, Missouri.

How does the height of this sculpture compare with that of **B**?

A Artist unknown, Greek. *Peplos Kore*, ca. 530 B.C. Marble, height approximately 48 inches. Acropolis Museum, Athens.

Comparing and Contrasting Full Figures

The figures in **A** and **B** were sculpted about 2,500 years apart. From the art of ancient Greece to Modern Art, each artist's style reflects an individual quality. Yet, the figures have a lot in common. For example, both sculptures are standing female figures. Notice, too, they have a puppet like stiffness about them. Neither figure appears relaxed.

The two figures also display some striking differences. The ancient sculpture was carved from a single slab of marble and has lost a part of one arm. However, the modern figure was molded in four hand-built parts of clay: the head; the neck and upper body; the skirt; and the hem of the skirt, legs, and feet. The center of each part is hollow. What differences can you point out between the clothing of the figures?

Artists portray the human form in many ways. The artworks in **A** and **B** show *figures,* or human forms, *in the round.* They are sculpted from head to toe as *full figures.* You can go around the figure to perceive the complete form.

Career *Link*

Viola Frey

California artist Viola Frey sculpts ceramic figures—both women and men—with some being more than 11 feet high! Her impressive, monumental figures command attention. They can even be intimidating. The seven-foot tall figure in **D** is from her series about grandmothers in flowered dresses and hats. The artist began her career in art as a painter and soon took up clay. She found that it allowed her to combine painting and drawing with sculpture.

Observe the proportions of people around you. Do they seem to be about like those in the guidelines? How do each person's proportions differ?

Guidelines

Anytime you create images of people, *proportion* becomes an important principle of design. Artists have guidelines, as in **C**, for drawing, painting, or sculpting typical proportions for full figures:

1. The height of most adults is about seven or eight times the length of the head. The ratio for children is different, as the body grows at a faster rate than the head.
2. The hands are about as large as the face.
3. The knees are positioned about halfway between the hip and the bottom of the feet.
4. The hip is about halfway between top of the head and the bottom of the feet.
5. The elbows are about parallel to, or even with, the waist.

Creating a Wire Sculpture

Create a Technique Sheet on a 9" x 12" sheet of paper by drawing nine horizontal lines, each 1 inch apart. Practice drawing the human figure in proportion. On a 12" x 18" sheet of paper, create several contour drawings of a figure in an action pose. Make your drawings at least 8 inches tall and show proportion. Finally, recreate your favorite drawing into a wire sculpture using pliable wire. Add a wooden base. Cover your sculpture with sculpting media and paint.

Sketchbook/Journal

Make several gesture drawings of figures in action. Make notes about proportions and wire sculpture.

Proportion and Full Figures

Lesson 3: Proportion and Faces

A Artist unknown, Egypt. *Head of Queen Tiy,* ca. 1391–1353 B.C. Yew wood with silver and glass, height 3 1/2 inches. Ägyptisches Museum und Papyrussammlung, © BPK, Berlin, 1998. Photograph by M. Büsing.

B Chuck Close. *Roy II,* 1994. Oil on canvas, 102 by 84 inches. Collection of Hirshhorn Museum and Sculpture Garden, Washington, D.C.

Three Views

Look at **A**, **B**, and **C** to observe different facial features—eyes, nose, mouth, and ears. Artists refer to the way these features relate to each other as *facial proportions*.

A good way to learn more about facial proportions is to ask a friend to be your **model**. Your model **poses** in a sitting or standing position for you as you sketch. Artists often sketch their models from three views.

A **front view**, as in **A**, shows the front side of the person or animal in the portrait. Artists often begin such a drawing by lightly drawing basic lines and shapes of the facial proportions. Next, the lines are changed to reflect actual qualities of the person. Finally, special qualities are added. These might be wrinkles around the eyes to show a sense of humor or a distinguishing birthmark on the cheek.

A **profile view**, as in **B**, shows the subject from a side view. Notice in **B** that you cannot see the other side of the face. Notice how the neck connects to the jaw through a shadow under the chin.

A **three-quarter view**, as in **C**, is positioned in between a front view and a profile. You can usually see both eyes, the nose, and the mouth. Notice that the size relationships of the vertical proportions remain about the same.

Rogier van der Weyden. *Lady Wearing a Gauze Headdress*, ca. 1435. Oil on wood, 18 5/16 by 12 1/2 inches. Gemaeldegalerie, Berlin.

Guidelines

Artists have guidelines for drawing, painting, or sculpting typical facial proportions. The proportions of the *portraits* in **A**, **B**, and **C** are similar, yet there are subtle differences among them. Find similarities and differences as you study the guidelines:

1. The halfway point between the top of the head and the chin is at the eyes.
2. The halfway point between the eyes and the chin is at the bottom of the nose.
3. The mouth is just above the halfway point between the nose and the chin.
4. The side edges of the mouth are even with the center of each eye.
5. The space between the eyes is about as wide as each eye.
6. The iris is partly covered by the eyelid.
7. The ears are about parallel to the bottom of the nose and the eyes.

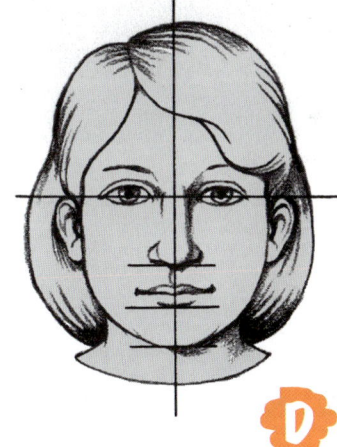

Career Link

Chuck Close

American artist Chuck Close lost the use of his hands due to a paralyzing illness in 1988. Despite this tragedy, the artist was determined to continue with his work. He devised a way to paint using his arm muscles. Close paints large colorful portraits, usually facial portraits of friends, as in **B**, from grids based on photographs.

Drawing Faces

Select a partner. Draw three rectangular boxes with a black felt-tip pen on drawing paper positioned horizontally. Draw an oval in each box and a line across the center of each oval. Draw your model from three different views: front, profile, and three-quarter views. Notice the light sources and, using pencils, add shading and shadows accordingly.

Sketchbook/Journal

Create drawings of a family member from all three views. Make notes about face and head proportions.

Proportion and Faces

Lesson 4: Creating a Self-Portrait

Get the Picture

A **self-portrait** is an artwork created by an artist that shows the likeness of the artist. Slightly more than 500 years ago, a young man—about your age—drew his self-portrait, in **A**. His name was Albrecht Dürer. He lived in Germany, where, as a teenager, he became an *apprentice* to study with a painter. Dürer was the first known artist to make a series of self-portraits. In fact, his *Self-Portrait at Thirteen* is the first record of his artwork. Would you say the drawing is an action figure or a formal self-portrait? In studying **A**, what personality traits might you assume about this artist?

As he grew older, Dürer studied the philosophy of art; that is, he asked questions about logic and wisdom, as they pertain to the visual arts. His studies inspired his writings about ideal proportions for the human figure.

You can create your self-portrait. It might be a close-up portrait of your head and shoulders, or it could be a full-length self-portrait. Your self-portrait may show you as an action figure working on your favorite hobby or playing a game. Or it might be a formal self-portrait, in which you show yourself posing.

 Albrecht Dürer. *Dürer at Thirteen*, 1484. Silverpoint on paper, 10 3/4 by 7 2/3 inches. Graphische Sammlung, Albertina, Vienna.

 Nicholas, Collins Intermediate. *Cool*. Oil pastels on paper, 12 by 18 inches.

Get Set

Materials you will need:
- small hand-held mirror
- #2 pencil
- drawing paper for practice
- 12" x 18" white drawing paper
- favorite drawing or painting media

How to Create a Self-Portrait

1. Study the proportions of your face in a mirror. Practice making some sketches of your facial features.

2. On 12" x 18" drawing paper, lightly draw your face, head, and shoulders as a self-portrait. Study the way your facial features relate to each other.

3. Use your favorite drawing or painting medium to complete your self-portrait.

Brekken, Webb Middle School. *Self-Portrait*. Charcoal and conté crayon on paper, 12 by 18 inches.

Creating a Past, a Present, and a Future Self-Portrait

Imagine how you looked as a young child or study photographs of you at that time. Observe photographs of one of your parents, grandparents, or another older family member. Using your favorite drawing or painting media, create a three-part self-portrait of yourself then, now, and in the future.

Sketchbook/Journal

Make thumbnail sketches of a friend or family member. Make notes about that person's character.

Be an Art Critic!

1. **Describe** Tell about special features in your self-portrait.
2. **Analyze** How would you describe the facial proportions of your drawing?
3. **Interpret** What mood does your self-portrait convey?
4. **Judge** Which parts of the self-portrait look most like you?

Creating a Self-Portrait

Lesson 5: Animals as Subjects

Artists and Animals

Animals have been companions to people for thousands of years. Wild animals, working animals, domestic animals—they all have a commanding presence in the history of humankind. For this reason, artists traditionally have shown a keen interest in portraying animals as their subjects. Animal subjects represent a variety of emotions and states of being, such as compassion, humor, fear, strength, independence, and loyalty. Artworks with animals as subjects can make us laugh, cry, shriek, and even feel differently about ourselves.

A Toko. *Cat and Spider*, ca. 1868–1911. Colors and ink on silk, 14 3/4 by 11 inches. The Metropolitan Museum of Art.

Animal Artworks— Old and New

You have learned about animal subjects in Prehistoric cave paintings, as on page 60. Those artworks remind us of the importance animals held with respect to the survival of humans. Ever since, all civilizations have interacted with animals in their shared *environments*, or surroundings.

The images in **A** and **C** were created by artists of the Modern era. How do you think each artist felt about the animal portrayed? How do the artworks make you feel?

B Ben, Alamo Heights Junior High School. *Scott.* Tempera on paper, 18 by 12 inches.

William Wegman. *A Certain Smile,* 1994. Polarcolor ER photograph. © William Wegman.

 Elizabeth, Alamo Heights Junior High School. *Abstract Fish.* Tempera on paper, 12 by 18 inches.

The cat in **A** bristles its whiskers at a spider as it peers around the edge of a screen. The nineteenth-century Japanese artist Toko sparks our curiosity. Is the cat merely observing, or is it ready to pounce? Notice the implied lines that define the shape of the cat. The artist created a soft, furry texture with broad swoops of the brush. Notice the intensity of the cat's eyes. What effect does the artist achieve with the wrinkle of the cat's nose?

William Wegman, creator of the photograph in **C**, is known for his unusual photographs featuring dogs as subjects. How does the title help you understand the meaning of the photograph? Explain how both the title and the slice of melon create emphasis. Try to imagine the task of persuading a dog to pose in such a way. What attributes would you need, as a photographer, to work with animals as subjects? If you had to explain why this photograph shows humor, you might find it difficult to do so. After all, a dog looks straight ahead with a melon slice in its mouth. Sometimes artists create humor through their artworks that words cannot easily describe.

Drawing an Animal

Collect magazine, newspaper, or personal photographs of your favorite animals. Pay close attention to the proportions of the animals. Draw portraits of your favorite animal from different viewpoints. Select your favorite two or three drawings, and create a design that incorporates these drawings. Create a background showing the animal's natural environment. Add color with your favorite medium.

Sketchbook/Journal

Make several thumbnail sketches of animals at a zoo or pets. Make notes about proportions.

Animals as Subjects

Lesson 6 STUDIO

Making a Ceramic Animal Vessel

 Artist unknown, Peruvian. *Stirrup Spout Vessel in the Form of a Seated Deer*, 3rd–6th century. Ceramic, height 11 inches. The Metropolitan Museum of Art.

 Artist unknown, Peruvian. *Vessel (Effigy in the form of a deer)*, 14th–15th century. Silver, height 5 inches. The Metropolitan Museum of Art.

Get the Picture

 Animals are a popular subject with sculptors, as well as artists of two-dimensional compositions. The sculptures in **A** and **B** show two sculptors' *interpretations* of the same animal, a deer. The sculptures were created in Peru about 500 years apart. They are both vessels, or hollow utensils for holding something. Many artworks are made in this way—designed with a specific purpose in mind, to be useful. They are known as utilitarian art. In addition to being visually pleasing, **utilitarian art,** also known as **applied art,** is functional. Applied art is different from **fine art,** which is created for the sole purpose of being viewed.

Read the credit lines for these artworks. Which of the vessels is older? Compare the different media the sculptors used. The deer in **A** is a *ceramic,* meaning it is hand-built of clay. The deer in **B** was *cast,* or duplicated, in silver by using a mold form of clay or wax. Notice that both of these examples of applied art are housed in a large museum in New York City—the Metropolitan Museum of Art.

Get Set

 **Materials you will need:**
- #2 pencil
- 9" x 12" white drawing paper
- ruler
- red or white clay
- old toothbrush
- plastic knife
- small plastic container
- found objects as clay stamps
- paper towels
- plastic bag
- glaze or watercolors

 Lesson 6

How to Create a Ceramic Animal Vessel

To help you with this Studio, refer to pages 260–263 for tips.

1. On 9" x 12" drawing paper, draw several designs for a functional ceramic animal vessel that will be about 8 inches high with a square base. Select your favorite one.

2. Roll out a 1/2-inch slab of clay.

3. Make a slab base by cutting out a 4-inch square of clay.

4. Build your animal vessel by connecting smaller slabs. Score the clay and attach the joints with slip. Remember to make your vessel functional.

5. Add a textured pattern by gently pressing found objects onto the surface.

6. After your vessel has been fired, glaze it or paint it with watercolors.

Miguel, Webb Middle School, *Untitled.* Glazed clay, 10 by 7 1/2 by 2 inches.

Drawing an Imaginary Animal

On white drawing paper, create an imaginary animal by combining parts of various animals. Create a background of black and white positive and negative space with black felt-tip pen or pencil.

Be an Art Critic!

1. **Describe** Point out the functional parts of your animal vessel.

2. **Analyze** How do the body proportions of your sculpture compare with the proportions of the animal in the photographs you collected?

3. **Interpret** How do you intend for your vessel to be used?

4. **Judge** In what room of your house might your vessel belong? Explain why.

Making a Ceramic Animal Vessel 147

Lesson 7 Still Life as a Subject

A Paul Cézanne. *Apples and Oranges*, ca. 1900. Oil on canvas, 29 1/8 by 36 5/8 inches. Musée d'Orsay, Paris.

One of the oldest subjects of painting is still life. A **still life** is the subject of an artwork that shows an arrangement of nonliving things, such as foods, cut flowers, bottles, and books. The still-life paintings on these pages were created by artists who arranged a group of objects on a surface and set about to portray the vision on a two-dimensional surface.

Still-Life Techniques

Have you ever heard the statement that you cannot mix apples with oranges? Apparently artist Paul Cézanne did not heed the warning. Read the title of **A**, and notice his selection of fruits as a subject. The warm, analogous color scheme of the apples and oranges contrasts starkly against the light and cool tints of the folded drapery beneath them. Notice the contrast of tints and shades within the folds of the drapery. What subtle colors can you see on the drapery? Cézanne created yet more contrast by placing dark shades of green in the patterned furniture beneath the light drapery. The folds of both fabrics create a rhythm that guides your eye to encircle the fruit.

Compare Cézanne's nineteenth-century style of painting with that of Anne

 Anne Vallayer-Coster studied art at the Royal Academy in Paris.
Anne Vallayer-Coster. *The White Soup Bowl,* 1771. Oil on canvas, 19¹¹/₁₆ by 24½ inches. Private collection.

C Matthew, Alamo Heights Junior High School. *African Work.* Colored pencils on paper, 12 by 18 inches.

Vallayer-Coster in **B**. Notice her selection of neutral colors to portray an everyday meal of soup and dark bread eaten by French peasant families. Imagine the warm dampness of the steam she created with thin, white paint. How do you think the soup bowl would feel in your hands? Notice the angle of the bowl, as though she painted it at eye level. She positioned the spoon handle and the steam to make the viewer curious to see the color and texture of the soup. Notice the way in which the folded drapery, or napkin, resembles the drapery in Cézanne's still life. How are the draperies alike? different?

The still-life subjects in **A** and **B** were a part of the artists' everyday lives. Think about a still-life subject that might represent a part of your everyday life.

Creating a Still Life

Bring several objects from home that tell something about you, and arrange them in a still-life composition. Make several thumbnail sketches of the still life from different viewpoints. With a black felt-tip pen, decorate a 1-inch border on a sheet of white drawing paper. Enlarge your favorite thumbnail sketch inside the border and paint it with the medium of your choice.

Sketchbook/Journal

Create several thumbnail sketches of plants or flowers in a vase that you would like to draw or paint. List other objects you would like to include in a still life.

Still Life as a Subject

Lesson 8 STUDIO: Creating a Cubist Still Life

Get the Picture

The abstract style of art called *Cubism* was developed in Paris by a group of artists during the early part of the twentieth century. **Cubism** is characterized by a separation of the subject into cubes and other geometric forms from multiple viewpoints. Cubists divide their subjects visually into shapes and forms and then recombine them so that each part of a subject is shown from a different viewpoint. Look again at the collage in **A** by Georges Braque. Does it resemble any table you have ever seen? Notice how the parts were broken into different shapes and then put together again in new ways.

Georges Braque and Pablo Picasso were founders of Cubism. They developed Cubist techniques in both two- and three-dimensional artworks. Some of their ideas were inspired by African sculpture, as in **B**, which shows a subject from multiple viewpoints. Braque and Picasso analyzed, broke down, and drastically changed visual concepts of the traditional subjects of portrait, landscape, and still life.

Get Set

 **Materials you will need:**
- several objects with some geometric form
- #2 pencil
- drawing paper for practice
- 12" x 18" white drawing paper
- tempera paint
- brushes
- paper towels
- oil pastels
- colored markers
- black felt-tip pen

 Georges Braque. *The Table,* 1928. Oil and sand on canvas, 70 3/4 by 28 3/4 inches. The Museum of Modern Art, New York. Acquired through the Lillie P. Bliss Bequest. Photograph © 1998 The Museum of Modern Art, New York City.

How to Create a Cubist Still Life

1. Observe and practice drawing several objects with geometric forms in pencil, using contour lines.

2. On a 12" x 18" sheet of drawing paper, draw each form three times from different viewpoints, this time overlapping them.

3. Use oil pastels, colored markers, and a black felt-tip pen to emphasize the different viewpoints and overlapping.

4. Fill in the negative spaces within and around the Cubist forms with a paint medium of your choice.

Vanessa, Driscoll Middle School. *Untitled.* Colored marker on paper, 12 by 18 inches.

Drawing a Cubist Portrait

Select a self-portrait or a portrait you would like to draw. Draw the portrait in a Cubist style lightly in pencil. Add color to your design using several of your favorite art media.

Sketchbook/Journal

Create several thumbnail sketches of fruits and vegetables in a Cubist style. Make notes about creating Cubist still lifes.

Be an Art Critic!

1. **Describe** How many different shapes and forms did you create in your Cubist still life?
2. **Analyze** How does your Cubist arrangement of shapes and forms show rhythm? unity? variety?
3. **Interpret** Describe the mood of your still life.
4. **Judge** What comments do you think Picasso or Braque might have made about your still life?

Creating a Cubist Still Life

Lesson 9: Landscape as a Subject

 Paul Gauguin. *Tahitian Landscape,* 1891. Oil on canvas, 26 11/16 by 36 3/8 inches. The Minneapolis Institute of Arts.

The first inhabitants of your community probably stood on the highest point to survey the land around them. Some artists paint such views of mountains, trees, fields, and other natural scenery as **landscapes,** as in **A** and **B**. Others paint views of the sea, called **seascapes,** or views of cities, known as **cityscapes.** All are views of natural or human-made environments. They may show weather conditions, seasons, or times of day or night that represent a variety of moods and emotions. Which landscape on these pages portrays a warm and peaceful afternoon on a quiet island? Which one shows a dramatic change in weather, along with possible feelings of hope and sudden excitement?

Complementary Colors in Landscapes

Study the landscape in **A**. Artist Paul Gauguin spent many years of his life painting on the island of Tahiti. There, he recorded the beauty of the people, vegetation, mountains, and seas of the island. For his canvases painted in the South Seas, Gauguin chose to use *complementary color schemes*—orange and blue, yellow and violet, green and red. The placement of such colors against each other, as in **A**, creates a vibrant intensity. Yet, combined with his choice of subject matter, the colors provide a calm and tranquil mood. Point out complementary colors in **A**. How does the painting make you feel?

 Eric, Ed White Middle School. *Arizona Highways*. Watercolor, 9 by 12 inches

 Charles Burchfield. *November Sun Emerging,* 1956–1959. Watercolor on paper, 37 1/2 by 31 3/4 inches. Courtesy of SBC Communications Inc.

Landscape as Expression

Artist Charles Burchfield painted landscapes, as in **B**, during the twentieth century. His love of the outdoors, combined with his inner spiritual quest, are evident in his paintings of joyous emotion. Notice the rhythmic pulsations in the November sky. The painter chose to emphasize his light source—the sun—in a physical, an emotional, and a spiritual sense. What message do you think he was trying to convey?

Think about your own environment. What thoughts does it bring to mind? What feelings does it bring about? How might you express these thoughts and feelings in a painting?

Painting a Landscape with Watercolor

To help you with this Studio, refer to page 257.

Practice drawing real or imaginary landscapes. Cut a sheet of 9" x 12" white watercolor paper into fourths. On each section, paint a wet-wash watercolor sky at a specific time of day. Include morning, noon, afternoon, and evening. When your papers dry, paint a dry-wash watercolor landscape on each of the four sections.

Sketchbook/Journal

Create several thumbnail sketches of different landscapes you have seen at different times of day. Try drawing horizon lines bent and straight. Make notes about creating landscapes.

Landscape as a Subject   153

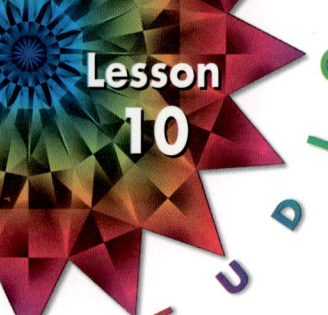

Lesson 10 STUDIO

Creating a Pointillist Seascape

Georges Seurat. *The Lighthouse at Honfleur*, 1886. Oil on canvas, 26 1/8 by 32 inches. The National Gallery of Art, Washington, D.C.

Get the Picture

Look closely at **A**. Now look even more closely to find thousands of tiny dots of color applied for your eye to blend. This technique, called **Pointillism**—or **Divisionism** by its creator Georges Seurat, became Seurat's style of painting during the nineteenth century. Using tiny dots of color instead of lines, Seurat painted pictures of people enjoying the circus, playing in the park, and bathing beside a river, as in **A**. Notice how he visually blended colors through the placement of dots. For example, to create the effect of violet, he placed red dots beside blue ones. How long do you suppose it would take you to carefully apply thousands of colored dots to a large canvas the size of Seurat's canvas? Seurat spent as long as two years on some paintings. His technique was so detailed that he completed only a few compositions in his lifetime.

Get Set

 **Materials you will need:**
- 9" x 12" white drawing paper
- 12" x 18" white drawing paper
- #2 pencil
- colored markers
- oil pastels and watercolors

How to Create a Pointillist Seascape

1. Collect photographs of different kinds of seascapes. Create several thumbnail designs of imaginary seascapes. Include scenes of the sea, beach, and sky.

2. On 12" x 18" sheet of drawing paper, lightly draw an enlarged image of your favorite thumbnail design of a seascape.

3. Use colored markers to draw Pointillist dots. Place yellows next to blues to create the impression of greens. Use the color wheel to help you visually blend other colors, too.

B Lisa, Wood Middle School. *Parade of Violets*. Tempera on paper, 12 by 18 inches.

Creating a Watercolor Resist

Draw lightly with pencil to create a seascape during a raging storm. Add short and diagonal lines, or parallel slashes, of oil pastel colors as a related Pointillist technique. Cover your entire drawing with watercolors to create an oil pastel, watercolor resist.

Sketchbook/Journal

Create several thumbnail sketches of seascapes you have seen or imagined. Make notes about creating seascapes and Pointillism.

Be an Art Critic!

1. **Describe** How did you show color in your composition?
2. **Analyze** Point out the foreground, middle ground, and background.
3. **Interpret** What meaning does your seascape convey?
4. **Judge** Would your seascape enhance the lobby of a commercial office building? Tell why or why not.

Creating a Pointillist Seascape

Lesson 11

Impressionism

 Claude Monet. *Arrival of the Normandy Train, Gare Saint-Lazare,* 1877. Oil on canvas, 23 1/4 by 31 1/4 inches. The Art Institute of Chicago.

What Is Impressionism?

The term *Impressionism* was first used in 1874 by a journalist ridiculing a landscape by painter Claude Monet called *Impression—Sunrise.* This public comment officially recognized what would become a significant art movement in France. A group of about twenty-five Parisian artists had grown weary of the strict rules and regulations posed by judges of art contests, such as the Salon. They were also tired of the dark and sometimes muddy colors from the palettes of *Realistic* painters. The new, free, and spirited group called themselves the *Independents* because their style was independent of the popular Realistic style.

The Independents soon became known as **Impressionists** because they painted or drew impressions—moments of everyday life—as they saw and felt them. They often painted or drew outdoors because they liked the way the changing light made their subjects appear. This style, called **Impressionism,** showed a new way of filling in spaces, with hundreds of strokes and dabs—straight, curved, thick, thin, broken, smooth, dotted, blurry, sharp, squiggly, and zigzag.

 Camille Pissarro. *The Place du Havre, Paris,* 1893. Oil on canvas, 23 1/2 by 28 2/3 inches. The Art Institute of Chicago.

Impressionist Techniques

The images you see in **A** and **C,** were painted by two of the early Impressionists, Claude Monet and Camille Pissarro. Notice in their paintings the blurry quality of the brushstrokes. Pissarro's painting of a Parisian street scene shows his thoughtful use of color and a remarkable understanding of the effects of light and atmosphere. Perhaps even more than conveying the effects of light, the artist emphasizes the busy energy of street life in Paris.

Monet had realized that his brushstroke was becoming much looser, and he began to emphasize simple brushstrokes, rather than to organize them into broad areas of color. He had also discovered that anything made a suitable subject for a painting, regardless of what conventional-minded people thought. In this composition, Monet conveyed a real sense of the interior of the train shed with the open space beyond. He achieved this sense of interior space partly through actual perspective techniques, but also through an Impressionist technique known as **atmospheric perspective.** Notice the soft, diffused light—a technique to show distance by using lighter tints for faraway elements. Monet sought to represent these elements as they appear in nature due to conditions of distance, air, and light. In this way, he and other Impressionists felt their artworks were realistic, yet different from the traditional Realistic art style.

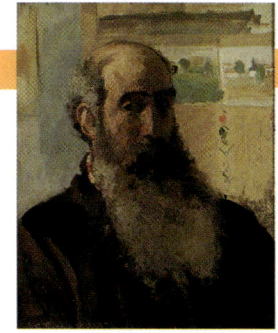

Camille Pissarro. *Self-Portrait,* 1873. Oil on canvas, 21 3/4 by 17 7/8 inches. Musée d'Orsay, Paris.

Career Link

Camille Pissarro

Camille Pissarro was an Impressionist who learned techniques from his contemporaries, such as Monet and Seurat, and influenced other artists, such as Paul Cézanne. Pissarro wrote in a letter to his son Lucien, "...We have to approach nature sincerely, with our own modern sensibilities." He was speaking of the Impressionist belief that what was real in nature was the play of light with color. This belief was reflected in Pissarro's painting throughout his career.

Creating an Impressionist Painting

Select a portrait, still life, landscape, seascape, or cityscape you would like to paint. You may find the design in your Sketchbook/Journal. Lightly sketch the design on drawing paper with pencil. Using tempera or some other water-soluble paint, add color to the design in an Impressionist style. Remember that you are trying to give special attention to the light source and the impression of what you see.

Sketchbook/Journal

Observe outdoors. Create several thumbnail sketches for paintings you would like to create in an Impressionist style. Make notes about Impressionism.

Impressionism

Lesson 12 STUDIO

Drawing as an Impressionist

Get the Picture

ART HISTORY

In 1877, an American artist named Mary Cassatt was working in Paris when she made a decision that would change the direction of her career—and therefore her life. Like Claude Monet and Camille Pissarro, she was frustrated with the conventional Salon because of its strict rules about how artists should paint and draw. She had heard about the rebellious Independents, later known as Impressionists, through her friend Edgar Degas. At the invitation of Degas, a member of the new group, she decided to exhibit her artworks with them. Cassatt was overjoyed! Finally she had found a circle of free-spirited painters who, like herself, wanted to portray their subjects with bright colors and loose brushstrokes.

Many of Cassatt's drawings, as in **A**, and paintings show indoor scenes. Yet, she still used bright colors to show the effects of light on her subjects. The subject of **A**, the artist's sister Lydia, was a favorite model. With chalk pastels, Cassatt drew her impression of Lydia sitting in a loge, or box seat, at the theater, observing the performance from the edge of her chair. The artist drew patterns of short, sharp strokes. These strokes combine to form oval shapes and curves—Lydia's face and hair, her shoulder and neckline, and the chair. Warm reds, yellows, and oranges shimmer in the light of the chandelier. Even Lydia's reflection in the mirror radiates with the light and colors that energize this pastel drawing.

A What do you notice about the way Cassatt drew her subject, Lydia? Notice the loosely drawn marks on the background.

Mary Cassatt. *At the Theatre (Woman in a Loge)*, ca. 1879. Pastel on paper, 21 13/16 by 18 1/8 inches. The Nelson-Atkins Museum of Art, Kansas City, Missouri.

Get Set

Materials you will need:
- 12" x 18" white drawing paper
- #2 pencil
- colored pencils
- oil pastels
- chalk pastels

158 Lesson 12

How to Create an Impressionist Drawing

To help you with this Studio, refer to pages 252–253.

1. Select a portrait, still life, landscape, seascape, or cityscape from your Sketchbook/Journal, or create a new sketch. Using pencil, lightly sketch the design on 12" x 18" drawing paper.

2. Use colored pencils, chalk pastels, or oil pastels—or a combination of all three—to provide color for your design in an Impressionist style. Give special attention to the light source in recording your visual impression of the subject.

 Nina, Driscoll Middle School. *Iris and Mexican Hat.* Oil pastels on paper, 12 by 18 inches.

Creating an Impressionist Portrait

Ask a friend to pose as you lightly sketch a portrait. With colored pencils, chalk pastels, or oil pastels, complete the portrait in an Impressionist style. Use some diagonal lines, as in **A**, to show texture.

 **Sketchbook/Journal**

Make notes about the differences between Impressionism and Realism. Draw examples of the points you make.

 **Be an Art Critic!**

1. **Describe** How did you use color and line in your composition?
2. **Analyze** What makes your drawing appear Impressionistic, rather than Realistic?
3. **Interpret** If you could visit the place in your drawing, how would it make you feel?
4. **Judge** How does the style of this drawing compare with other styles you have explored? Which do you prefer?

Drawing as an Impressionist

Lesson 13: Expressionism

Gabriele Münter. *Portrait of Marianne von Werefkin*, 1909. Oil on cardboard, 31 7/8 by 21 5/8 inches. Städtische Galerie im Lenbachhaus, Munich, Germany.

What Is Expressionism?

It can be said that all styles of art are expressive. Realistic artists express views of how subjects actually look. Cubists express understanding of subjects from many viewpoints. Impressionists express impressions of subject and light at a given moment. Indeed, all artists express themselves. But notice that the word *expressive*, in these examples, does not begin with a capital *e*. Only artworks in which the main idea is to express a definite or strong mood or feeling are considered to be of a style called **Expressionism.**

Two major art movements of the twentieth century fall within the bounds of this style. In Germany during the early part of that century, a group of artists called *The Blue Rider* worked together to create a style of using simple designs and brilliant colors to express their thoughts, moods, and feelings. This style of art became known as **German Expressionism,** to which you were introduced in Unit 3. You can find an example of German Expressionism in **A**.

The second Expressionist art movement occurred in the United States during the middle of the twentieth century. **Abstract Expressionism,** as the painting style is called, is also known as *action painting*. Look at the artwork in **B** to see why. Envision the painter applying paint freely to a large canvas to suggest her ideas, feelings, and emotions.

German Expressionism

German artist Gabriele Münter was a founder of The Blue Rider. She recalled in her diary the transformation of her artwork from an Impressionist to an Expressionist style. "After a short period of agony I took a great leap forward, from copying nature—in a more or less Impressionist style—to abstraction, feeling the content, the essence of things."

Look again at Münter's *Portrait of Marianne von Werefkin,* who was also a member of The Blue Rider. Find areas where Münter applied abstract techniques, such as omitting details. What do you notice about her choice and placement of colors?

The title of this artwork may spark your imagination.

Joan Mitchell. *George Went Swimming at Barnes Hole, But It Got Too Cold*, 1957. Oil on canvas, 85 1/4 by 78 1/4 inches. Albright-Knox Art Gallery, Buffalo, New York. Gift of Seymour H. Knox, 1958.

This bold and radical way of using color stemmed from Münter's interest in yet another art movement called **Fauvism**. Artists in this group lived and worked in France from 1905–1907. Their bold color schemes and radical color placement, as in **A**, startled viewers so much so that these artists were called "wild beasts," or **Fauves**. Members of the Blue Rider were interested in color techniques of the Fauves.

Abstract Expressionism

"I carry my landscape around with me," commented American artist Joan Mitchell about the closeness she feels to nature. Read the title of **B**. How do the artist's words combine her love of nature with a sense of humor? Consider the artist's comments about water as you study the image in **B**: "The lake is with me today. The memory of a feeling. And when I feel that thing, I want to paint it."

Mitchell's paintings exemplify techniques of the Abstract Expressionist movement, such as slashing, swooping, and active brushstrokes, or dripping, spattering, and pouring paint on canvas. These techniques helped artists express their feelings about life after the end of World War II.

Expressive Painting in Fauve Colors

On 12" x 18" white construction paper, create a sketch in an Expressionist style. For example, you might choose to sketch a German Expressionist portrait or an Abstract Expressionist landscape. With tempera paint, add color in a Fauve style. Give special attention to bright colors placed in unusual ways. Leave blank paper as negative space between colors and shapes. Crumple your painting and then press it flat with your hands. Brush black drawing ink over the entire surface of the painting. When your paper is dry, put it on a boardlike surface and run water over the top. The excess ink will wash off the painting and sink into those areas not painted.

Sketchbook/Journal

Create several thumbnail sketches of people and places that arouse an emotion within you. Make notes about colors you might use to express your feelings in a larger composition.

Expressionism

Lesson 14: Surrealism

René Magritte. *The Mysteries of the Horizon,* 1955. Oil on canvas, 19 1/2 by 25 1/3 inches. Private collection.

"The mind loves the unknown. It loves images whose meaning is unknown, since the meaning of the mind itself is unknown."

—René Magritte, 1959

What Is Surrealism?

Did you ever wake up from an amazing dream and write down what you remembered about it? Some artists record their dreamlike thoughts through their drawings, paintings, and other artworks. In this style of art, known as **Surrealism**, artists include some realistic images but make them appear strange and dreamlike. They create a feeling or mood that stems from their memory or imagination. The mood can be humorous, frightening, mysterious, or a combination of these and other qualities.

Techniques

Perhaps you have arrived at a strange place in the dark and were surprised to see the reality of it the next morning. Everything seems to appear different at night. Shapes and forms take on distorted proportions. Moonlight and flashlights reflect off objects, casting dark shadows. Is it any wonder that many Surrealist painters have chosen to show nighttime scenes?

Strange dream-world scenes characterize Réne Magritte's paintings. Notice in **A** the mysterious mood he achieved with a nighttime sky looming over a daytime landscape—or is it a moonscape? Or could it be that three crescent moons shining at night create a daytime landscape? three moons? *You* decide what makes this composition seem so strange. What are the men thinking? Are they real? Do they know each other? Are they brothers? triplets? Notice Magritte's use of cool colors and neutrals, popular color choices among Surrealists. What other Surreal qualities do you see in **A**?

Some Surrealist artworks are filled with bright colors. Notice how artist Lee Smith chose bright colors to contrast against a dark sky. Like Magritte, this artist uses paint to show color, space, and texture. Read the credit line in **C** to discover other materials, such as the three-dimensional airplanes flying near the bottom of the composition. Planes flying near the ground? Or is that actually the ground? Why are those people moving around in space? Or is that the ground they are on? Notice how the artist guides your eye around the composition with the diagonal lines of the light rays. What other Surreal qualities do you see in **C**?

B

Career Link

Lee N. Smith

Lee Smith, the artist of **C**, is an adventurer of time and space. He travels through the shifting landscape between memories and dreams. Smith is a painter, whose Surreal compositions tell stories about his childhood adventures in open fields behind his home. A self-taught artist, Smith shows his dreamlike memories of games, ceremonies, and rituals that he and his friends enjoyed as they played in the wide-open spaces. His unusual placement of figures and objects are dramatically unreal. His color selections reveal his vivid imagination. However, the mood of his compositions is always true to the way he felt as a child.

Think about some Surrealist scenes you might create in a composition. You might make a list of people, objects, and animals as they would appear in a Surrealist setting. For example, consider fish in the sky, dogs in the sea, and clocks in the desert.

 Lee N. Smith III. *Intruder in the Port,* 1993. Oil and 3D construction on panel, 78 by 96 by 7 inches. Private collection.

Creating a Surrealist Scene in Mixed Media

On 12" x 18" drawing paper, create a design of a Surrealistic scene. Add color to your design, using colored pencils. Leave some blank space around each shape and color you use. Add detail to your drawing, using a black felt-tip pen and shading techniques.

Sketchbook/Journal

Make several thumbnail sketches of other Surrealist scenes you envision. Note the Surrealist techniques you used.

Surrealism 163

Lesson 15

Making a Surrealist Painting

Get the Picture

Salvador Dali, a leading twentieth-century Surrealist, focused on portrayals of visions from dreams and the subconscious. **Symbols** in his paintings represent words, messages, or ideas. If you could have talked with Dali, what questions might you have asked about symbolism in ? *The Elephants* was a study for a backdrop for a 1960s opera, *The Spanish Lady and the Roman Cavalier.* How does this fact help you understand Dali's suggestion of a red curtain in the foreground? Notice the cool color scheme he chose, in comparison to the warm colors of Melissa Miller's composition in **B**. How does her fantasy painting make you feel? How does the title help you understand the mood? What comparison can you draw about the proportions of figures in both paintings?

A Salvador Dali. *The Elephants,* 1961. Pencil, watercolor and gouache, 27 1/2 by 27 1/2 inches. Indianapolis Museum of Art, gift of Mr. and Mrs. Lorenzo Alvary. Photograph © 1975, Indianapolis Museum of Art.

Get Set

 **Materials you will need:**
- 9" x 12" drawing paper
- #2 pencil
- 12" x 18" white drawing paper or illustration board
- tempera or acrylic paints, paintbrushes, water container
- chalk pastels

B Melissa Miller. *Clowns,* 1983. Oil on linen, 56 by 76 inches. Private collection.

164 Lesson 15

How to Create a Surrealist Painting

To help you with this Studio, refer to pages 253 and 256–257.

1. Make several thumbnail sketches showing Surreal elements, such as symbols, fantasy, humor, mystery, strange landscapes, cool colors, bright colors, or neutrals.

2. Select your favorite thumbnail sketch, or a combination of thumbnail sketches, and enlarge the composition on a 12" x 18" sheet of drawing paper.

3. Use tempera or acrylic paints and chalk pastels to add color to your composition.

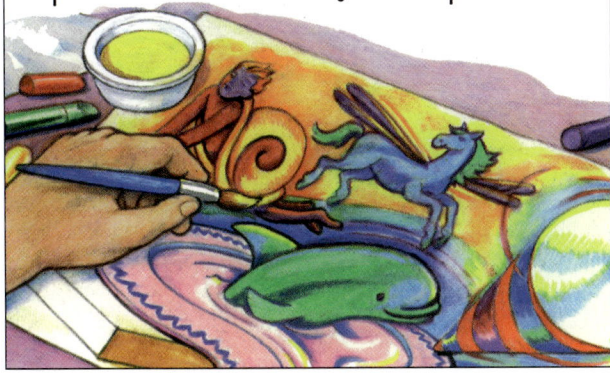

Curtis, Alamo Heights Junior High School. *Bookworm.* Mixed-media on paper, 12 by 18 inches.

Creating a Fantasy Animal Drawing

Choose one animal and create a fantasy drawing around it. For example, you might show a zebra swimming or flying. Think about ways the background can help express your fantasy. Use chalk pastels or crayons to add color to your composition.

Sketchbook/Journal

Jot down words that describe a fantasy place you have imagined. Draw a sketch of the place.

Be an Art Critic!

1. **Describe** Tell what is happening in your composition.
2. **Analyze** What techniques did you use to show fantasy?
3. **Interpret** What meaning might you give to this dreamlike composition?
4. **Judge** What person do you know who might especially like your fantasy composition? Explain why.

Making a Surrealist Painting

Lesson 16

Pop Art

"I suppose I would still prefer to sit under a tree with a picnic basket rather than under a gas pump, but signs and comic strips are interesting as subject matter."

—Roy Lichtenstein, 1963

What Is Pop Art?

Pop art, short for *popular art,* is a style of art that developed in the United States and England during the 1950s and 1960s. Pop artists took as their subject matter the products and images of popular culture, such as comic strip images, as in . Other Pop artworks featured advertisements, billboard posters, and other images related to commercial and brand-name products. Pop artists also created humorous interpretations of popular objects, as in **B** and **C**.

 Roy Lichtenstein. *Nurse,* 1964. Oil and magna on canvas, 48 by 48 inches. Private collection. © Estate of Roy Lichtenstein.

Techniques

Pop artists often used scale to help them emphasize a concept. **Scale** refers to the size of an object in relation to an ideal or normal size. It may also refer to the size of an object in relation to other objects or to its environment. You have learned about scale through *size relationships.* Which one of the fine-art examples on these pages shows a monumental, or huge, scale? How would it feel to look up at this sculpture? Why do you think the artist used such a monumental scale?

 Claes Oldenburg. *Clothespin,* 1976. Cor-ten steel, height 45 feet. Centre Square, Philadelphia.

James Rosenquist. *Telephone Explosion,* 1983. Oil on canvas, 78 by 66 inches. Courtesy of SBC Communications Inc. © James Rosenquist/Licensed by VAGA, New York, New York.

Another example of emphasizing an object to convey a popular idea or concept is shown in **C**, by James Rosenquist. What is happening in the painting? Notice how lines help guide your eye to the focal point, the telephone. Observe the smiling faces that likewise emphasize the telephone. Was Rosenquist suggesting girls like to talk on the telephone or that such a notion is a stereotype perpetuated by advertising?

Look back at **A**. Notice the thousands of tiny dots spaced as though they were applied by a machine. In about 1957, Roy Lichtenstein shocked his viewers with his adaptation of the printing techniques of newspapers, particularly comic strips. He explained about his decision to turn to Pop art as a reaction to some other Modern Art movements: "…Everybody was hanging everything. It was almost acceptable to hang a dripping paint rag; everybody was accustomed to this. The one thing everyone hated was commercial art." Then, referring to his own success and that of other Pop artists, he added, "Apparently they didn't hate that enough either."

Making Pop Art

From at least three viewpoints, create drawings of an item in today's popular culture. From ideas in the drawings, create a papier mâché sculpture. Make an armature, or framework, using crumpled newspaper and tape. Add several layers of newspaper strips that are saturated with papier mâché paste. Spread one or two layers of paper towels onto the wet sculpture. When your sculpture is dry, add detail and color with tempera paint. Found objects, such as yarn, string, and buttons, can also help you show detail.

Sketchbook/Journal

Draw a sketch of your sculpture. Write about the cultural popularity of your object and why you chose to feature it as the subject of your artwork.

Talk About Art

"The only thing I know is that I paint because I need to...."

— Frida Kahlo
1907–1954

Less than a century ago in Mexico, there lived a young girl who would become an artist known throughout the world. Her full name was Magdalena Carmen Frida Kahlo y Calderón. She was called Frida Kahlo. Kahlo was interested in the artistic qualities of her father, a photographer. At age 19, she was severely injured in a traffic accident, which would affect her health for the rest of her life. That year, she taught herself to paint on a lap easel in her bed while she recovered. She liked to hang mirrors around the bed so she would have a ready subject. In fact, most of Kahlo's paintings, as in **A** and **B**, include self-portraits.

When Kahlo's strength returned, she showed her paintings to some well-known artists in Mexico. One of them was the popular muralist Diego Rivera, whom she married in 1929. This union would be a stormy, yet a passionate, relationship. At about this time, she immersed herself in traditional Mexican culture. She decorated their home with Mexican folk art and wore Mexican clothing. In 1931 she painted their wedding portrait, in **B**. Indeed, Kahlo was much smaller than Rivera. But notice the scale she established by exaggerating Rivera's size and minimizing her own. How would you say the sizes of their feet, for example, compare with each other's? As another humorous touch, she portrayed her husband as being the only artist of the two, and disguised her own feisty personality and enormous talent as an artist.

Kahlo's art is often considered Surreal, even though she felt it was not. She explained that she based her subjects and

 Kahlo's "trademark" became the unibrow she painted in her self-portraits.

Frida Kahlo. *Self-Portrait (The Frame)*, ca. 1938. Oil on aluminum and glass, 11 1/8 by 8 inches. Collections Mnam/Cci-Centre Georges Pompidou.

style on her real-life experiences, rather than on dreamlike ones. If you study her paintings, you will find that she indeed used many of the techniques familiar to Surrealists—symbols, fantasy, humor, mystery, strange landscapes, cool colors, bright colors, and neutrals. However, if you

Frida Kahlo. *Frida and Diego Rivera*, 1931. Oil on canvas, 39 3/8 by 31 inches. San Francisco Museum of Modern Art.

read about her life story, you will know that many of her real-life experiences of pain and suffering were truly surreal. Her triumph over physical and emotional challenges gave her the strength she needed to continue her work as an artist. In 1984, thirty years after her death, the Mexican government decreed her art to be a national patrimony, among the heritage of male artists, including Rivera.

Framing Your Self-Portrait

Draw or paint a self-portrait in a style of your choice. As a part of the design, draw or paint a frame in your composition. Your frame should show objects that are especially familiar to you and your culture.

Be an Art Critic!

Look at B to answer these questions:

1. **Describe** What is happening in this portrait? What kinds of colors, shapes, and lines do you see?
2. **Analyze** How does each figure help you understand the other one?
3. **Interpret** How do you think Kahlo feels about Rivera?
4. **Judge** Do you think Rivera liked this portrait? Why or why not? How do you feel about the composition?

Talk About Art 169

Portfolio Project

 **Materials you will need:**
- pencil
- 18" x 24" sheet of drawing paper
- tempera paint, oil pastels, crayons
- paintbrush
- water container

Developing Individual Style

1. List ways you would describe your own art style.

2. Based on your description of your own art style, draw a sketch of you and one or more of your family members enjoying an activity together.

3. Using a pencil, lightly enlarge your design on an 18" x 24" sheet of drawing paper.

4. Add color with two or more media.

Gallery

 Ben, Barbara Bush Middle School. *Fish Stories.* Tempera and marker on paper, 18 by 24 inches.

 Jason, Ray Corbett Middle School. *The Fishing Hole.* Watercolor on paper, 18 by 24 inches.

Portfolio Project 171

Art Links

MUSIC

Cataloging Musical Tastes

No single style of art rules public taste in the United States today. Examine the art you see around you in everyday life—in magazines, banks, doctors' offices, and so on. You are likely to see examples of realism, impressionism, pop art, and many other styles. The same holds true for music, as you can tell by visiting any large music store or just flipping through stations on a radio dial.

Take a look through the tape and CD collections of a few people (with their permission). If possible, choose at least one person younger than 20, one about your parents' age, and one about your grandparents' age. See what generalizations you can make about their tastes. Write a paragraph or two describing the kinds of music each person likes and name at least one other album he or she might enjoy. Then interview the people about their musical tastes. Do they describe the music the same way you have done? Are they interested in the album you have named?

DANCE

Analyzing Different Dance Styles

Just as there are many styles of art, so there are many types of dancing—classical ballet, modern dance, folk dancing, American musical theatre, jazz, and so on. Two styles of dance may have moves in common, yet the eye can usually tell one style from another within seconds. How?

Explore this question with a friend. Each of you collect a number of videotapes that show different styles of dancing. Prepare the tapes so you can start in the middle of a dance, and then play 10 to 30 seconds of dancing that contains no explanation or context. As you watch your friend's clips, jot down the styles you can identify. Then show your notes to your friend, and see how many she or he can classify. Afterward, discuss how you identified each style. What did your eyes see that marked each one? Make a chart of dance styles, and list the traits that make each style what it is.

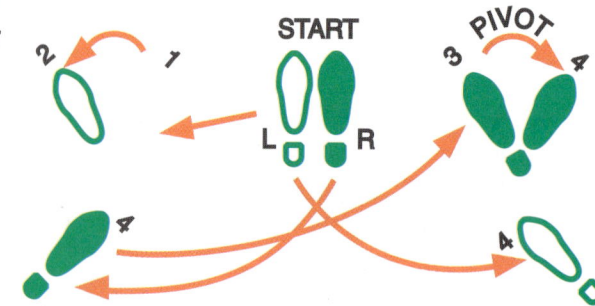

THEATRE AND MEDIA

Classifying Movies by Subject

In theatre, as in the visual arts, certain themes and subjects keep appearing. The Greeks had two categories of theatre—tragedy and comedy; each focused on its own range of subjects. A tragedy generally told the story of a great hero who falls from grace due to some character flaw. A comedy generally told a story that poked fun at news of the day and highlighted petty human foibles.

Have these categories endured? With a group of friends, make a list of plays and movies you have seen—the longer the list the better. Include movies you have seen on TV if you like. Then see if you can divide your list into comedies and tragedies. If not, how would you describe the movies that do not fit into either category? Suppose you were making up your own system for classifying all movies and plays by subject. What would the categories be? Write a brief description of each one.

LITERATURE

She said.... I said....

Exploring Point of View

A realistic painting feels unified only if the light source is consistent: all the shadows must fall the same way. In a work of fiction, "point of view" casts a similar "light." Even if a story is told in the third person, the author stands somewhere to tell it. Compare these sentences:

> ▶ Susan wondered if Bob would ever say "I'm sorry." But Bob had no idea she was angry—he was just so excited about the game.
>
> ▶ Would Bob ever say the words? Susan gave him a hard stare; but he just grinned and started babbling something about some dumb game.

Both examples are written in the third person, but in the first example, the author is on no one's side and knows how both characters feel. The second example is written from Susan's point of view.

Choose a passage from a novel written in the third person. Decide what the point of view is, and then rewrite the passage using a different point of view. How much do you have to change? How do your changes affect the feeling of the passage?

ArtLinks 173

Unit 4

What Have You Learned?

Explore the Language of Art

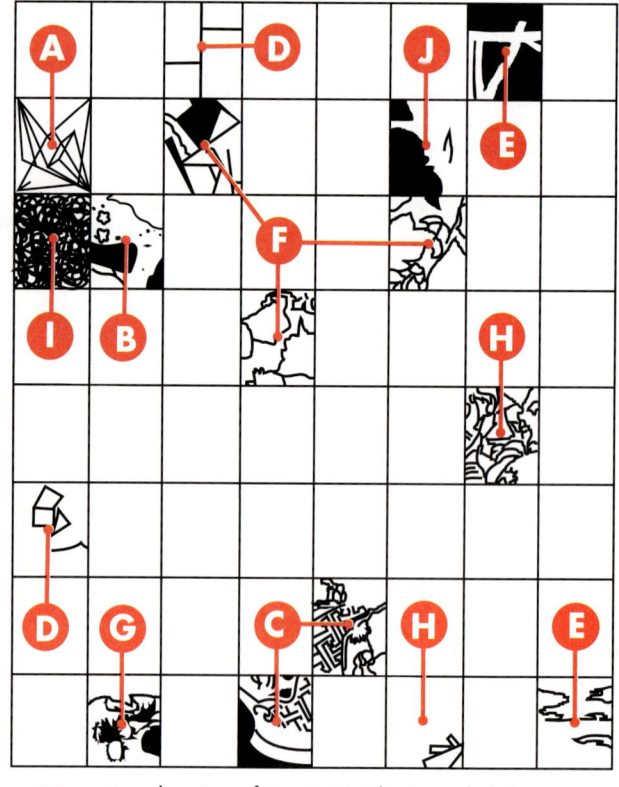

A Pat Steir. *The Brueghel Series (A Vanitas of Style)*, 1982–1984. Oil on canvas, 64 panels: each 28½ by 22½ inches. Courtesy Robert Miller Gallery, New York.

B Line drawing of Pat Steir's *The Brueghel Series*

174 Unit 4

Can You Find...?

Where Am I?

Match each art term below with the letter in the illustration of Pat Steir's painting on page 174.

1. color intensity
2. bold brush strokes
3. pattern of lines
4. organic shapes
5. patterns
6. texture
7. geometric shapes
8. overlapping
9. neutral colors
10. negative shape

How Am I?

Using the language of art, respond to the following questions.

1. Describe what the 64 panels in this composition show.
2. How do the various art styles help to unify the composition? Which elements of art provide variety?
3. Why did the artist use various styles to create this painting?
4. What is the mood of this artwork? What does this artwork remind you of?

And the Subject Is...?

Find the term that *does not belong* in each art subject. Indicate in which subject the term belongs and explain why.

5. **Beings:** people, animals, profile, emotions, landscape, full figure, self-portrait, facial proportion.
6. **Places:** seascape, profile, cityscape, interior, environment, weather conditions, time of day, mountains.
7. **Objects:** still life, symbol, drapery, gesture, furniture, tree, food, vessel.

Look back through this unit. Find examples of artworks that combine the following subjects. Explain why you selected each example.

8. **Beings and places**
9. **Places and objects**
10. **Beings and objects**
11. **Beings, places, and objects**

- *How do the subjects and styles work together to create a mood in each example you selected?*

What Have You Learned?

Write About Art

A Artist unknown. *The Flying Horse.* Eastern Han dynasty, 2nd century A.D. Bronze, 13½ by 17¾ inches. Photograph © Robert Harding Picture Library.

B Jaune Quick-to-See Smith. *The Family Tree,* 1986. Pastel on paper, 30 by 22 inches. Collection of Bernice and Harold Steinbaum. Courtesy of Steinbaum Krauss Gallery, New York.

C Deborah Butterfield, *Untitled (Eclipse),* 1986. Steel, 80 by 110 by 24 inches. Private collection, courtesy Edward Thorp Gallery, New York.

In Your Own Words

Compare and contrast **A**, **B**, and **C**.

1. What is similar?
2. What is different?
3. What media were used to create each artwork?
4. Imagine the sounds and movements in **A**, **B**, and **C**. How might these horses represent cultural symbols?
5. How do these three images of horses compare with the horse in *Guernica* on page 133?

Re-View

Do You Know the Artist?

Match the artwork and artist at the left with the theme and medium at the right.

1. Toko, *Cat and Spider*   Surrealist scene/Oil
2. Mary Cassatt, *At the Theatre*   Portrait/Color photograph
3. Albrecht Dürer, *Dürer at Thirteen*   Self-portrait/Silverpoint drawing
4. Claes Oldenburg, *Clothespin*   Abstract Expressionist landscape/Oil
5. Viola Frey, *Grandmother Series: July Cone Hat* Full figure portrait/Ceramic sculpture
6. Joan Mitchell, *George Went Swimming at Barnes Hole,…* Animal scene/Silk painting
7. John Biggers, *Three Quilters (Quilting Party)* Pop art portrait/Oil and magna
8. William Wegman, *A Certain Smile*   Female portrait in 3/4 view/ Pastel on paper
9. Roy Lichtenstein, *Nurse*   Monumental object/Sculpture
10. René Magritte, *Mysteries of the Moon*   Group portrait/Conté crayon

Put It All Together

"Whatever the artist makes is always some kind of self-portrait."
—Marisol

TALK AND WRITE How Does a Work of Art Speak?

A Marisol Escobar. *The Family,* 1962. Painted wood and other materials in three sections, overall: 82⅝ by 65½ by 15½ inches. The Museum of Modern Art, New York. Photograph © 1996 The Museum of Modern Art, New York.

1. Describe Describe the subject of *The Family*. Look carefully. How would you describe the expressions of the figures? What is the setting? Describe the objects and symbols you see.

2. Analyze How did the artist use the elements of art and principles of design to represent the subject? Analyze the visual qualities of the artwork by writing three or more words that describe each example of the elements and principles listed below:

> **Example:**
> line— *curved, horizontal, bold, implied,* and so on

pattern	contrast	space
color	texture	emphasis
shape	value	

How do these elements and principles work together? How is variety achieved? What provides unity? Explain how two and three dimensions create depth in this assemblage.

3. Interpret What is the meaning of this artwork? What might each figure be thinking about? What does this assemblage remind you of? How does this artwork make you feel?

4. Judge How do the subject and the style work together to make this assemblage special? Explain. How might you represent your family?

In Your Journal
Reflect on your art-making process.

- How did you generate ideas for your subjects?
- How did you develop and refine your ideas in your artworks?
- What style and medium did you most enjoy? Why?
- How did you reflect your own style in your artworks?

What Have You Learned?

Unit 5

Henri Matisse. *Interior with Egyptian Curtain*, 1948. Oil on canvas, 45³/4 by 35¹/8 inches. The Phillips Collection, Washington, D.C.

A World of Places and Objects

If someone asked you about your favorite place, how would you describe it? Is it somewhere you have visited or imagined, such as a faraway land? Or is it nearby—perhaps a cozy little nook beside a window? Artist Henri Matisse created a painting of one of his favorite places, shown on the facing page. What clues inform you it is indoors? The composition is colorful and filled with pattern and light. Notice the still-life arrangement of fruit on the table. Matisse captured the inner beauty of these objects to help the viewer appreciate the way they fill space in a pleasing way. See how his interpretation of a curtain on the right side calls attention to its exotic appeal. Can you imagine a palm tree more symmetrically positioned in a window? Such scenes are recorded by painters through memory, observation, or imagination. They are special places with objects of beauty—inspired by the artist's imaginative eye.

Places and objects in art can be as serious as a war memorial sculpture in our nation's capital or as whimsical as a colorful wall mosaic in a neighborhood. They can be indoors or outdoors, large or small, hard or soft. They can be utilitarian art or fine art; they can be made of found objects or of more traditional media.

As you study this unit, you will become familiar with places and objects as they are seen through the eyes of artists. Some lessons focus on an artful object, while others are about an artful place. Many lessons include both an object and a place together. As Matisse said about his own paintings, "The object is not interesting in itself. It's the environment which creates the object."

What objects will you show in your artworks? Think about how the places surrounding those objects might help create a mood for your compositions. Look through your Sketchbook/Journal to find drawings of objects that you have created. What is special about those objects? What drawings of places did you include that also hold special meaning for you? The Studio activities in this unit offer opportunities for you to expand upon the ideas and feelings these drawings convey.

At a Glance

Does this scene look like a place you might like to live? Why?

How would you describe the climate in this place?

How do you think the artist feels about this place and the objects in it? Tell why.

Lesson 1

Murals as Visual Stories in Communities

Murals and Messages

For at least 30,000 years, artists have sought out places to showcase their artworks. Before they were introduced to canvases and paper, for example, artists often created a visual story, or **mural**, by painting images directly onto walls and ceilings in caves. Photographs of these murals show us stories about ideas, beliefs, and values of long ago. Perhaps you have seen murals in your own community. They may be painted on billboards, sides of buildings, walls, and ceilings. They often tell visual stories about modern culture and its history or convey messages, as do advertisements or public safety announcements.

A common purpose of a mural is to convey a theme that has a political or social message. For example, Mexican murals painted during the early twentieth century often portray the revolution of the people of Mexico against their government. Where have you seen a mural that conveys a political or social message?

Murals tell other kinds of stories too. They might show a religious event from beginning to end or ways people celebrate a special day. Think about the kinds of messages you have seen in murals. How would you describe them? Were they historical, social, or political? Did they show a religious event or a celebration? What other messages might murals convey?

Some murals are created for entertainment, for humor, or to call attention to something unusual. The

A How does the car in this mural help you understand its size relationships?

Kent Twitchell. *Edward Ruscha Monument,* 1978–1987. Mural, height 70 feet. Los Angeles, California.

artist of **A**, Kent Twitchell, drastically changed an urban environment with his enormous 70-foot–high wall painting by commanding attention to it in an entertaining way. The title of the mural, *Edward Ruscha Monument,* offers clues about the artwork's meaning. During the Pop-art movement, California artist Edward Ruscha created humorous artworks that challenged the impersonality of billboard advertisements. What makes this mural so humorous?

B How would you describe the theme of this mural designed by the muralist Judy Baca?

A **muralist** is an artist who designs a mural and manages a team of artists who help paint it. Muralists work with a theme— that is, the artist's interpretation of a broad or abstract topic, such as nature, love, beauty, or humor. Compare the murals of Twitchell and Judy Baca. How are their themes different? Which do you prefer?

Career Links

Judy Baca

If you drive on a freeway in Los Angeles, California, you may see one of Baca's large murals painted on a concrete wall. The mural in **B** is an example of such a creation she designed to show beauty in nature. For more than five summers, Baca supervised 215 teenagers in completing the half-mile mural. She was hired in 1969 by the Cultural Affairs Division of the City of Los Angeles as a resident fine artist. In this position, she created a youth art program that later became a model program for her mural projects.

Creating a Mural for Your School

Conduct research about the history of your school by interviewing members of the community and researching information in publications and on the Internet. Use pencil and drawing paper to make a sketch of a mural for your school. On craft paper, divide the design into several parts, and assign each part to a group of students. Use acrylic-based paints to complete the colorful mural.

Sketchbook/Journal

Make notes about the events in your mural. Describe how they support a theme. Sketch other events in your community's history. Note how those events might be portrayed in a mural.

Murals as Visual Stories in Communities

Lesson 2
Mosaics as Objects of Expression

Mosaic— a Timeless Medium

You may recall the Roman **mosaic** you studied on page 107, which is housed today in The Metropolitan Museum of Art in New York City. A mosaic is made by fitting together small pieces of colored glass, stone, paper, and other materials called **tesserae**. These found objects are glued onto a flat surface, such as wood or cement. The negative space surrounding each shape is filled with a plaster called *grout*. As a medium, mosaic is timeless. Many modern artists create mosaics. As in Roman mosaics, modern designs are created for sidewalks, furniture, and other surfaces, such as the wall in **A**.

A Modern-Day Mosaic Mural

The mosaic in **A** is also a mural because it appears on a wall. Muralist Isaiah Zagar works by gluing small fragments of found objects—broken mirror pieces, brightly colored clay shards, and pieces of glass and tile—to exterior walls. His artworks enhance the beauty of their surroundings in Philadelphia, the "City of Brotherly Love." What kinds of tesserae can you identify in **A**? Zagar arranged hundreds of tesserae to create

A This mural adorns a wall of a house occupied by, you guessed it, two writers.

Isaiah Zagar. (Detail) *Pemberton Street Mosaic,* 1997. Mixed-media mosaic, 12 by 25 feet. Philadelphia, Pennsylvania.

patterns of swirling rhythms. Find at least three colors of grout between the tesserae. How does this color selection help guide your eye around the composition? Notice the two facial portraits near the center. How does the title of the artwork offer a clue about the portraits? What message might a mural on the side of your home suggest about the talents and activities of family members who live there?

 Isaiah Zagar stands as the focal point of his own mural atop his art studio in Philadelphia.

Isaiah Zagar. *Sculptured Roof Garden,* 1997. Mixed-media mosaic, 10 by 15 feet. Philadelphia, Pennsylvania.

C Bryan, McDonald Middle School. *Native American Mosaic.* Torn construction paper on paper, 24 by 18 inches.

Artist Link

Isaiah Zagar

Isaiah Zagar began his artistic journey in 1969 in Philadelphia, when he decorated the walls of his own art gallery with a rambling mosaic. He enjoyed the process so much that he decorated a wall in his studio with his swirling rhythmic patterns of tesserae. Neighbors were so moved by his work, they commissioned him to create a mosaic for a wall in their neighborhood church. Several mosaic murals later, he became known as the artist with a mission to change condemned and broken-down walls of Philadelphia into concrete canvases. During the past thirty years, Zagar has decorated more than two dozen local structures with his mosaic murals. The mosaic mural of whole objects in **B** is the artist's ongoing project above his studio.

Designing a Mosaic Mural

On a sheet of black construction paper, draw lightly with pencil to create a design for a mosaic mural showing an imaginary dragon in its environment. Cut and tear scraps of colored pages from magazines to create tesserae, and arrange them on your drawing. Glue them into place, working from the center of the design outward and leaving black spaces around each tesserae.

Sketchbook/Journal

Draw several sketches of a mosaic to use to create a tabletop mosaic. Make notes about the techniques of making mosaics.

Mosaics as Objects of Expression

Lesson 3
Outdoor Sculptures as Objects of Adornment

Places for Outdoor Sculptures

While some artists create murals and mosaics to enhance outdoor spaces, others envision ways in which large sculptures can tell visual stories outdoors. **A** and **B** show examples of outdoor sculptures. They are traditionally larger than indoor sculptures and are surrounded by a lot of open space. How do the sculptures appear similar? What differences do you see?

Some outdoor sculptures are *portable structures;* that is, they can be moved from one location to another. The sculpture in **A**, by Niki de Saint-Phalle, is an example of a portable sculpture: It is transported for exhibition from one city to another. The various mirrors add interest to the sculpture and may alter its meaning. Imagine how placing such a sculpture in a dark forest could change the mood of the artwork. Where might you place this portable sculpture in your community? How might its presence alter the mood of the place?

Seppo Aarnos sculpted **B** as a *permanent installation*. He designed it especially to adorn an outdoor space belonging to a specific place of business. Notice the abstract shapes near

A The shiny texture of this cheerful monument to the sun can help elevate the spirits of viewers who peer into its mirrored surface.

Niki de Saint-Phalle. *Oiseau sur l'arche,* 1993. Mosaic of mirrors, approximately 18 by 12 1/3 by 5 1/2 feet. Paris, France.

the top of the sculpture. They represent the skylines of two metropolitan areas in Texas, where the business is located. How would you describe the texture of this sculpture? What mood does the sculpture convey to employers and visitors entering the place of business?

Think about the kinds of outdoor sculpture that enhance your community. Are they designed as portable structures or as permanent installations?

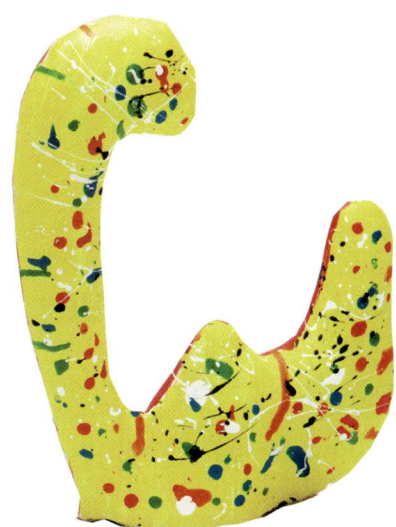

 Rosalinda, Crockett Intermediate. *Crockett Wildcats.* Plaster sculpture, neon tempera, approximately 10 by 12 by 3 inches.

B The initials of the corporation that commissioned this sculpture are CSI. Find each letter in the sculpture.

Seppo Aarnos. *CSI, Inc.,* 1997. Stainless steel, height 16 feet. Fort Worth, Texas.

Materials for Outdoor Sculptures

Almost any material that is weatherproof can be used to build the *armature,* or skeletal framework, of an outdoor sculpture. Armatures are often made of iron, copper, bronze, or other metals. Some sculptors coat their armatures with weatherproof paints. Others rely on the natural elements to create a rusted surface on iron or a **patina,** an attractive greenish film, on copper or bronze. The sculpture in **B** is made of stainless steel. How would you describe its texture? Notice the shiny textured mirrors that Niki de Saint-Phalle chose to apply over a strong, metal armature in **A**. When the sun strikes either of these sculptures, they reflect light. This effect helps visually energize the mood of the artwork.

Creating an Outdoor Sculpture

Suppose your school district asked you and your classmates to create an outdoor sculpture for your school to show appreciation of the arts. What materials might you use? What meaning would your sculpture hold? Make a list of materials you will need; include found objects, paint, glue, and foam core. You may wish to build your sculpture outside in the place you intend to display it.

Sketchbook/Journal

Create several sketches of designs for outdoor sculptures. Include a design for a permanent installation to enhance your favorite place, as well as a design for a portable structure. Make a list of places to display the sculpture. Make notes about the media you would consider using for such a construction.

Outdoor Sculptures as Objects of Adornment

Lesson 4 STUDIO: Creating a Maquette for a Bronze Sculpture

Get the Picture

What might inspire an artist to design a 7-foot, 8-inch bronze about the pain and suffering of war? Sculptor Glenna Goodacre had one major reason: She wanted to honor the 265,000 women who served as support during the Vietnam War. From among that group, 11,000 American military women, nearly all volunteers, helped the sick and wounded.

The outdoor bronze sculpture shows three Vietnam-era women caring for a wounded soldier. There is no rank among the women, and their clothing shows they could be either soldiers or civilian volunteers. The woman who cradles the soldier across her lap is a nurse. Goodacre covered the top of the soldier's face so he would appear anonymous. The standing woman looks for help—perhaps from a medevac helicopter or a spiritual source. Why do you suppose the woman who kneels, looking down at the soldier's helmet, is often considered to be the heart and soul of the sculpture? Goodacre says many veteran women have told her, "That was me. That's how I felt."

To create the sculpture, Goodacre created a small model made of clay, called a **maquette.** This model serves as a plan for a larger sculpture. Goodacre used the *lost wax casting technique* to create both the maquette and the larger bronze sculpture. This process involves several steps, one in which a wax form is melted away from a ceramic mold—hence, the term *lost wax.*

 "To think that my hands can shape the clay that heals the heart. I'm proud of my sculpture." — Glenna Goodacre

Glenna Goodacre. *Vietnam Women's Memorial,* 1993. Bronze cast, height 92 inches. National Mall, Washington, D.C.

 In this image, the sculptor, Glenna Goodacre, molds a clay maquette as a model for a larger sculpture.

Get Set

 **Materials you will need:**
- 12" x 18" white drawing paper
- clay utensils
- #2 pencil
- clay

How to Create a Clay Maquette

To help you with this Studio, refer to page 263.

1. Make a sketch of a volunteer in your community whom you would like to honor. Show the volunteer helping others.

2. Include in your sketchbook a public place to exhibit your outdoor sculpture of this "unsung hero"—old or young, male or female. Begin to create a clay maquette by building a slab foundation.

3. Roll, coil, flatten, and twist some clay to create the form of your unsung hero. Remember to score the parts and join them with slip.

4. Add other people and objects to your maquette to show your volunteer in action.

Creating a Papier Mâché Maquette

Use papier mâché to create a maquette of a team of volunteers in the process of helping others. As you plan your maquette, think about balance and proportion.

Sketchbook/Journal

Make a sketch of an outdoor exhibition place where you envision a larger sculpture of your maquette. Describe the volunteer you portrayed in your maquette and make notes about the mood you intend to convey.

Be an Art Critic!

1. **Describe** Tell about the textures you created for your maquette.
2. **Analyze** How do the people and objects relate to each other in size and movement?
3. **Interpret** How does the mood of your maquette reflect the visual story you are telling about a volunteer?
4. **Judge** In what place in your community might a larger sculpture based on your maquette best be exhibited? Tell why.

Creating a Maquette for a Bronze Sculpture

Lesson 5

Furniture as Art

Furniture Building— a Traditional Artform

When you walk into a room, you can often establish a sense of place simply by studying the furniture there. Who sat in that chair? What conversations took place around this table? What sentimental treasures could be lurking inside the cabinet? The kinds of furniture that surround people in homes, businesses, and other structures tell visual stories about places and the people who use them.

Until two hundred years ago, furniture was built by hand. Villagers used wood and other materials readily available on farms to make their own furnishings. Most furniture designs were simple and crude. Handcrafted and ornately designed furniture was affordable only to people of wealth and high rank.

Toward the end of the eighteenth century, during the Industrial Revolution, machines replaced the labor and skill of many artists in Europe and the United States. Furniture builders were called upon mainly to create designs of chairs, tables, and other objects for machines to mass-produce. Furniture factories sprang up, employing assembly-line workers to operate the machines. Producing furniture by machines made a wider variety of styles and pieces available to the general public. Prices for manufactured furniture and other mass-produced items were affordable to many families. As a result, handmade furniture became rare, and the value for such artworks grew.

 How would you use this chair? What mood might it convey to those who sit in it?

Barbara Brozik. *Deco Chair*, 1997. Acrylic on wood, carved, and gold leafed, 42 by 18 by 18 inches.

B Barbara Brozik is inspired by childhood memories of her mother's antique furniture collection.

Career Link

Barbara Brozik

Barbara Brozik, furniture designer and builder, lives and works in Georgia. Her line of furniture reflects her playful, colorful style. "I think of my work as a painting or sculpture which is functional. You can really use it. Sit on it. Write on it. Set things on it. . . . Enjoy it." Many of her one-of-a-kind furniture sculptures show animal patterns, repeated geometric shapes and forms, and nature motifs. Each item has its own design, form, and pattern, yet together, the forms create a sense of unity in any room. Like other artists, Brozik often obtains commissions from customers to design and build artworks to their specific likes and needs. She also creates furniture to display in shops and galleries for prospective buyers.

Furniture Building in Modern Times

Today's handcrafted furniture found in the United States and other countries is often designed and built by artists. Why do you suppose such furniture is more expensive than furniture made in a factory? *Deco Chair,* in **A**, is a one-of-a-kind design, built by the hands of designer-builder Barbara Brozik. How does this chair compare with furniture manufactured by machines? What uses might you find for this artwork? What mood does it convey?

Beneath the glossy surface of *Deco Chair,* a thin layer of gold- and silver-leaf metal shimmers against a royal burgundy hue. Look closely at the texture the artist achieved with brushstrokes. The armature of this sculptural chair is a wood base, which the artist assembled by cutting, fastening, and gluing parts together to achieve a pleasing form. Would you likely find a *Deco Chair* in your school? at home? Explain.

Designing Furniture as Art

Make a list of types of furniture, and draw thumbnail sketches of your favorite items. Use your imagination to create unusual, yet practical, designs. Work with a partner to follow your best design by building a model. Use cardboard, foam core, matte board, and adhesive materials. Add color to your model by using paint, discarded wallpaper, fabric, and other media.

Sketchbook/Journal

Create several thumbnail sketches of chairs or other kinds of furniture at home. Show your favorite qualities, such as comfort, functionality, beauty, and originality. Make notes about furniture design; include your own ideas about design.

Furniture as Art 189

Lesson 6: Design of Everyday Objects

The Art of Industrial Design

Name three objects in your immediate surroundings that are a result of the Industrial Revolution. You should find that most objects you name originated from a design created so that a machine can make the product. The artful objects in **A** represent a wide variety of designs. Some of these designs belong to a type of art known as **industrial design,** or the plan of an object manufactured for mass distribution, usually by large companies. What items on the poster originated with an industrial design? What items do you think were crafted by hand?

Industrial design objects, such as a container or tool, perform a physical function. Art objects with a physical function are used by someone doing something in them or with them. For example, find the rollerskate in **A**. What is its physical function? Like other objects with a physical function, footwear must be designed to operate well, be functional, and look good. Name some other items of industrial design that you see on these pages.

 This poster is a large greeting card sent to friends of the designers who created it. Each object holds inspirational meaning to a designer. Why do you suppose the design of the poster has no focal point?

Chris Pullman, art director; Gaye Korbet and Chris Pullman, designers. *Seasons Greetings from WGBH Design,* 1985. Courtesy of WGBH, Boston.

Career Link

Industrial Designer

An **industrial designer** is an artist who plans the appearance and form of useful objects. Industrial designers work with scientists and engineers to design objects, such as computers, telephones, cars, toys, and kitchen appliances, to be made in factories. These are mass produced to make many identical products from the same design. After the products have been purchased and tested in the market, industrial designers create plans to improve them.

These everyday objects are examples of industrial design.

B

Planning for an Industrial Design

For each design project, an industrial designer must answer questions, such as:

- Who will use the product? What are the kinds of industrial products the customer currently uses?
- For what purpose will the product be used? For example, will a new bicycle be used to win races? as transportation to school? to ride on mountain trails?

The industrial designer conducts research to answer questions. These answers may help to strengthen the new design. Some designers interview potential customers. A designer may also conduct a written survey. A survey about a new bicycle design that improves upon an existing bicycle might include questions such as these:

- Do you currently own a bicycle?
- What brand of bicycle do you use?
- What features do you like about your current bicycle?
- What features do you dislike about it?
- What features would you like to have on a new bicycle?

Designing a Product

List your ideas for improving a product already in the marketplace, such as a telephone, computer, kitchen appliance, or car. Conduct research in a library, and ask friends questions to help you form your list. Make sketches of the front and side views of your product. Transfer your design sketches to a 12" x 18" sheet of white drawing paper that is folded in half. Show a different point of view on each half. Include any measurement notations that might be helpful to a manufacturer. Draw over pencil lines with black felt-tip pen, and add color with colored pencils or markers.

Sketchbook/Journal

Create a design for a new product. Make notes about who would use the new product and how it would be used.

Design of Everyday Objects

Lesson 7 STUDIO: Creating a Model for a Prototype

Get the Picture

The lamp in **A** is a product of a modern industrial design. Notice that it sends out soft light. What kinds of uses might the designer have intended? Where would this kind of lighting be most appropriate? The bulb is sandwiched between two heavy handcast glass blocks that can be placed on a floor or tabletop. For dramatic effect, you could stack them—or even step on them! What other art objects can you envision in a room with this lamp? Think of a special place for it. Who might use it there? What mood do you think it would convey in your special place?

Creating an industrial design for a product, such as the lamp in **A**, involves three elements: a good imagination, careful planning, and a **model**. Industrial designers create **prototypes**, or working models, of products that will be mass produced later.

Some industrial designers prefer to experiment by creating a variety of models in preparation for designing a prototype. For example, a designer might use clay to create two or more models of a new telephone design. From those models the designer, or group of designers, would select a design for the prototype.

 Harri Koskinen, designer. *Block Lamp*, 1996. Hand-cast glass, 4 by 4 by 6 inches. The Museum of Modern Art New York Design Store.

Get Set

Materials you will need:
- your drawing from the Studio on page 191
- pencil
- modeling clay
- blank card for *credit line*

192 **Lesson 7**

How to Create a Model for a Prototype

1. Revisit your drawing of a design for a product of the future that you created on page 189. Feel free to add any features that might add humor and intrigue to your design.

2. Use modeling clay to create a prototype model for your design.

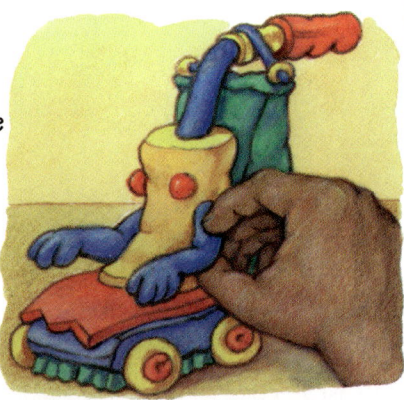

3. Give your model an original title, and display it for others to observe and critique.

Gracy Walters. *Handy Vacuum Cleaner*, 2010. Modeling clay, 6 x 4 x 2 inches. Portfolio.

Creating a Paper Model

Create a paper model for a prototype based on your drawing of a product of the future. Use tagboard as your material. Scissors, glue, and tape may be helpful tools.

Sketchbook/Journal

Write a list of the kinds of materials you would choose to for a prototype of your model. Make notes about observations you may have about your model.

Be an Art Critic!

1. **Describe** What kinds of special features does your model show?
2. **Analyze** How is the form of your model different from existing products?
3. **Interpret** What do the lines of the form tell about the purpose and meaning of your model?
4. **Judge** As you made the model, what information did you gain that may help you create a prototype? Do you think you improved the product?

Creating a Model for a Prototype

Lesson 8

Found-Object Assemblages

About her attraction to gold paint, Nevelson commented: "Gold . . . reflects the great sun."

Louise Nevelson. *Dawn*, 1962. Wood painted gold, 94 1/2 by 75 1/2 by 7 3/4 inches. Private collection.

The Art of Assemblage

"That's a heap of junk!" Artists sometimes hear such words concerning the materials they intend to assemble as a work of art. To the imaginative eye, a "heap of junk" may become an enchanting robot or a dazzling wooden wall of shapes and forms. That heap of found objects, redesigned and configured as an assemblage, can transform a space into a place of beauty or humor.

Unity and Variety in Assemblages

Try to envision the assemblage *Dawn* before artist Louise Nevelson painted it gold. What varieties of shapes and forms do you see in it? What kinds of colors, textures, and patterns do you suppose it had? How does a single color of paint help unify the sculpture?

Now look at **C**, *Case Alien,* by David Strickland. Notice that this assemblage is made of tractor parts. What kinds of elements do you notice that provide variety? What two distinctive qualities unify the sculpture? How would you describe the mood of *Case Alien?* Describe an ideal place—indoors or outdoors—for the assemblage to be exhibited.

B

Louise Nevelson collected found objects to create large assemblages.

C

This artist arranged tractor parts to create a whimsical and humorous assemblage.

David Strickland. *Case Alien,* 1991. Metal machinery parts and glass, 104 by 46 by 63 inches. Private collection.

Artist Link

Louise Nevelson

As a child in New England during the early 1900s, Louise Nevelson, in **B**, loved to collect found objects. She scavenged pebbles, sticks, marbles, and other trinkets, and then arranged them in little boxes. As an adult, during the 1960s, Nevelson became known for the assemblages she created—large wooden walls made of dozens of individual boxes filled with hundreds of carefully arranged found objects. Many of these objects came from fragments of furniture or woodwork rescued from old houses. Milk boxes, lettuce crates, hats, and scores of other items were assembled and then painted black, white, or gold. In this way, she brought unity and harmony to her composition.

Train your eye to look for creative possibilities in what might be considered junk. Start a collection of found objects that you can transform into an exciting assemblage.

Assembling a Robot from Found Objects

Create several thumbnail sketches of ideas you have for a robot. Working with a group of two or three classmates, build your robot from objects, such as cardboard boxes, plastic cylinders, and foam forms. Add small found objects as details. Use paint, colored paper, and other media to give your robot color and unity.

 **Sketchbook/Journal**

Create a sketch of your robot. Make a list of duties it can perform.

Found-Object Assemblages

Lesson 10: Pottery as a Global Artform

Decorative and Functional Pottery

If someone asked you to name the most readily available art material in the world, what would you say? Certainly the medium of clay would enter into the discussion. Clay is made of fine particles of minerals found in the earth. Most clay particles come from the decomposition of older rocks, while others are formed by the grinding action of glaciers. In every part of the world, you can find objects made of clay called **ceramics,** or **pottery,** that have been hardened by intense heat.

Both **A** and **B** are examples of both decorative and useful pottery. As functional and decorative *vessels,* they are beautifully designed and decorated objects that can hold liquids or solids. The bowls in **A** were used for storing meal, seeds, and other dry foods in the desert of Arizona. Ancient, seafaring Greeks stored liquids which were used in the stirrup jar in **B**. Notice the handles as grips for thirsty sailors. Motifs for decorative designs by Greek artists were often drawn from nature. A common design on pottery was a dark octopus with spiraling tentacles. How does the decorative design of **A** compare in subject matter with that of **B**? How do the lines and shapes in the stirrup jar compare with those in Nampeyo's bowls?

 Nampeyo, Fannie Nampeyo, and Dextra Quotskuyva. *Polychrome Ceramic Pottery,* ca. 1900–1980. Private collection.

 Artist unknown, Mycenaean culture. *Stirrup Jar with Octopus,* ca. 1200–1100 B.C. Terra-cotta, 10 1/4 by 3 5/16 inches. The Metropolitan Museum of Art.

Stages in Creating Pottery

In Unit 3 you explored the process of building with clay. As clay dries it becomes delicate. This occurs in the **greenware** stage. Historically, greenware was then **fired,** or baked, over hot coals. Today most potters use an electric or gas kiln, to fire greenware. When the pots cool, potters paint decorative designs on them. Some artists use a thin layer of transparent paints made of minerals called **glazes.** When the glazed pot is refired, the minerals fuse to the clay. The potters of **A** and **B** used glazes to decorate their vessels. Notice how the designs create positive and negative spaces.

Fannie Nampeyo carried on her mother's tradition of creating hand-built Hopi pottery.

Jose, Webb Middle School. *Untitled.* Glazed clay, 9 by 7 1/2 by 5 inches.

Nampeyo

About a century ago, an archeologist in northern Arizona discovered an exciting part of our nation's history. In 1885 a prehistoric village was uncovered. Among the relics found were the pottery bowls similar to the ones in **A**. In addition to preserving the bowls, museum curators wanted modern-day potters to carry on the tradition of the artful designs.

Nampeyo was the finest potter in a nearby Hopi village. She was authorized to record the designs and forms of the ancient pottery bowls. As a creative artist, Nampeyo soon altered and adapted the designs, and added her own variations of the ancient themes. She became well known and taught her craft to her daughters, granddaughters, and great-granddaughters. These potters also changed Nampeyo's style somewhat, varying the stylized motifs, such as reptiles, birds, and feathers.

Creating a Hand-Built Pottery Vessel

To help you with this Studio, refer to pages 260–261.

Roll a chunk of wedged clay into a small sphere with your hands. Make a pinch pot by pushing your thumb into the sphere's center and pinching the clay evenly to form edges. Score the top edge of the pinch pot and add slip to it. With your hands, roll several coils of clay and wrap them around the top of your pinch pot, scoring and applying slip between the layers of clay. With a rolling pin, make a slab of clay and cut it to form a lid for your vessel. Add decoration to the damp clay by pressing relief prints with found objects. When the greenware has been dried and fired, add color with glazes or watercolor.

Sketchbook/Journal

Draw sketches of several designs of functional pottery that you would like to build. Make notes about the process you would use to build your clay vessel.

Pottery as a Global Artform

Lesson 11

Art as Clothing Design

A Artist unknown, Japanese. *Nuihaku*, ca. 18th century. Hand-painted, stenciled gold leaf with silk floss embroidery, length 64 inches. Museum of Art, Rhode Island School of Design. Gift of Lucy Truman Aldrich.

Expressive Eastern Clothing Designs

Look closely at the intricate designs of clothing in **A** and **B**. They are examples of fine craftwork and artistic expression from Japan and Pakistan. The Japanese robe in **A** is a Nuihaku, or a loose-fitting garment with embroidery and *gold-leaf decorations,* which are applied thin layers of gold. Nuihakus may be worn by women and men, including rulers, young warriors, and lay priests. Sometimes entertainers wear the silk robes on stage. Notice the long-tailed bird motif with linked good-luck diamonds. In a word, how would you describe the Nuihaku? What other kinds of colors, patterns, and textures have you seen in Japanese clothing design?

Compare the embroidered designs in **B**, *Wedding Blouse,* with those in **A**. Observe how each artist used the technique of silk embroidery to achieve a different effect. The festive Pakistanian clothing in **B** is bejeweled with mirrors, sequins, and thousands of embroidered silk geometric and organic shapes. If you have a magnifying glass, try counting the handmade stitches in even one square inch of the fabric. How long do you suppose it took to sew the entire garment? Notice the designer's sense of pattern in this artwork. How does the color scheme provide for both unity and variety?

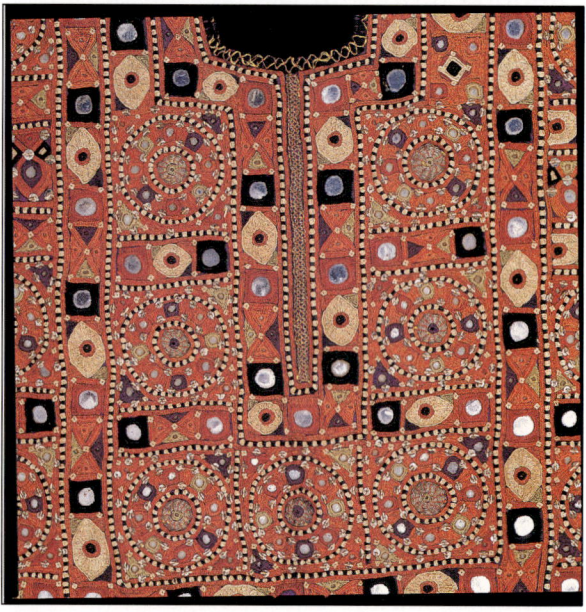

B Artist unknown, Pakistani. *Wedding Blouse: Gaj,* early 20th century. Embroidered silk and cotton, with sequins and mirrors, 20 1/2 by 42 inches. Museum of International Folk Art, Santa Fe, New Mexico.

The Art of Clothing Design

Do you know how the clothes you wear are designed? The art of planning designs for clothing is called **clothing design** or **fashion design.** Fashion design allows opportunities for artists to express their creative ideas in cloth. Each year the art of fashion design presents new styles and lines of clothing. What predictions might you make about next year's clothing styles? How have styles changed during the past five years?

For what purpose might a costume designer create costumes?

Career Link

Clothing and Costume Designers

Clothing designers make drawings for shirts, blouses, skirts, pants, and other garments. Some designs are selected to be sewn as an outfit and presented at a fashion show for clothing manufacturers. If a manufacturer likes the outfit and the way it looks when it is modeled, the design might then be mass-produced in many sizes in a factory. These items are then sold in specialty shops and large department stores. Other clothing designs are for one-of-a-kind "high fashion" garments that can be specially created for a customer.

Costume designers create plans for the clothing you see for actors, dancers, and musicians on the screen and stage. The artist in **C** is a costume designer. Notice the costume she has created from her sketch. It is a historic costume, which required research about its period in history. Some costume designers use computers to help them plan their design. How might this electronic medium for design provide new opportunities for a costume or clothing designer?

Chloe, Ed White Middle School, *Style Plus Fashions: Always in Season.* Marker on paper, 9 by 12 inches.

Creating a Clothing Design

On a computer or a sheet of paper, create several thumbnail sketches of clothing designs you would like to wear. Redraw your favorite two designs to create a sales advertisement. Use your favorite media to add color.

Sketchbook/Journal

Practice drawing a friend or family member modeling a clothing design you create. Make notes about the types of fabric, colors, and patterns in your design.

Art as Clothing Design

Lesson 12
Creating a Repoussé Wall Hanging

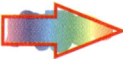 How did the artist reverse the bird motif on some of the squares?

Artist unknown, Peruvian. *Breastplate*, ca. A.D. 1000–1470. Hammered and repoussé gold, 13 1/3 by 8 1/2 inches. The Art Institute of Chicago.

Get the Picture

The gold breastplate in **A** is an example of decorative and utilitarian art made more than five hundred years ago by an artisan in the Chimu culture of Peru. The artist formed it by using the **repoussé** technique of hammering a sheet of gold over a wood form. Notice that the bird shape is repeated as the main theme. This recurring element is called a **motif.** What meaning do you suppose the bird shape held for the artist? Imagine the relief of the bird shape as it appeared on a wood block. The artist placed a sheet of gold metal over the block and hammered gently to define the motif. This procedure is known as **tooling.**

Notice the shape and form of the entire breastplate. Why might it have been thought to protect a ruler during battle? In what ways does this armor seem like other protective coverings you have seen? How is it different? Name some other cultures whose artists designed protective coverings for soldiers to wear during battle.

Get Set

Materials you will need:
- repoussé tools
- metal stylus
- hard rubber or thick felt mat
- 2 sheets of 6" x 6" copper-colored aluminum metal
- white drawing paper
- soft marking pencil, grease pencil, or chalk
- hole-punching tool and hammer
- yarn, leather, or another decorative cord

How to Create a Repoussé Wall Hanging

To help you with this Studio, refer to page 264.

1. Place a sheet of metal on a mat and experiment with tools to create a variety of textures.

2. Draw a sketch of your favorite animal motif for your repoussé wall hanging. Create a textured environment in the background.

3. Use a soft marking pencil, grease pencil, or chalk to transfer the design to another copper-colored sheet of metal.

4. Tool the copper square to show your motif.

5. Punch two holes in the upper corners of your wall hanging, and attach it to a decorative cord. Display your artwork on the wall.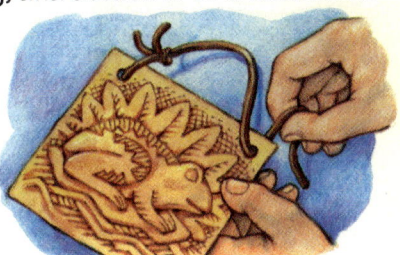

B

Marta, Ed White Middle School. *Pescado (Fish)*. Tooled copper, 9 by 12 inches.

Tooling a Copper Design

Find a design for your motif in your Sketchbook/Journal. Transfer the design to copper, and tool the motif. Rub India ink onto the background for an antique effect.

Sketchbook/Journal

Draw some sketches of motifs for another repoussé design. Make notes about how to create repoussé designs.

Be an Art Critic!

1. **Describe** Tell about the different textures of your wall hanging.
2. **Analyze** How do the textures help create emphasis?
3. **Interpret** What special meaning does the animal motif hold for you?
4. **Judge** Where and how will you display your wall hanging? Explain.

Creating a Repoussé Wall Hanging

Lesson 13: Art as Functional Decoration

 These earrings were found in the tomb of Tutankhamen.
Artist unknown, Egyptian. *Duck-shaped Earrings,* 18th dynasty. Gold with glass, calcite, and colored faience, length 4 1/2 inches. Egyptian Museum, Cairo.

 This knife belonged to a chief of the Chimu cultural group, who used it for ceremonial purposes.
Artist unknown, Peruvian. *Ceremonial Knife,* Pre-Columbian. Gold with inlaid stones, 15 1/2 by 6 1/4 inches. The Museum of Gold, Lima, Peru.

Art and Adornment

You have read about pottery and other kinds of *utilitarian art,* often called **applied art.** These artworks are judged not only for their beauty but for how well they perform their functions. The objects in **A**, **B**, and **C** are examples of applied art intended to decorate spaces and places around them. Each of these artworks has a functional use, as well as a decorative one.

Crafts Around the World

Decorative art has always been popular around the world. Today, as in the past, artists create useful objects by hand. These are known as **crafts.** The artists use gems, metals, and other raw materials as their media. These **craftspeople** fashion artworks such as jewelry, metalworks, beaded objects, stitchery, weaving, and ceramics.

Look closely at the pair of earrings in **A**. They were **crafted,** or made skillfully by hand, in Egypt about 3,000 years ago. Notice the duck head and hawk wings the artist chose to feature. How does the design of these earrings compare with modern-day designs for jewelry? What conclusions can you draw about how nature was considered in ancient Egyptian culture?

"I am rich in silver. I am rich in gold." These words are from an Inca poem. They celebrate the wealth of the Inca civilization

This *Beaded Zemi* shows likenesses to artworks in Africa, Europe, South America, and the Caribbean.

Artist unknown. *Beaded Zemi*, ca. 1515. Wood, cotton, shell, and glass, height 12 1/2 inches. Collection of Museo Nazionale Preistorico ed Etnografico "Luigi Pigorini" Rome, Italy.

that flourished in the Andes Mountains of South America at about the same time the Renaissance took place in Europe. With an abundance of gold mined from the mountains, Incan artists developed expertise in gold-working techniques. The Peruvian knife, in **B**, is an example of decorative and functional art. The handle was crafted from gold as adornment when the knife was not in use as a tool. How does the dual purpose of the handle compare with some modern-day keychains, watches, and other functional objects of adornment?

The *Beaded Zemi,* in **C**, shows artistic components from Africa, Europe, and the Caribbean. Some say the sculpture is a South American spiritual image. Others claim it was fashioned after a chief of the Taíno culture, a group that disappeared from the Caribbean Islands about 500 years ago. What kinds of materials can you identify in this sculpture? What function and meaning might you attribute to the figure? How do beaded objects from your culture compare with *Beaded Zemi* in function and adornment?

Creating Decorative Art

Find an old picture frame, box, small milk carton, or another container. Collect a variety of small found objects that represent your life, and plan how you will use them to decorate your container. Glue the objects to your container in a decorative design. Use paint or nontoxic permanent markers to add additional decoration to your applied artwork.

Sketchbook/Journal

Write about the significance of each found object to your life. Draw sketches of the objects.

Art as Functional Decoration

Lesson 14: Talk About Art

"What I dream of is an art of balance, purity, and serenity."

Henri Matisse, 1869–1954

Henri Matisse was a twenty-year-old law clerk recovering from appendicitis when he first began to think about becoming a visual artist. Perhaps it was his mother's gift of a box of colorful paints that inspired Matisse to become an artist. At any rate, he soon abandoned law to launch a career as a visual artist that would last a lifetime.

Matisse enrolled in the École de Beaux-Arts, a well-known art school in Paris, France. He learned the techniques of working in a variety of art media. Exploring the visual arts in this way gave his life deeper meaning. Painting, he said, opened for him "a kind of paradise" that was unlike the ordinary world. In fact, his goal became to give the viewer of his artworks the calmness he felt as he painted. He wanted his work to relieve some of the everyday stress of a busy world. What would you say to Matisse if you could discuss the way his painting in **B** makes you feel?

Notice the bright colors in **B**. Matisse was an originator of *Fauvism*, the French art movement deriving its name from a term meaning "wild and dangerous beast." Along with other *Fauves*, he acquired this reputation because he used bold and vivid color in his artworks. Images of faces were painted, for example, greens and violets, which enraged many traditional art critics. Matisse persisted with this new method of using color in unexpected ways and at the same time enhanced the rich patterns of lines and shapes in his compositions. About the art critics,

 Henri Matisse. *Self-Portrait,* ca. 1900. Oil on canvas, 25 1/4 by 17 3/4 inches. Private collection.

he commented: "I have always sought to be understood and, while I was taken to task by critics or colleagues, I thought they were right, assuming I had not been clear enough to be understood. This assumption allowed me to work my whole life without hatred and even without bitterness toward criticism, regardless of its source."

Henri Matisse. *Interior with Egyptian Curtain,* 1948. Oil on canvas, 45 3/4 by 35 1/8 inches. The Phillips Collection, Washington, D.C.

Throughout his career Matisse strived to simplify his compositions. For example, he felt that shading and perspective often weakened the effect of line, color, and pattern. By exploring techniques to flatten his shapes and colors, he challenged the way painters had traditionally expressed their views since the Renaissance.

Be an Art Critic!

Look at B to answer these questions:

1. **Describe** Tell about the kinds of lines, shapes, and patterns you see. Point out the focal point of the composition. Where do you see positive and negative spaces?

2. **Analyze** Point out both realistic and abstract qualities of the objects in this painting. Discuss the type of balance the artist used. How does Matisse's use of contrast help define shapes?

3. **Interpret** What mood did Matisse intend for this painting? What clues in the scene offer a sense of place?

4. **Judge** Describe the music you would select for this place. Would you like to visit there? Explain why or why not.

Creating a Sequel to an Artwork

Imagine that you are visiting the place depicted in **B**. You open the window to observe a sudden windstorm. Paint your impressions of the place and objects as they might appear under that condition.

Talk About Art

Portfolio Project

Materials you will need:

- Sketchbook/Journal
- three 12" x 18" sheets of white drawing paper
- black marker
- black construction paper
- #2 pencil
- paper cutting tools
- tempera paint
- tape

Creating a Triptych

A **triptych** is a picture or a carving in three panels, or parts.

1. Select several designs from your Sketchbook/Journal that show three of the following characteristics: color, mixed media, abstract expression, a mask design, a relief sculpture design, an industrial design, or a clothing design.

2. Use a pencil to re-create three of your designs on three 12" x 18" sheets of white drawing paper or black construction paper.

3. Transfer your other drawings to the other parts of your triptych. Add color with oil pastels or tempera paint, or carefully cut out your design.

4. Tape the three images together. Give additional meaning to your triptych by adding written descriptions about your feelings and observations around the edges of the composition.

Gallery

A Josue, Webb Middle School. *Eagle Triptych.* Cut construction paper on poster board, 36 by 22 inches.

B Robert, Webb Middle School. *Bird of Paradise.* Cut construction paper on poster board, 36 by 22 inches.

Portfolio Project 209

Art Links

MUSIC

Identifying Music in Everyday Life

Famous paintings and drawings are frequently used to decorate everyday objects, such as T-shirts, calendars, and umbrellas. Famous pieces of music, too, are often used to adorn or promote various products.

Listen for music in everyday situations and jot down tunes that you have heard in other versions and situations. For example, you may hear hit songs with new words used in TV ads. You may hear famous folk songs piped into a supermarket as background music. Make a list of songs that have been adapted for use in commercials or as background music. Select one or two of these and listen to the original version, if possible. What do you think about changing a song this way and using it for a new purpose? Write a paragraph explaining your position for or against this practice. Compare your position with your classmates' views.

DANCE

Inventing a Dance

People create art in their everyday lives when they make greeting cards, paint their cars with flamelike designs, decorate their homes, and so on. Folk art may end up in a gallery, but it is often anonymous: we do not know the artist's name. The same is true for social dances—the kind of dances people do for fun. New dances are constantly springing up, but we rarely know how these dances came to be or who created them. Often, no one person is responsible.

Explore the way a new dance springs up. Choose a song you like and invent four to six dance steps to go with it. Teach your dance to some of your friends. Let them adapt the steps to music they like and then teach the dance to some of their friends, and so on. Ask the sixth or seventh person down the chain to teach the dance to you. Is it the same dance you created? How has it changed?

THEATRE AND MEDIA
Creating a Reality-Based Dramatic Scene

Some modern artists make exact replicas of ordinary people and scenes. Sculptor Duane Hanson, for example, puts realistic sculptures of ordinary people dressed in real clothes in public places. Some modern television shows go one step further: they offer "reality" itself as drama. Courtroom shows, for example, feature real judges hearing real cases.

Create a dramatic scene based on real life. Get together with a friend and select a subject you tend to argue about—in a friendly way, of course—a sports team, a song, or a clothing fashion, for example. Tape-record yourselves discussing the topic again. Turn the most dramatic five minutes of your conversation into a written script and perform it for some friends—but change roles, each of you speaking the other person's "lines." Afterward discuss the scene with your audience: did it feel like "theatre"? Why or why not? What did you learn that you might use as an actor?

LITERATURE
Writing a 60-Second Story

Many visual artists use their talents to design the packages and ads for products that we buy. Writers sometimes use their storytelling talents to make commercials, public service announcements, and the like. The best television ads deliver a story complete with setting, characters, and plot in just 60 seconds.

See if you can write a 60-second story that could be used as an ad or public service announcement. For example, you might script an ad about the dangers of smoking. Write a script that would take less than 60 seconds to perform. Exchange scripts with a friend and give each other feedback: What could you do to make your script a better story? What could you do to make it a better ad? Would the same changes that make it a better story also make it a better ad, and vice versa? Why or why not?

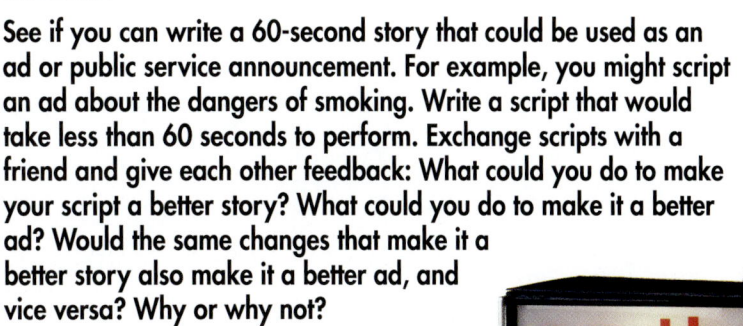

ArtLinks 211

Unit 5

What Have You Learned?
Explore the Language of Art

 Romare Bearden. *Morning of the Rooster*, 1980. Collage on board, 18 by 13¾ inches. Courtesy Estate of Romare Bearden/ACA Galleries New York, Munich.

TALK AND WRITE **Can You Find . . . ?**

Where Am I?

Match each art term at the right with the letter in the illustration of Romare Bearden's collage in B.

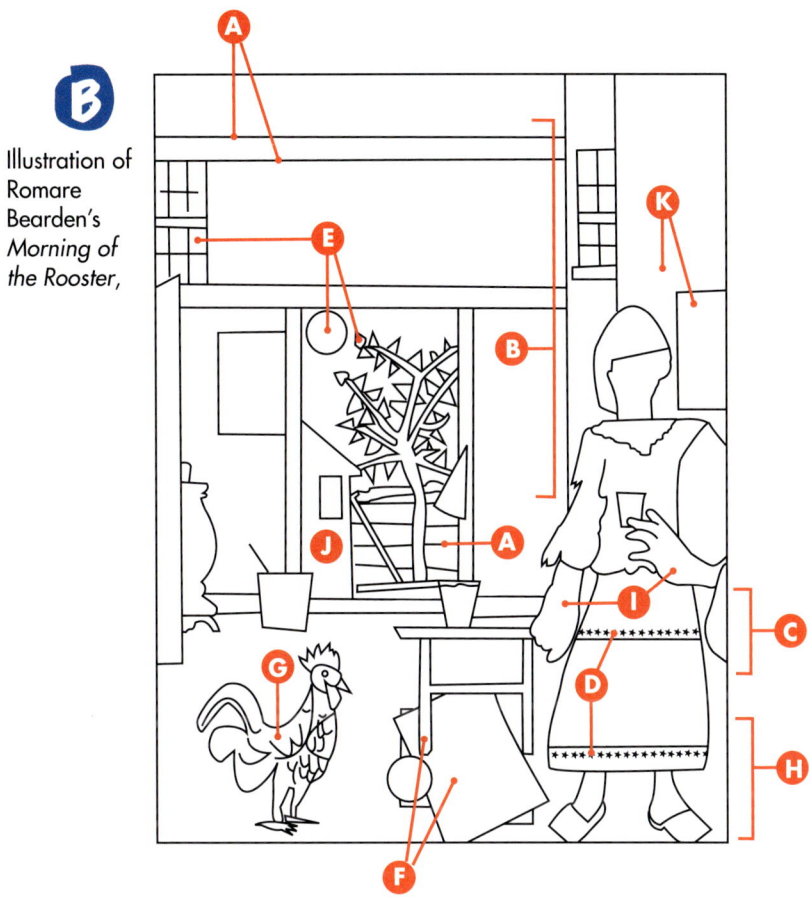

Illustration of Romare Bearden's *Morning of the Rooster,*

1. distortion
2. geometric shapes
3. organic shape
4. texture
5. middle ground
6. negative space
7. foreground
8. pattern
9. parallel lines
10. overlapping
11. background

How Am I?

Using the language of art, respond to the following questions.

1. Describe the place and objects you see in this collage. What lines and shapes do you see?

2. How are the elements of art used? Which principles of design provide variety?

3. What is happening in this artwork? What is the mood? Imagine the sounds and smells. What does the scene remind you of?

4. How did the artist create this collage?

5. Why do you think the artist chose to show this special place and these objects in his artwork?

What Have You Learned? 213

Write About Art

A Simon Rodia. *Watts Towers* (seven towers total), 1921–1954. Scrap metal and mosaic, height range 11 to 100 feet. Los Angeles, California. Photograph © L. Willinger/SuperStock.

B Christo and Jeanne-Claude. *Running Fence, Sonoma and Marin Counties, California, 1972–1976.* Woven nylon fabric, stretched between steel poles, supported by steel cables, 18 feet by 24½ miles. © 1976 Christo. Photograph by Jeanne-Claude.

C Andy Goldsworthy. *Sand Brought to an Edge to Catch the Light,* August, 1991. Shore of Lake Michigan. © Andy Goldsworthy. Photograph courtesy of the artist.

TALK OR WRITE — In Your Own Words

Compare and contrast A, B and C.

1. What is similar?
2. What is different?
3. How was each artwork created?
4. Imagine the sound and motion in each artwork. How does each artwork interact with its environment?

Re-View

WRITE — Do You Know the Artist?

Match the artist and artwork at the left with the subject and medium at the right.

1. Barbara Brozik, *Deco Chair*   Clothing design/Embroidery
2. Louise Nevelson, *Dawn*   Outdoor mural/Mixed media mosaic
3. Henri Matisse, *Interior with Egyptian Curtain*   "Combine Painting"/Mixed media
4. Niki de Saint-Phalle, *Oiseau sur l'arche*   Full-figure portrait/Mural
5. Kent Twitchell, *Edward Ruscha Monument*   Group sculpture/Bronze cast
6. Robert Rauschenberg, *Bed*   Furniture/Acrylic on wood
7. Mycenaean culture, *Stirrup Jar with Octopus*   Still life/Oil
8. Glenna Goodacre. *Vietnam Women's Memorial*   Terra-cotta jar/Ceramics
9. Isaiah Zagar, *Sculptured Roof Garden*   Outdoor sculpture/Mirror mosaic
10. Unknown, Pakistani, *Wedding Blouse*   Assemblage/Found objects

Put It All Together

"I try to find things to paint which I feel have been overlooked, . . . and neglected subjects." — Wayne Thiebaud

TALK AND WRITE How Does a Work of Art Speak?

 Wayne Thiebaud. *Apartment Hill,* 1980. Oil on linen, 65 by 48 inches. The Nelson-Atkins Museum of Art, Kansas City, Missouri (Purchase: acquired with the assistance of the Friends of Art).

1. **Describe** Artist Wayne Thiebaud is a figurative painter known for his colorful paintings of objects, such as mass-produced food and household items. What has the artist shown as the subject in *Apartment Hill?* Identify and describe the objects and shapes you see.

2. **Analyze** How did the artist use the elements of art and principles of design to reflect the subject? What elements help your eye move around the composition? Analyze the visual qualities of the artwork by writing three or more words that describe each example of the elements and principles below.

   Example:
   line— *curved, horizontal, implied,* and so on

   pattern   space   light   color
   background   emphasis   tints   shape
   contrast   balance   texture   foreground

3. **Interpret** What is the mood of this artwork? How might it feel to pass by the hill on the street below? to live there? What does this painting remind you of?

4. **Judge** What makes this painting special? Explain. What other information would you like to learn about this artwork?

In Your Journal
Reflect on your art-making process.

- How have the artists in this unit helped you discover new ways of exploring places and objects in art?
- Reflect on your favorite places and objects. How did you include these in your artworks?
- What places and objects would you like to explore in future artworks?

What Have You Learned?

Unit 6

Georgia O'Keeffe. *From the Lake No. I*, 1924. Oil on canvas, 37 1/8 by 31 inches. Des Moines Art Center, Iowa.

A World of Expression and Meaning

Have you ever been at a loss for words? Most everyone has had to struggle to find the right way to discuss an idea or a feeling. Georgia O'Keeffe often turned to her favorite art process—painting—to help her express ideas and feelings. She had only to pick up a paintbrush as an invitation to create colors and shapes. They helped her convey meanings about ideas and feelings her own words sometimes could not express. Notice the cool colors and abstract shapes of her painting on the facing page. Feel the rhythm of the water. What words would you use to describe this composition?

When artists express themselves, they use *symbols* to represent their ideas and feelings. **Expression** is an artist's way of using symbols that are meaningful to her or him. For example, a dancer dressed in orange and red colors may tiptoe across a stage in short, rapid steps to symbolize flames. Such a performance may have a special meaning to the dancer and various other meanings to members of the audience. Likewise, a visual artist may use symbols, represented through line, shape, color, form, texture, and space, to express meaning on canvas or other media. Viewers may think about the *intended meaning* of the artwork, or what the artist meant to express. Why did the artist create the work? What emotions does it convey? What experiences in the artist's life may have motivated such an expression? Based on their own experiences, viewers may arrive at meanings of their own.

An important part of expression is **originality,** an artist's unique way of showing ideas and feelings. Consider that given the same instrument, two musicians will create two entirely different tunes. Given the same list of words, two poets will create two distinctively different poems. Why do you think this happens? Why aren't all tunes and poems just about alike? Some of the artworks in this unit share the same subject, but they are distinctly different works of art. As you explore these artworks, you will discover ways in which each artist used original thoughts and ideas to express individual meaning.

As you examine and critique the artworks in this unit, you will find Studio activities to help you express your own ideas and feelings. What stories will you tell? How will the symbols you choose help show your intended meanings?

At a Glance

What is happening in this image?
How does the credit line help you understand the subject?
How do the colors make you feel about the water?

Lesson 1: Expression Through Nature

 Georgia O'Keeffe liked to fill a large canvas with the colors and shapes of one flower. How does the scale of this poppy create emphasis?

Georgia O'Keeffe. *Red Poppy,* 1927. Oil on canvas, 7 by 9 inches. Private collection.

Styles and Expression

These paintings of poppies show that style is an important part of expression. *Styles* include all the features that make an artwork different from other artworks. For example, the different styles of **A** and **B** show the originality of each artist. Both styles also have features that make the artworks similar to other artworks.

Some art critics say Georgia O'Keeffe's paintings of nature show a *realistic* style. They claim that you can almost reach out and touch the poppy in **A**. Other critics see *abstract* qualities in many of her artworks because of their simplified and flattened shapes. The artist herself said that she painted exactly what she saw. Which style do you think *Red Poppy* reflects?

Victor Gatto's expression of poppies, in **B**, is an example of **Folk Art,** a style usually created by people who have not received formal art training. Folk Art generally reflects a culture or tradition. As you explore the Folk Art painting in **B**, describe the qualities of the artist's surroundings.

 Victor Joseph Gatto was forty-eight when he decided to become an artist. In what ways might this be reflected in the meanings of his paintings?

Victor Joseph Gatto. *Poppies,* ca. 1950. Oil on canvas panel, $15^{3}/4$ by $19^{3}/4$ inches. Collection of Dr. Kurt Gitter and Alice Rae Yelen.

Artist Link

Georgia O'Keeffe and Victor Joseph Gatto

If you ask any artist to recall the time when she or he decided to become an artist, many cite a special moment. They may describe a conversation or an event in which visual expression became an important part of their lives. This realization can come to artists at any age.

At the age of twelve, Georgia O'Keeffe declared to a friend that her life's goal was to become an artist. Perhaps she was inspired during private art lessons she had taken on Saturdays growing up. For many years as a young girl, O'Keeffe practiced drawing, painting, and sculpting with other young artists. As she grew older, she attended art schools and studied with skilled art teachers. She developed friendships with artists who enjoyed discussing problems and solutions involving their own and others' artworks. In these ways, O'Keeffe learned about the techniques, history, and philosophy of art.

Artist Victor Joseph Gatto, at age forty-eight, attended an outdoor art show in the Greenwich Village community of his hometown New York City. Realizing his own talent for visual expression, he began to create energetic, colorful paintings inspired by the world around him and his rich imagination. This turning point fueled a passion for painting that launched his career as a Folk Artist.

C Sara, Salado Intermediate School. *Lavender Paradise.* Oil pastels on paper, 12 by 18 inches.

Expression Through Color and Shape

Select an emotion you often feel, such as happiness, sadness, or anger. Write a description of the colors and shapes that best represent the emotion. Create several thumbnail sketches of abstract designs in nature that express the emotion you have selected. Re-create your favorite design on a sheet of 12" x 18" white paper, and add color using watercolor or other media.

Sketchbook/Journal

Create and label several other thumbnail sketches that express different emotions. Make notes about expressing your emotions through color.

Expression Through Nature

Lesson 2: Expression of Self

A Miriam Schapiro. *My History*, 1997. Paper, acrylic, fabric on paper, 33 3/4 by 25 1/4 inches. Collection of Eleanor and Len Flomenhaft. © Miriam Schapiro. Courtesy of Steinbaum Krauss Gallery, New York City.

Mixed Media for Expression

An artwork created by using more than one medium is called a **mixed-media** work. The collage in **A** is an example of a mixed-media composition by artist Miriam Schapiro. What do you think the artwork is about? What does the shape of the artwork represent? How is symbolism used in the artwork?

Notice the individual sections that resemble blocks of a quilt. Each one holds an object or symbol that represents special meaning to the artist. For example, needlework and embroidery items honor women who have created artworks through the ages. What symbols do you see that represent Schapiro's Jewish heritage? Do you recognize the photograph of Mexican artist Frida Kahlo on the right side? Schapiro considers Kahlo a symbol of strength and creativity because of her triumph over pain and suffering. What other symbols do you see? How do you suppose they relate to the meaning of the title—*My History*?

Types of Mixed Media

A popular type of mixed media is *collage*, as in **A**, which often consists of a painted background with flat items attached. Still photographs are sometimes parts of mixed-media collages. You may remember reading about the "combine paintings" of Robert Rauschenberg, and the found-object assemblages by Louise Nevelson and David Strickland. These are examples of three-dimensional mixed media. More recently, video installations, like those of Bill Viola that you saw in Unit 2, as well as some computer artworks, have been referred to as mixed media.

 Rondo is a musical term that involves a lively rhythm with a recurring theme. How does that information help you understand the femmage in this photograph?

 Elizabeth, Salado Intermediate School. *Jazz.* Colored markers on paper, 9 by 12 inches.

Artist Link

Miriam Schapiro

Miriam Schapiro refers to each of her mixed-media collages as a **femmage.** Femmage is a type of collage that includes traditional fabric art made by women. Aprons, handkerchiefs, hot pads, lace, and other needlework fabrics add meaning to her femmages. "I have such regard for people who make work that is called 'crafts,'" she explained. "Because of the way I use fabric, I have always wanted to be part of their world. I feel a closeness to them."

Unity and variety are strengths of Schapiro's femmages. She invites the viewer to explore the composition through the rich variety and interesting placement of mementos. Line, color, and shape express a feeling of oneness within Schapiro's work. Notice also the techniques she uses to show movement. How do the rhythmic lines in **B** help bring unity to the photograph?

Creating a Self-Portrait in Mixed Media

Select a fine-arts area, such as music, theatre, or dance, that you enjoy. Create four thumbnail sketches of you performing in costume in this artform. Re-create your favorite two sketches, each on a sheet of 9" x 12" white paper. Use colored pencils or markers to add patterns to each background. Add interest to your self-portraits by cutting and gluing various colors and patterns of fabrics.

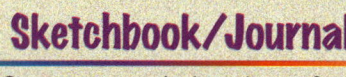

Sketchbook/Journal

Create several sketches of designs for a quilt showing you as a visual artist, a dancer, a musician, and an actor. Make notes about mixed media.

Expression of Self

Lesson 3: Expressive Points of View

 Piet Mondrian painted several versions of this tree. How would you describe his point of view?

Piet Mondrian. *The Red Tree*, 1908. Oil on cloth, 27 1/3 by 38 2/3 inches. Gemeentemuseum Dan Haag, Netherlands.

 This painting is seen from a bird's-eye view. Look for the hunter.

Andrew Wyeth. *The Hunter*, 1943. Tempera on Masonite™, 33 by 33 7/8 inches. The Toledo Museum of Art, Toledo, Ohio. Elizabeth C. Mau Bequest Fund.

Point of View

A **point of view** is the angle from which a viewer sees an object or a scene. Artists may choose a point of view to express their feelings about a subject. Notice the compositions in **A**, **B**, and **C**. They each show the same subject—a tree. Now consider how their differing points of view change the way you think or feel about the tree. How might point of view help artists express meaning in their compositions?

Three Points of View

Artists often work from one of three points of view. Any one of these points of view can change the way a viewer thinks and feels about a subject. The most common point of view is a *straight-on view*, as in **A**. This image shows the tree from a familiar angle. If you look back at all the images in this book, you will see that most of them show a straight-on point of view. Such a view encourages the viewer to focus on other aspects of the composition.

Sometimes, as in **B** and **C**, the artist intends to show a subject from a more dramatic angle. In these images, the viewer's eye is pulled quickly into the composition. Notice how features of the tree, such as the shapes of leaves and branches, stand out. What mood do you feel each artist conveys?

The composition in **B** is an example of a *bird's-eye view*. Can you explain why? The trunk of a sycamore tree, which appears large at the top, recedes almost immediately to the forest floor, where we see the tiny figure of a hunter. Notice that in this example a leaf can be the same size as a human figure! This point of view is an effective way of making the viewer forget that the image is a flat, two-dimensional composition.

C Artist Georgia O'Keeffe was inspired to paint this image as she stargazed through tree branches on the ranch of her friend D.H. Lawrence. How does her point of view affect your understanding of her experience?

Georgia O'Keeffe. *The Lawrence Tree,* 1929. Oil on canvas, 31 by 39 1/4 inches. Wadsworth Atheneum, Hartford, Connecticut.

The point of view from beneath, in **C**, is often called a *ground-level view* or *worm's-eye view*. We see the images as a worm or an ant might see them. Using a worm's-eye point of view can help an artist express feelings about the power of the subject. Notice the bright stars that almost twinkle on the canvas. How do they help establish the mood of this painting?

D Andy, Driscoll Middle School. *From Above.* Colored markers, 9 by 12 inches.

Working from a Worm's-Eye View

Imagine yourself the size of a bug or a worm. Create a drawing of yourself in the center of tall buildings, in a forest, or in some imaginary environment. Add color, using colored pencils or markers.

Sketchbook/Journal

Create several thumbnail sketches from a worm's-eye view and several from a bird's-eye view. Make notes about drawing from different points of view.

Expressive Points of View

Lesson 4 STUDIO

Creating an Abstract Cityscape

Get the Picture

Sometimes artists work from more than one point of view in a single composition. The image in is an example of such an expression. Its subject is an abstract cityscape of recognizable objects. The artist simplified and flattened shapes of buildings and other objects in this unusual, yet expressive composition. These symbols are shown from more than one point of view. How would you describe the points of view in **A**? Explain how the technique of using more than one point of view makes you feel about the composition. How does the title of the artwork indicate that a part of the composition is shown from a bird's-eye view?

Now explore the composition to discover the artist's many abstracted shapes. Notice the fence-like structure, windows, doors, and sides of buildings in this city. Identify a variety of objects in the image. Notice how the blue spiral shape guides your eye to a focal point near the center. How would you describe the focal point? What natural element might the blue area represent? How does the title help you understand the blue area? What other objects do you see in this abstract cityscape? How might you interpret their meanings?

Have you ever thought of a cityscape as a self-portrait? Now that you have closely examined **A**, consider that artist Friedensreich Hundertwasser intended this cityscape to represent an image of himself! The tightly wound blue spiral

A This abstract composition is one man's expression of a cityscape, and it shows his feelings about the place. What mood does the image convey?

Friedensreich Hundertwasser. *808A End of Waters on the Roof,* 1985. Woodcut in 28 colors, 20 1/2 by 25 3/8 inches. © 1998 Gruener Janura AG, Glarus, Switzerland.

symbolizes the artist. Even the eye in the center is symbolic of the artist's eye. What emotions do you think the artist wished to express? What meaning do you suppose he intended as he created this expression of an interior of a cityscape? How does the composition make you feel?

Get Set

 **Materials you will need:**

- photographs of cityscapes
- 12" x 18" white drawing paper
- ruler, #2 pencil
- tempera paint and brushes
- mixing tray

How to Create an Abstract Cityscape

1. Examine several photographs of metropolitan cities.

2. Make a list of objects you see in the sky and near the ground.

3. Create lightly in pencil an abstract design of your favorite city by simplifying the shapes of the objects in your list. You may wish to use more than one point of view.

4. Add bright colors to your design using tempera paint.

Creating a Cityscape Collage

Create a design that combines a city of the present with a city of the future. Glue cut and torn construction paper and tissue paper to fill in the large areas. Add detail to your design using colored pencils, markers, and oil pastels.

 **Sketchbook/Journal**

Create several thumbnail sketches of cityscapes. Make notes about abstract design and how you planned your artwork.

 **Be an Art Critic!**

1. **Describe** Tell about the shapes you created for your abstract design.
2. **Analyze** Did you use one or more than one point of view? Explain how your selection affects the design.
3. **Interpret** How would you describe the mood of your abstract cityscape?
4. **Judge** Where do you imagine your cityscape displayed? In which special building might it be showcased?

Creating an Abstract Cityscape

Lesson 5
Expression Through Commercial Arts

Graphic Design

If you have ever created a poster for a school or community event, you were creating an expression through graphic design. **Graphic design** is the art of communicating messages with images and lettering. It is often used in the commercial arts, such as advertisements, signs, book jackets, and jewel cases for music CDs and CD-ROM software. **Logos** are often created by **graphic designers**, who are commissioned to design symbols to visually represent cities, businesses, clubs, or other groups.

The computer is the medium of choice for today's graphic designer. On a high-powered computer, graphic designers create animated figures, place them in backgrounds of *virtual reality,* and relay messages suited for the Internet, television, or electronic games.

Multimedia, a combination of technology-related media used to create compositions, is a huge success in the highly competitive world of electronic games and Internet advertisements. Movies are considered *multimedia presentations* because of their combination of sound, film, and graphic design. These media are often combined with digital animation to produce web page designs, television commercials, and full-length motion pictures.

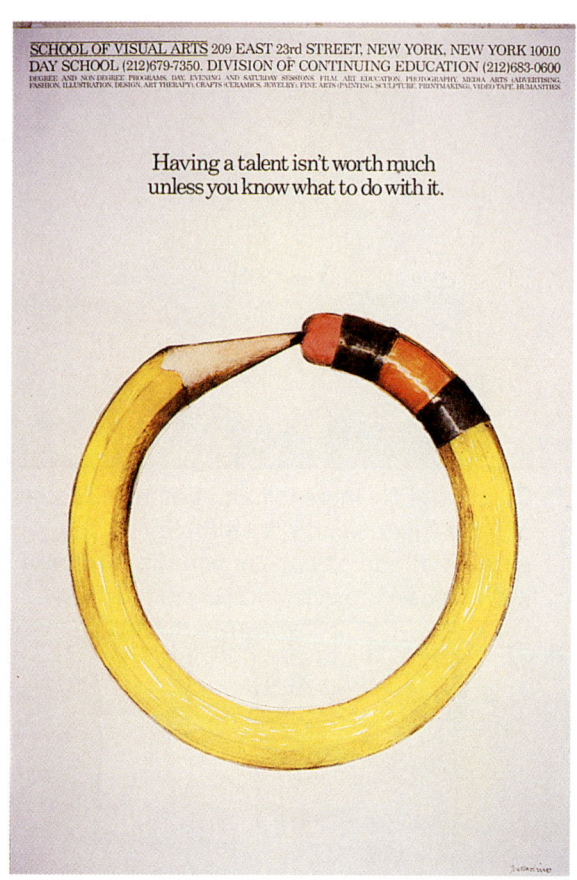

 Tony Palladino. Untitled, 1978. Pencil and watercolor on paper, 29 1/2 by 45 inches. Courtesy of School of Visual Arts, New York City.

 Jesse, Edgewood Middle School. *My NBA Dream.* Colored markers on paper, 12 by 18 inches.

226 Lesson 5

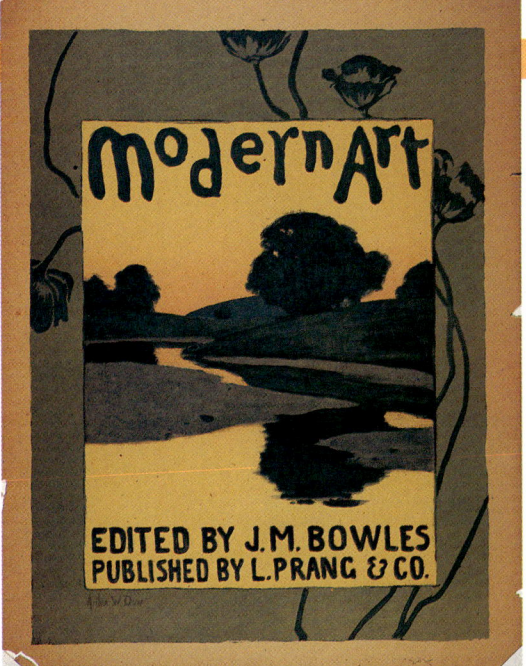

Arthur Wesley Dow. *Modern Art*, 1895. Color lithograph on paper, 20 by 15³/₄ inches. National Museum of American Art, The Smithsonian Institution, Washington, D.C.

Posters as Graphic Designs

Posters have long been a popular form of graphic design. During the 1860s, posters that advertised special events became popular in Europe and the United States. Some announced that the circus was coming to town; others advertised concerts or plays. Many of the colorful posters were so attractively designed and held such sentimental meaning that people hung them in their homes and businesses as artworks.

The poster in **A** is designed to entertain and give information. The first message you might get is from the **illustration,** or informative drawing. In most graphic designs, as in **A**, the illustration commands your attention. Indeed, it is hard to miss the humorous treatment of the pencil—its lines, shape, and colors! Describe the illustration in **A**. What is its message? Notice the use of negative space. How does it affect the subject? What aspects of the poster let you know that the designer intends a serious meaning in a humorous way?

Artist Link

Arthur Wesley Dow

The poster in **C** was a gift in 1985 to subscribers of a publication entitled *Modern Art*. The graphic design for the poster was created by a popular art teacher and graphic designer, Arthur Wesley Dow, whose instruction at the Art Students League in New York City influenced many well-known artists. Dow's woodcut for *Modern Art* was reproduced in a twenty-inch–high color *lithograph*, an artwork made through a printing process. His deep interest in Japanese art is apparent in the design of this poster. Notice the peaceful mood of the lines and shapes of the trees reflected in the still water. How would you describe the color selections?

Creating a Poster

Think about a goal you would like to achieve, such as graduating from college, having an exhibition of your artworks, or excelling in a sports event. Gather information—words, and illustrations—and establish a date, place, and time to include in a poster announcing a celebration of your achievement. Create several thumbnail sketches for your poster. On 12" x 18" poster board, lightly draw your best design. Use cut-out letters, colored markers, and other materials to complete your poster design.

Create a poster on a computer using a suitable drawing software application. Or scan the design you created, and make enhancements using the computer tools.

Sketchbook/Journal

Collect posters and other advertisements from magazines and newspapers, and paste them into your Sketchbook/Journal. Make notes about each of your favorite designs.

Expression Through Commercial Arts

Lesson 6

Expression Through Symbols

Totems as Symbols

Does your school have a *mascot*—a person, animal, or object that represents the school? A mascot serves as a symbol of the school and its students. At athletic games and contests, the mascot is a symbol of good luck.

Totems are used in a similar way. Totems are symbols that represent clans and other subgroups of a culture. Various cultures around the world, such as some in Australia and Polynesia, use totems to symbolize their beliefs and practices. The totems in **A** and **B** are from different cultures on different continents. The credit lines can help you learn more about them. How are they similar? What do their symbols tell you about their culture?

Traditional and Modern Totems

The totem in **A** represents the Native American Tlingit cultural group located on the Northwest coast of the United States. This massive carved post, called a *totem pole*, is typical of most Native American totem poles that show family histories. Such sculptures were traditionally built to memorialize important events, to mark land ownership, or to honor the dead. What kinds of symbols do you see in **A**? What type of balance does the totem pole show? If you were a member of the Tlingit cultural group, where might you display this totem pole?

 Artist unknown, Tlingit culture. *Tlingit House Post*, date unknown. Carved and painted wood, height 89 3/4 inches. University of Pennsylvania Museum, Philadelphia.

The group of abstract totems in **B** were created by a modern sculptor, Francisco Matto. Find the six symbols on the flat boards. What do they represent? Describe the artist's use of both organic and geometric shapes. How does the variation in the size of each sculpture add interest to the overall composition? What story might you tell about each of the totems?

B Francisco Matto. *Lamb, Mask, Venus, Universal Man, Snail,* and *Covenant Tablets,* 1979. Carved wood totems, painted with oil, height 71 to 83 inches. Courtesy of Cecilia de Torres, Ltd., New York City.

C Amanda, Ed White Middle School. *Animal Farm Totem.* Colored construction paper, approximately 13 by 4 by 3 1/2 inches.

Career Link

Francisco Matto

Francisco Matto, a sculptor from Uruguay, began his art career in 1926, teaching himself how to paint. During a trip to Argentina he started collecting **Pre-Columbian artworks**, paintings and sculptures created before Columbus's voyage to the Americas in 1492. These, and other artworks from Africa and Oceania, inspired him to include the kinds of signs and symbols you see in **B**.

In 1939 Matto visited Joaquín Torres-García, a well-known art educator and artist in Uruguay, and showed him some paintings he had created on wood. Torres-García encouraged him to continue painting and sculpting in the same style. This connection was the beginning of a friendship that produced a school for artists whose artworks reflect a similar abstract style. The school, *El Taller* [Workshop] *Torres-García* was an established art education center for almost 20 years (1944–1962). It was highly regarded throughout South America. Members of the *Taller* expressed themselves through painting, sculpture, ceramics, wood and iron reliefs, furniture, murals, and architectural projects.

Creating a Totem

Create a design for a totem that includes the sketches of the heads of at least three of your family members, friends, or favorite animals. Use cut construction paper and paper sculpture techniques to make each of the heads for your three-dimensional totem. To create a pole, form a cylinder using a sheet of 12" x 18" construction paper and add a cardboard base. Glue or tape the paper heads, one on top of the other, to the pole.

Sketchbook/Journal

Draw several sketches of ideas for totems that you would like to make for the facade of your school. Make notes about totems and how you made yours.

Expression Through Symbols

Lesson 7: Masks for Expression

 Artist unknown, Teotihuacán culture. *Funerary Mask*, ca. A.D. 400–600. Rock and shell mosaic, 8 1/2 by 7 3/4 inches. National Museum of Anthropology, Mexico City, Mexico.

Purposes of Masks

No one knows when people first started wearing masks and using disguises. Masks traditionally have been a part of cultures all over the world. They are often used as symbolic decorations in dances, dramas, and ceremonies. They help wearers temporarily change their appearances, often becoming players in a theatre of fantasy. Look at the masks in **A**, **B**, and **C**. Where does your imagination take you as you view each one?

Meanings of Masks

If you have ever worn a mask, you have experienced the way it changes how you look and feel for a short while. Perhaps you raised or lowered your voice to help hide your identity. Each of the

How would you describe the balance of this Peruvian mask created during the Inca Empire?

Artist unknown, Peruvian. *Inca Mask*, date unknown. Gold with paint, 21 1/4 by 12 1/8 inches. Museo Arqueológico Larco Herrera, Lima, Peru.

C This ceremonial mask from Zaire is a symbol of the spiritual world.

Artist unknown, African. *Kifwebe Mask,* date unknown. Wood fiber, pigments and feathers, 14⁷⁄₈ by 8¹⁄₈ inches. © Royal Museum of Central Africa, Tervuren, Belgium.

Notice the facial proportions of the mask. How would you describe the texture? How do you suppose the mask was used by the Incas? What meaning do you think the artist intended in creating the mask?

African artists have created a multitude of expressive masks, each with its own special purpose and meaning. Many African masks are intended to help the people of the specific cultural group relate to the spiritual world. Like the ceremonial Kifwebe mask from Zaire, in **C**, many African masks are richly carved, portraying dramatic facial features in an abstract style. The whitish color of the carved lines and shapes in **C** symbolize milk, a reminder of nourishment and good health. The fabric around the face is handwoven, and the fibers beneath it are called *rafia.* How might you interpret the expression of this mask?

masks on these pages was worn to hide the identity of the wearer. Each one holds a special meaning or tells a story about the culture it represents.

A **mask** is a symbol that represents ideas, beliefs, and/or values of the artist or cultural group with which it is associated. It may be used in tribal ceremonies. It may be believed to protect the tribe from unknown forces of nature and other harmful threats. The mosaic mask in **A** was worn during funerals of members of the Toltec cultural group in Mexico. Why might a mask have been an important visual symbol in such a ceremony?

Look again at the mask in **B** made in Peru during the time of the Inca empire, which comprised a group of lands and peoples ruled by one government. This empire was founded about A.D. 1200 by Quechua Indians. This mask is among the few surviving gold and silver artworks of that time.

Creating a Mosaic Mask

Create several practice sketches for a mask of geometric shapes. Draw an enlargement of your design with pencil on a sheet of 9" x 12" black construction paper. Cut a variety of small pieces of construction paper and colored magazine scraps, and glue them onto the design to create a mosaic effect. Cut out slots for the eyes and nose. Attach a string or an elastic headband.

Sketchbook/Journal

Make several thumbnail sketches of ideas for animal masks you would like to create. Make notes about mosaic masks.

Masks for Expression

Lesson 8 STUDIO: Creating a Papier Mâché Animal Mask

Artist unknown, North American. *Horned Toad Mask*, ca. 1996. Papier mâché, 10 by 10 by 7 inches. Private collection.

Get the Picture

You have seen masks made of mosaic, gold, and wood. Notice the mask in **A**. It was made of **papier mâché**, a sculpting technique made of newspaper and liquid paste. Paper strips or torn bits of paper are pasted in five or six layers to make papier mâché. After the paste-soaked paper has dried, the form is stiff and hard. The artist then applies paint to the mask.

Artists often use an **armature**, or support, to help form their papier mâché masks. The armature can be made of a variety of materials, such as clay, cardboard, or wood. For large papier mâché sculptures, a chicken-wire armature or a large balloon is used. Artists use an armature to help the inside of the wet paper become dry and to reduce the weight of the artwork. What type of materials might have been used to build the armature of **A**?

Notice the *facial proportions* of **A**. They are about the same as those of an actual horned toad. The colors of paint the artist selected are similar to, but not exactly the same as, the colors of a horned toad. Even so, this mask could loosely be considered a realistic portrayal of a horned toad.

Get Set

Materials you will need:
- #2 pencil
- 9" x 12" white drawing paper
- 12" x 18" cardboard
- heavy paper, scissors, stapler, paste, glue
- newspaper or paper towel strips
- papier mâché paste
- colored tissue paper
- thinned glue
- tempera paint and brush

B Lena, Marshall Middle School. *The Rainbow Mask*. Papier mâché, approximately 12 by 11 by 3 inches.

Lesson 8

How to Create a Papier Mâché Animal Mask

To help you with this Studio, refer to page 263.

1. With colored pencils or markers, create several thumbnail sketches of animal masks.

2. With pencil, enlarge your favorite mask design onto a larger piece of cardboard as an armature.

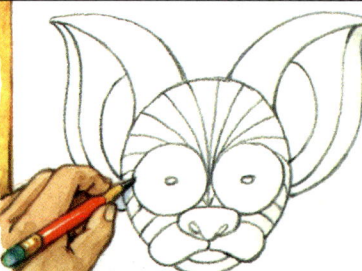

3. Build up facial features with pieces of cardboard or other heavy paper. Attach the pieces with paste, tape, or staples.

4. Cut slits for the eyes and nose.

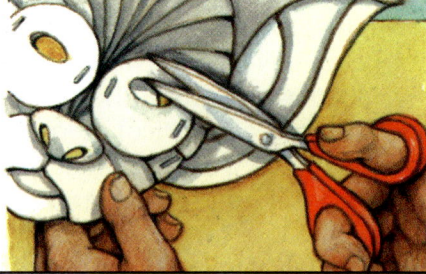

5. Apply at least three coats of newspaper strips with papier mâché paste, allowing each coat to dry before applying the next coat.

6. Add color to your dry mask. Use strips of tissue paper with thinned glue, along with tempera paint.

Making a Paper Mask for a Festival

Create a design for a mask that covers only the areas surrounding the eyes and nose for a local festival. Transfer your design onto tagboard and cut it out, creating holes for the eyes and nose. Add color by using your favorite color media. Attach a wooden or rolled-paper dowel to one side of the mask as a handle.

 ### Sketchbook/Journal

Create thumbnail sketches of other masks you might want to create. Make notes about papier mâché and mask-making. Write a short, step-by-step description of how you created your mask.

Be an Art Critic!

1. **Describe** Tell about the form you used to build your armature.
2. **Analyze** Compare the proportions of your mask's facial features with those of your own.
3. **Interpret** Discuss the meaning of your mask. What feelings and ideas does it represent to you?
4. **Judge** Where will you wear your mask? How does it make you feel to wear it?

Creating a Papier Mâché Animal Mask

Lesson 9: Expression Through Humor

Humor in Illustrations

Illustrations, pictures created for printed works, such as books and magazines, are often intended to have a humorous or satirical meaning. Norman Rockwell, the artist of , is often considered an **illustrator**—an artist who creates pictures for printed works. The illustration of a man viewing an Abstract Expressionist painting, in **A**, is an example of Rockwell's humor. What do you suppose the man viewing the painting is thinking about it?

 Norman Rockwell. *The Connoisseur,* 1962. Oil painting for the cover of *The Saturday Evening Post,* January 13, 1962.

Meanings and Humor in Cartoons

Cartoons, drawings intended to be humorous, often mean something different to each person. The **cartoonist,** an artist who creates a cartoon, also intends for it to have a humorous or satirical meaning. Read the **caption** below the cartoon in **B**. Based on what you know about an architectural model, consider cartoonist Leo Cullum's intended humor. Do you think most people would think this cartoon is funny? Why?

The illustration in **A** and the cartoon in **B** are meant to entertain or amuse. What do you think about the artists' humor? Think of your favorite illustration or cartoon, and then ask yourself how it expresses humor.

"It's just the architect's model, but I'm very excited."

 Leo Cullum. "It's just the architect's model, but I'm very excited." 1997. Ink, 4 by 5 inches. © The New Yorker Collection 1997 Leo Cullum from cartoonbank.com. All rights reserved.

Career Link

Cartoonists

In addition to creating cartoons, cartoonists express themselves in other ways. Some examples are through comic strips, adventure cartoon books, greeting cards, and animated cartoons for television and movies. Some produce drawings for advertisements and editorial cartoons. These are intended to persuade the viewer to accept a particular way of thinking about a product or an issue. Other cartoonists illustrate stories in an amusing way to help the reader understand what the story is about. Traditionally, cartoonists have drawn with pencil, charcoal, pen and ink, and other hand tools. More recently, some cartoonists prefer to draw and paint using the computer.

Cartoonists may work for magazines and newspapers. Some of them are *syndicated*; that is, an organization sells their work to many different newspapers for publication. Many cartoonists work on a free-lance basis, often having a studio in their homes. These artists sell their cartoons to various publications. Regardless of their location or type of employment, all cartoonists must have a rich imagination, a sense of humor, and an understanding of language.

What kinds of cartoons do you like best? Do you have a favorite cartoon character or hero? In creating your own cartoon, think about how you can express your message through an image and just a few words.

Kazim, Zachry Middle School. *Squirrel Seasons.* Colored pencil on paper, 12 by 18 inches.

Creating a Cartoon Strip

Collect your favorite cartoon strips and make notes about how cartoonists use elements of art and principles of design. On white drawing paper with colored pencils, create a fictitious superhero of the past, present, or future. Write a cartoon script with four short sentences about his or her adventure. Draw the outline of each cartoon strip frame with black felt-tip pen. Outline each figure with pen and color the shapes with colored pencils or other color media.

Consider drawing your cartoon on the computer. Print your cartoon strip and add it to your Portfolio.

Sketchbook/Journal

Arrange some of the cartoons you collected on pages of your Sketchbook/Journal and glue or tape them in place. Make notes about cartoon strips.

Expression Through Humor

Lesson 10: Creating a Caricature

Chuck Jones. *Love Is In the Hare,* 1998. Limited edition giclée, 20 by 15 inches. © Warner Bros.

Get the Picture

Eh, what's up doc? You probably recognize that question as coming from a well-known cartoon character, Bugs Bunny, in **A**. But do you know the name of the cartoonist who is responsible for making Bugs and his friends jump, skip, hop, skid, screech, and otherwise move in a variety of ways? The cartoonist's name is Chuck Jones, shown in **B**. He is known for his **animated cartoons,** or motion pictures made from a series of drawings that make the characters appear as though they are moving. This effect is achieved through slight progressive changes in each drawing.

As he animates the cartoon characters, Jones often exaggerates their proportions. Study the facial features of Bugs Bunny and his partner. How does the exaggerated length of their teeth and the sizes of their eyes, cheeks, and feet express the humor of their character? This technique—exaggerating features of a person or an animal through drawing—is called **caricature.**

Get Set

Materials you will need:
- 9" x 12" white drawing paper
- #2 pencil and a black felt-tip pen
- colored markers, felt pens, pencils

Career Link

Chuck Jones

Chuck Jones, in **B**, has animated more than thirty cartoon figures that are known throughout the world. In addition to Bugs Bunny, you may recognize his animations of Wile E. Coyote, Roadrunner, Daffy Duck, Porky Pig, and Dr. Seuss characters. As an animator, Jones worked from the original images and redesigned them for the screen. Jones gave them movement and rhythm through his animation.

How to Create a Caricature

1. Look into a mirror as you lightly sketch a contour drawing self-portrait in pencil.

2. Use black felt-tip pen to draw over some of the lines in the pencil drawing, but this time exaggerate one or more of your expressive facial features for humor.

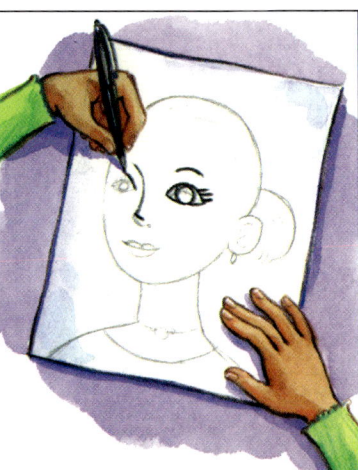

3. You may wish to exaggerate the shape of your face slightly too.

4. Use your favorite drawing or painting media to complete your caricature.

Creating a Caricature of a Famous Person

Collect photographs of movie stars, athletes, or other public figures you admire. Create caricatures of one or two of them. Use black felt-tip pen for outlining and colored chalk to fill in shapes.

Sketchbook/Journal

Cut out caricatures from magazines and newspapers. Glue them into your Sketchbook/Journal. Practice drawing caricatures of your family, friends, or pets. Make notes about caricatures.

Be an Art Critic!

1. **Describe** Tell about what is happening in your caricature.

2. **Analyze** How does the caricature compare to the way you actually look?

3. **Interpret** Does the caricature express something about you that you find humorous? Explain.

4. **Judge** Show your caricature to friends who know you well. Do they think it resembles you in a humorous way? Why or why not?

Creating a Caricature

Lesson 11 Art Museums and Galleries

 The facade of this modern-day art museum was fashioned in the style of the Italian Renaissance.
The San Diego Museum of Art, San Diego, California.

Keepers of the Culture

Many communities in the United States have **art museums,** structures designed to protect and exhibit artworks. Art museums are sometimes described as keepers of the culture. Why do you think they are described in this way?

The art museum in **A** is located in San Diego, California. What features do you notice about the structure? The museum's architectural style resembles that of Italian Renaissance structures. Notice the three figures resting in the *niches,* or nest-like enclaves. They were fashioned in the style of the Italian Renaissance sculptors Donatello and Michelangelo. Above them are coats-of-arms of Spain, America, California, and San Diego. The seashell above the doorway is a reference to San Diego (Spanish for *Saint James*). According to legend, Saint James was transported to the coast of Spain on a shell while the early Spaniards were carried to the New World in heavy sailing ships called galleons. What kind of message does the entryway convey to visitors?

The *floorplan* of most art museums includes **art galleries,** rooms devoted to the exhibition of artworks. Each gallery may be organized by artist, style, or period. For example, an art museum might have a gallery for the paintings of Mary Cassatt, another for Cubism, and another for Renaissance art.

Commercial Art Galleries

Commercial art galleries are places of business that arrange exhibitions of artworks to promote and sell the works of certain artists. Many commercial art galleries are situated near other art galleries, art museums, theaters, and music halls. This section of a community is called an *arts district.* The art gallery in **B** is located in the arts district of Santa Fe, New Mexico.

B How would you describe the building material used to create this structure and most others in Santa Fe?

Nedra Matteucci's Fenn Gallery, Santa Fe, New Mexico.

Career Link

Docents, Educators, Curators and Conservators

Inside art museums throughout the world, you will find employees working behind the scenes to display, protect, and preserve the artworks within the museum. Most of these workers are employed by the museum, while others volunteer their time.

A **docent** is the person who welcomes you to the museum. It is a docent's responsibility to guide visitors through the museum and answer questions about the artworks, artists, and museum.

The museum **educators** are teachers. They train the docents as well as give tours of the museum. Museum educators provide information about the museum to local schools and the general public.

A **curator** selects artworks to be displayed at the museum. This person may travel the world looking for artworks to acquire for the museum's permanent collection or for an interesting exhibition. The curator then arranges to have the exhibition brought to the museum for an extended period of time. Traveling exhibitions bring variety and added interest to art museums.

A **conservator** explores and studies ways to protect artworks from damage and decay. The work of a conservator requires detailed records and involves studies of new ways to preserve artworks for future generations.

C Casey, Ed White Middle School. *The A-Maze-ing Art Museum.* Cardboard box, mixed media, 23 by 30 by 5 inches.

Creating a Model of an Art Gallery

Work with a partner to construct a model of an art gallery in an art museum or as a commercial space. Use a cardboard box as a structure. Use tape or glue to attach interior cardboard walls as dividers between areas. Paint the walls as backdrops for two-dimensional artworks. Decorate small containers as *pedestals*, or stands, for sculpture. With tagboard, make benches for viewers and a desk/counter for the gallery staff. Decorate the exterior of your art gallery.

Sketchbook/Journal

Make a list of art museums and galleries in your community or find some on the Internet. Visit a museum or commercial gallery, and make notes about how the exhibits are arranged in person or on the Internet.

Art Museums and Galleries

Talk About Art

"I found I could say things with color and shapes that I couldn't say in any other way—things I had no words for."

—Georgia O'Keeffe
1887–1986

During her lifetime of ninety-eight years, Georgia O'Keeffe, in **A**, saw some of her nine hundred works of art exhibited in major museums. As this American artist gained an international reputation, she received many awards for her dedication to her career, including the highest honor a civilian can receive—the United States Medal of Freedom. Today many of the paintings she created hang in the Georgia O'Keeffe Museum in Santa Fe, New Mexico.

O'Keeffe lived in nearby Abiquiu, New Mexico, for most of her adult life. Her favorite subjects were desert landscapes and still lifes. Colorful hills, white bones, driftwood, a door on her adobe house, and a big sky fill her canvases. *The Lawrence Tree,* on page 223, shows a nighttime view of that same desert sky. Each of her paintings expresses a sense of independence and strength.

Some art critics feel that many of O'Keeffe's best works were created while she lived in New York City. Her dramatic paintings of skyscrapers express the sense of excitement she felt about the city. During the summer months in New York City, she rode a train upstate to Lake George. She especially liked being alone there or with only her husband by her side. O'Keeffe filled her days drawing and painting in the quiet and peaceful countryside. Her free spirit renewed itself— away from people who disturbed her concentration—and, she said, made her feel "like a hobbled horse."

A Laura Gilpin. *Georgia O'Keeffe,* 1953. Black and white photograph. ©1979, Amon Carter Museum, Fort Worth, Texas. Bequest of Laura Gilpin. P1979.230.4297

The painting in **B** shows O'Keeffe's abstract vision of Lake George. *From the Lake No.1* shows sharp, curving, and swollen forms reflecting the stormy rhythm of the lake. Notice the tints and shades of greens and blues painted in the foreground. Perhaps they suggest the cold, turbulent water below. In the background, at the top of the canvas, shades of gray look like steam rising from the water.

 Georgia O'Keeffe. *From the Lake No. I*, 1924. Oil on canvas, 37 1/8 by 31 inches. Des Moines Art Center, Iowa.

In this unit you have explored three expressive paintings by Georgia O'Keeffe. What have you learned about her preference of subjects? How would you describe her style? Would you classify her work as abstract, realistic, or both? Explain.

Creating a Swirl Painting

Use string, tissue, and ribbons as tools to help you create a swirl painting of water. Dip them in tempera paint, and drop, drag, and pull them across a sheet of paper. Think about how the water feels, sounds, and smells. Use a color scheme to help you express the meaning you intend.

Be an Art Critic!

Look at B to answer these questions:

1. **Describe** What do you see? Tell about the way O'Keeffe used tints and shades to help establish the mood.

2. **Analyze** Consider the way O'Keeffe's lines and shapes relate to each other. Notice her use of sharp points with fluffy shapes. How does this combination of elements help create rhythm?

3. **Interpret** How does the abstract quality of the subject help you understand the meaning O'Keeffe intended? What feelings do you think she had for the water?

4. **Judge** How does this painting of water make you feel about the subject? Why do you think she chose to paint this image? Where would you display the image?

Portfolio Project

 **Materials you will need:**
- pencil, ruler, scissors
- white drawing paper
- tagboard
- tempera paint and brush
- container of water

Creating an Art Exhibition

Select several artworks from your Portfolio to exhibit.
Then work in groups to carry out the tasks in the two checklists:

1. Checklist: Planning the Exhibition

Planning the Exhibition
A. Locate a place for the exhibition.
✓B. Make tagboard frames for two-dimensional artworks.
C. Design ways of displaying or hanging artworks.
✓D. Make cards for credit lines.
E. Create and display posters and flyers for the exhibition.
F. Make a guest list and invitations.
G. Plan refreshments for the opening reception.

2. Making a Tagboard Frame

3. Making a Card for a Credit Line

Sam Nio
Hill Country Landscape, 2000.
Tempera on paper, 17 x 22 inches.
Portfolio.

4. Checklist: Preparing for the Exhibition

Preparing for the Exhibition
A. Complete all the tasks on the planning checklist.
B. Send the invitations.
C. Display artworks and prepare the refreshments.
D. Host the opening reception.

242 Unit 6

Gallery

Artist: Samara
Title: Zilker Park
Medium: crayon on paper
Size: 9 by 12 inches
Date: January 1999
School: Kealing Jr. High

Artist: Matt
Title: Egyptian Pot
Medium: Ceramics and Paint
Size: 2" x 4"
Date: January 1999
School: Collins Intermediate

Portfolio Project 243

Art Links

MUSIC

Feelings from Sounds

An artist uses lines, shapes, and colors to communicate feelings and ideas. A musician uses rhythms, melodies, and lyrics. Many works of classical music, however, have no lyrics. Do classical composers express meanings and feelings without words? If so, how?

Listen to at least a few minutes of three very different classical works. For example, you might try Beethoven's *Fifth Symphony,* Mozart's *Requiem Mass,* and Debussy's *Afternoon of a Faun.* As you listen, jot down any feelings, moods, and ideas that come to mind or move through you. Then think about the overall feeling of each work. Is it triumphant? sad? excited? lazy? What pictures does the music bring to mind? After hearing all three compositions, describe what you think each composer was trying to express.

DANCE

Dancing with Objects

Many visual artists today use mixed media in their compositions. Modern dance companies also incorporate many different media into their choreography. Slides or film images are often projected onto the stage. Objects, masks, costumes, sounds, and words are also frequently integrated into the dance. Is the dance still just a "dance," or is it something else?

Choose a large object such as a picture, a ladder, a hose, a chair, or other object that you can obtain easily. Start moving around it and interacting with it until you begin to make it a part of your movements. Have a friend observe you. Afterward, discuss as a pair how the object affected your "dance."

THEATRE

Masking Feelings

We often think of a mask as a device for hiding one's feelings. Yet in many tribal cultures, masks are used to express particular feelings, such as the mask-wearer's relationship to a spirit world. Theatre companies throughout history have used masks as a way to reveal character. What effect does wearing a mask have on a performer?

Make two cardboard masks—one that expresses joy and another that expresses sorrow. Stand in front of a mirror with a mask in each hand. Begin acting, first with one mask over your face and then with the other. How does each mask affect your expression and influence what you say or feel? Discuss your experiences with a partner and prepare a joint statement.

LITERATURE

Writing a "Stream of Consciousness" Passage

Some abstract painters like Jackson Pollock work quickly and let intuition guide their choices about color and shape, keeping their conscious mind out of it. Some writers also tap pure intuition to create literary works by pouring out words in a "stream of consciousness" technique without editing or judging. Even writers who revise later may use this technique at an early stage to discover meanings they wish to express.

Try this technique yourself: Get a blank sheet of lined paper and start writing whatever thoughts come to mind. Do not stop until the entire page is filled with your "stream of consciousness" writing. When you are stuck, write "I'm stuck" or "I'm not sure what to say." Just do not stop writing until the page is full. Then read what you have written. Circle interesting ideas and feelings you have expressed. Are you surprised by some of your own insights? Circle those ideas in red ink.

ArtLinks

Unit 6

What Have You Learned?
Explore the Language of Art

Marc Chagall. *I and the Village*, 1911. Oil on canvas, 6 feet 3⅝ inches by 59⅝ inches. The Museum of Modern Art, New York. Mrs. Simon R. Guggenheim Fund. Photograph © 1996 The Museum of Modern Art, New York. © 1998 Artists Rights Society (ARS), New York/ADAGP, Paris.

TALK AND WRITE Can You Find . . . ?

Where Am I?

Match each art term at the right with the letter in the illustration of Marc Chagall's painting in **B**.

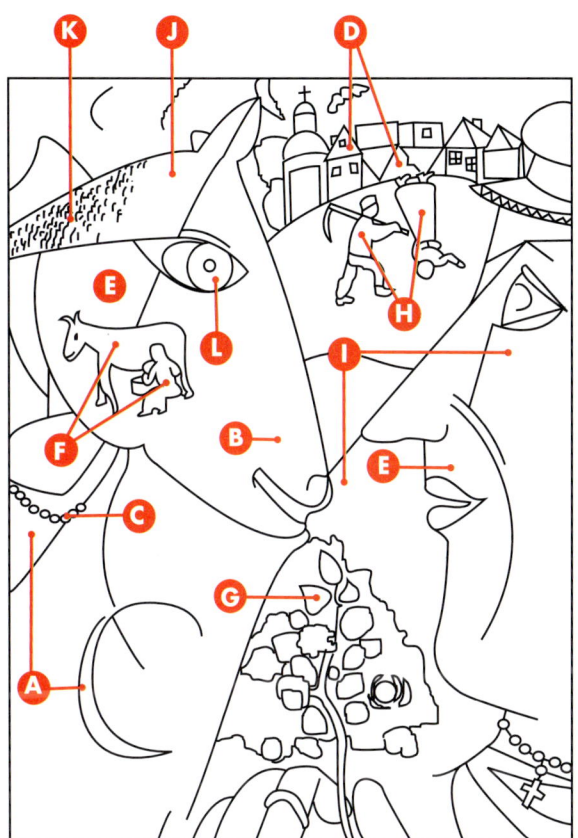

 Illustration of Marc Chagall's *I and the Village*.

1. contrast
2. pattern
3. organic shape
4. texture
5. implied line
6. color balance
7. floating images
8. neutral color
9. color intensity
10. overlapping shapes
11. emphasis
12. geometric shape

How Am I?

Using the language of art, respond to the following questions.

1. Describe how the pairs of figures in *I and the Village* interact with each other. What is happening in this painting?

2. How do the elements of art and principles of design work together in this painting? What provides unity?

3. What is the mood of this artwork? Why do you think so?
   What do you think Chagall wanted to express about himself and the village? What does this painting remind you of?

4. According to Chagall, "Our whole inner world is reality—perhaps more real than the apparent world." How does this statement by the artist help you understand this painting?

What Have You Learned?

Write About Art

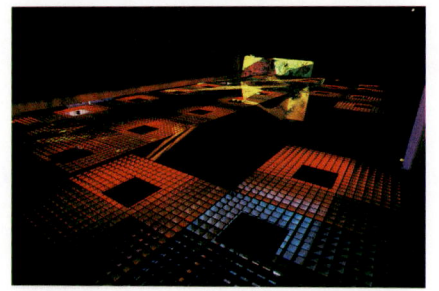

A Carmen Lomas Garza. *Birthday Party,* 1989. Oil on canvas, 36 by 48 inches. Collection of the artist. Photograph: Wolfgang Dietze. From *Family Pictures,* © Carmen Lomas Garza. Reprinted with permission from the publisher, Children's Book Press, San Francisco, California.

B Thana Lauhakaikul. *Celebration,* 1983–1985. Mixed-media installation with projected light and sound, 3 by 16 by 25 feet. Photograph courtesy of Chronicle Books.

C Marc Chagall. *Birthday (l'Anniversaire),* 1915. Oil on canvas, 31¾ by 39¼ inches. The Museum of Modern Art, New York, acquired through the Lillie P. Bliss Bequest. Photograph © 1996 The Museum of Modern Art, New York. © 1998 Artists Rights Society (ARS), New York/ADAGP, Paris.

TALK OR WRITE — In Your Own Words

Compare and contrast A, B and C.

1. What is similar?
2. What is different?
3. Explore each artwork closely. What sounds might you hear from each one? What movement might you see?
4. What is the mood of each artwork? How might the figures in **A** and **C** be feeling?
5. What makes each artwork special?

Re-View

WRITE — Do You Know the Artist?

Match the artist and artwork at the left with the theme and media at the right.

1. Norman Rockwell, *The Connoisseur*
2. Arthur Wesley Dow, *Modern Art*
3. Piet Mondrian, *The Red Tree*
4. African culture, *Kifwebe Mask*
5. Friedensreich Hundertwasser, *808A End of Waters on the Roof*
6. Victor Joseph Gatto, *Poppies*
7. Georgia O'Keeffe, *The Lawrence Tree*
8. Teotihuacán culture, *Funerary Mask*
9. Miriam Schapiro, *My History*
10. Tlingit culture, *Tlingit House Post*

Totem pole/Carved and painted wood
Femmage composition/Mixed media
Folk art landscape/Oil painting
Abstract cityscape/Woodcut
Ceremonial disguise/Mosaics
Magazine cover/Oil painting
Landscape/Oil on canvas
Star-gazing/Oil on canvas
Ceremonial disguise/Wood fiber, pigments, feathers
Poster/Color lithograph

248 Unit 6

Put It All Together

"My experimental TV is not always interesting, but not always uninteresting—like nature, which is beautiful—not because it changes beautifully, but simply because it changes."
—Nam June Paik

TALK AND WRITE: How Does a Work of Art Speak?

A Nam June Paik. *Couch Potato*, 1994. Mixed-media videosculpture, 74 by 67 by 91 inches. Courtesy Carl Solway Gallery. Photograph by Tom Allison and Chris Gomien.

1. **Describe** What has the artist shown? Look carefully at this life-size assemblage. Identify as many objects as you can. Describe the theme of this artwork.

2. **Analyze** How is the subject reflected in the elements of art and principles of design? Analyze the visual qualities of the artwork by writing three or more words that describe each element or principle below.

   Example:
   line— *curved, horizontal, implied,* and so on

   pattern   color   shape   form   value
   balance   texture   rhythm   space   emphasis

   Follow how your eye moves around the composition. Identify the shapes, forms, colors, lines, and textures. What unifies this composition?

3. **Interpret** What is the mood of *Couch Potato*? What might the figure be thinking about? What meaning might the artist be expressing in this artwork? How do all of the objects work together to emphasize the meaning?

4. **Judge** Korean American Nam June Paik is a musician, scientist, artist, and engineer, and is the foremost pioneer of video art. He is known for making his art from TVs, radios, video pictures, and music. How do you, as the viewer, interact with this technological assemblage? What makes this artwork special? Explain.

In Your Journal

Reflect on the expressions and meanings of artworks.

- How have the artworks of others influenced your art skills and your knowledge of art?
- How have your choices of media, subjects, and styles helped you express your ideas and feelings in your artworks?
- What other ways of expression would you like to explore through your artworks? Explain.

What Have You Learned?

Think Safety

Read these safety rules and be sure to follow them when you create artworks.

1. **Keep art materials away from your face** to prevent eye irritation and skin rashes.

2. **Do not breathe chalk dust or art sprays.** These materials can be harmful to your lungs.

3. **If you are allergic to a specific art material, notify your teacher.** If you experience an allergic reaction to any art materials, move away from the materials immediately and notify your teacher.

4. **Read the labels on art materials.** Look for the word **nontoxic** on labels. This tells you the materials are safe to use. Another label to look for is a small square bearing the words "Health Label."

5. **If you use a sharp-pointed object,** such as a clay tool or scissors, point it away from your body. Take care not to puncture your hand, and be considerate of other students' safety.

6. **Use only new meat trays and egg cartons.** Used ones may carry harmful bacteria.

7. **Clean up after you finish an artwork.** Take special care to wash tools you want to save, such as paintbrushes and water cans. Return art materials to their proper places. Wash your hands with soap.

Technique Handbook

Making a Sketchbook/Journal

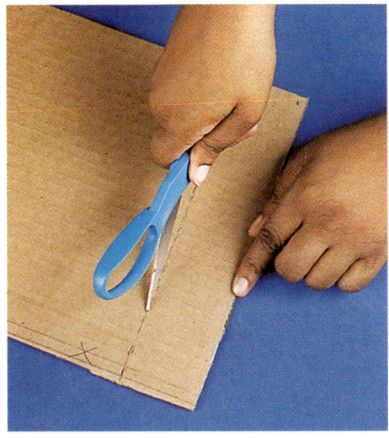
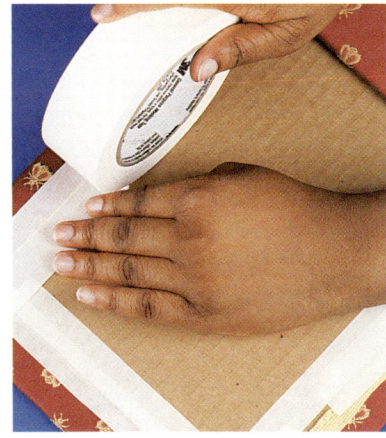
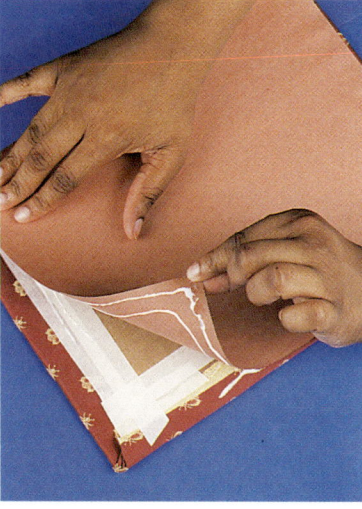

1. Find two sheets of cardboard about 10" x 13". Score the front cardboard panel 1" from the left side so that it will fold.

2. Cut two pieces of fabric 1" larger than your cardboard. Wrap the cardboard with the fabric pieces and tape or glue the edges to the back side.

3. Cover the taped or glued edges of the fabric using a sheet of construction paper.

4. Carefully use a hammer and nail to punch holes in a zigzag pattern along the spine of your Sketchbook/Journal. Use your cover as a template to punch the same holes through a stack of 9" x 12" drawing paper.

5. Weave raffia, yarn, or string in and out of the holes to bind the pages together. Tie a knot to secure. Fasten a button, bead, feather, or other decorative object over the knot.

Portfolios

Portfolio

Making a Portfolio

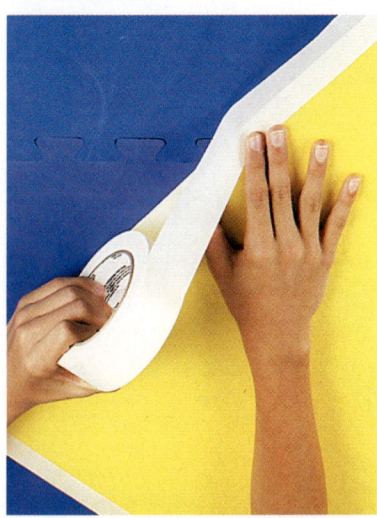

1. Staple or tape two sheets of poster board along three sides.

2. Cut a 6-inch piece of poster board the width of the open side. Tape the piece to the back of the open side, fold over the top and crease to create the flap. Staple a 5' piece of yarn to the flap as a wraparound tie closure.

3. Design your Portfolio using markers, oil pastels, or a collage technique. Use your imagination! Be sure to write your name on your Portfolio.

Drawing

Drawing with Crayon and Oil Pastels

1. Use the tip of the crayon or edge of the oil pastel to make a variety of lines, such as straight, curved, wavy, and cross-hatched. Put short lines or dots of different colors side by side to create an Impressionist effect.

2. To make thicker lines, peel the paper off the crayon or oil pastel. Then draw thick lines with the side. You may want to break the tool in half. This will keep your lines from being too thick.

3. To shade basic forms, press down firmly for a brighter color and press lightly for a softer color. Shade gradually from dark to light. Add black, a complementary color, or a darker color over a lighter one to make a darker shade. Mix colors by putting one on top of another. Blend several colors with your fingers or a tissue.

Drawing with Chalk Pastels

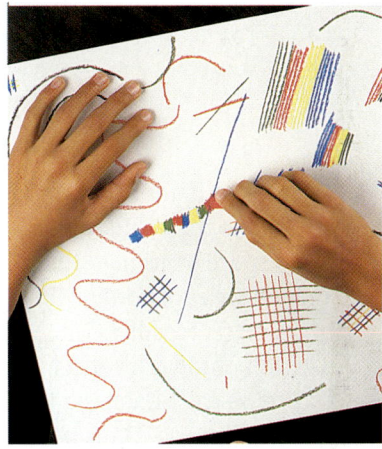
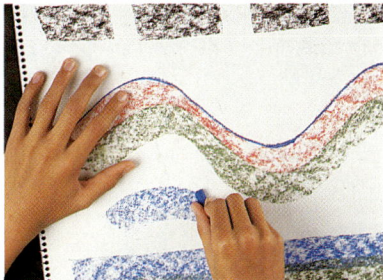

1. Use the tip of the chalk pastels to make a variety of lines, such as straight, curved, wavy, and cross-hatched. Place short lines or dots of different colors side by side to create an Impressionist effect.

2. To make thicker lines, draw with the side of the chalk.

3. Mix colors by putting one on top of another. Blend the colors with your fingers, a tissue, shading stump, or tortillon.

4. To create highlights or lighter areas, use a kneaded eraser or eraser of similar quality.

• • • • •

Drawing with Colored Pencils

1. Use the tip of colored pencils to make a variety of lines, such as straight, curved, wavy, and cross-hatched. Put short lines or dots of different colors side by side to create an Impressionist effect.

2. To make thicker lines, place the pencil at an angle and draw with the side of the pencil lead.

3. To shade basic forms, press down firmly for a brighter color and lightly for a softer color. Add black or complementary colors to make a darker shade. Mix colors by putting one on top of another. Or, blend colors with a shading stump.

Portfolios

Drawing with Pen and Ink

1. You will need the following basic materials to draw with pen and ink:
- Technical pens come with different sized tips, or nibs, which allow you to draw lines of different thicknesses. You can also fill these pens with the color of ink you wish to use.
- If you use a ball point pen, you can create crisp, clean lines. Put several lines together to create thicker lines.
- Always use smooth paper with ink. Rough paper will absorb the ink more quickly and give your drawing an uneven look.

2. Use these suggestions when drawing lines with a pen.
- Always sketch your design in pencil first, and then go over the lines with pen.
- If your design includes circles, use a compass and a pencil to create them. Then go over them very carefully in pen. Or, use patterns of circles cut from poster board or thick paper.
- To fill in spaces between lines you have drawn, work from one side to the other so as not to smear the ink.

3. To create different visual effects, follow these suggestions.
- Fill in a space by using a ruler to draw a series of parallel lines that get closer together. This creates a light-to-dark effect.
- You can use cross-hatching to create shading too. Draw parallel lines and then add another layer of lines going the other way. Space the lines out or put them closer together for lighter or darker areas.
- Create shades by stippling, or making points or dots with the tip of the pen. Gradually add more dots to create darker tones.
- Draw parallel curved lines to suggest curved forms.

• • • • •

Gesture Drawing

1. Pretend your eye is the lens of a stop-action camera. Notice the movement, pose, shape, weight and form of a figure preferably in action. Draw the figure, using quick, rhythmic, scribbling sketches for one to three minutes. **Hint:** You can quickly draw geometric shapes to capture the different forms that make up the human figure, such as an oval for a head, the torso and hips; and cylinder shapes for the neck, arms and legs.

2. As you learn skills in gesture drawing, add more detail by showing shadows and other dark areas, light areas, gesture lines that contour around parts of a figure in action, and thick and thin lines. Try drawing on large newsprint, using charcoals, pastels, chalks, felt tip pens and other drawing media.

Technique Handbook

Contour Drawing

1. Focus on the top of an object and draw a contour line, or outline, with your drawing tool in the air. Keep your eye on the contours at all times. Continue drawing in this way to show the outside and inside contours, folds, wrinkles, and creases.

2. Place your drawing tool at the top of the paper, and begin drawing the contour. Keep your drawing tool on the paper at all times. Draw slowly with your hand and forearm in a fluid motion. Concentrate so that your drawing tool will record the contour lines at the same time you see them.

To create a blind contour drawing, cover your drawing paper with another sheet of paper so you cannot see your drawing in progress. If your drawing tool should go off the paper, look at your drawing and find a new starting point.

3. To create a modified contour drawing, look at your drawing from time to time to see if you are using the proper proportions. Try to avoid lifting your drawing tool in order to create a continuous line.

Portfolios 255

Painting

Mixing Colors with Tempera or Acrylic Paint

1. To mix a tint, put some white paint on your tray. Add a small dot of colored paint and mix the two together. Keep adding very small amounts of color until you get the tint you want.

2. To mix a shade, start with a color. Add a small dot of black paint and mix the two together. Keep adding very small amounts of black until you get the shade you want. Be careful not to use too much black.

3. Dip the bristles of your paintbrush into the paint. Push down on the paintbrush for thick lines. Be careful not to spread the bristles. Use the tip for thin lines. Try holding the brush at different angles when you paint. Remember to wear an art smock to keep your clothes clean.

4. Clean your paintbrush every time you switch colors. Dip the brush in water until it is clean. Wipe it on the side of the water container. Blot the brush on a paper towel. Move to your next color.

5. Wash your paintbrush when you have finished painting. Use warm, soapy water. Then rinse it. Blot the paintbrush on a towel. Put the paintbrush into a jar, bristles up.

Technique Handbook

Painting with Watercolor

Note: Prepare your paints by brushing a large drop of water onto each color of paint. For best results, use watercolor paper for your compositions.

1. To use a drybrush technique: Gently squeeze the bristles of your brush to remove all excess water. Add paint to the tip of it, and make a variety of brush strokes.

2. Practice mixing colors as they appear on the color wheel. Try mixing two primary colors to create secondary colors. Mix primary and secondary colors to create intermediate colors. **Hint:** Begin with a light color, such as yellow, and add only a small amount of a darker color, such as red or blue.

3. Add water to a color to create tints of it. This allows the white paper to show through the paint. Add black or a complementary color to create shades of a color. **Hint:** Begin with a color, such as green, and add only a small amount of black or the complementary color.

4. To plan a white space in your composition, try one or more of these methods:
- Paint around a space, leaving the paper white.
- Use white crayon or white oil pastel to create a resist.
- Mask a white area to prevent the paint from covering the paper.

5. Use a wet wash, also known as a wet-on-wet technique, to create sky and ground areas. Wet a broad brush and paint over your paper with clear water. Then charge your brush with the color you wish your sky to be. Pull your brush horizontally across the top, and work your way down to the horizon line without recharging your brush. Rinse it, select a color for the ground, and begin a similar process. Lift your paper vertically to allow the wet wash to blend.

6. Allow your wet wash to dry before you paint details, such as grass, trees, flowers or birds. When this phase of your painting is dry, add even more details, using watercolor paints, crayons, or oil pastels. You can experiment with how watercolor reacts when mixed with sand and salt. When the painting is dry, create highlights by scraping some paint away with a scraping tool. **Hint:** For interesting results, try soaking your dry painting in a large sink for about two minutes. The paint remaining on the paper may serve as your background for yet more detail.

Portfolios

Printmaking

Making a Monoprint

1. To make a monoprint, cover a sheet of paper or a hard, slick surface with acrylic paint. Use a pencil or pen to draw a design into the paint.

2. Place a sheet of clean paper on top of your design. Smooth it down gently with your hands. Carefully peel the paper off. Let the paint dry.

• • • • •

Making a Stamp Print

1. To make a stamp print, cut a shape from a material such as cardboard or a clean meat tray. Attach twisted masking tape to the back for a handle. Dip the face of the printing block in acrylic paint. Carefully, but firmly, press the block onto a piece of paper.

2. Lift the stamp to see the print.

Technique Handbook

Make a Relief Print

 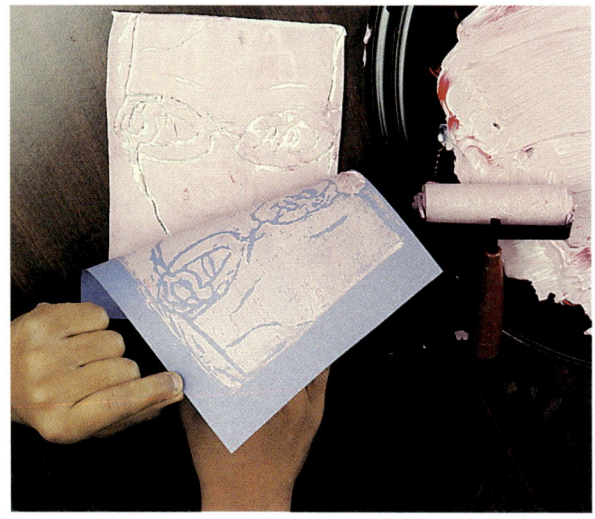

1. To make a relief print, use a pencil to draw a design on material such as a flattened piece of clay or a clean meat tray. Cover a roller, or brayer, with waterbased printers' ink or acrylic paint. Roll the ink or paint evenly over your design.

2. Place a clean sheet of paper on top of your design. Rub the paper gently with your hands. Carefully pull the paper off your design. Let the ink or paint dry.

 **Collage**

Making a Collage

2. Glue the cutouts, one at a time, to the background.

1. Decide on an idea for your collage. Will it show shape and color? Will it contain photographs? Then collect what you will need. Cut out shapes of colored paper or photographs from old magazines. Arrange your cutouts on a piece of construction paper. Move them around until you find an arrangement you like. Be sure you cover most of the paper.

3. Add any found objects that enhance your design.

Portfolios 259

 # Clay

Working with Clay: Setting Up

1. Cover your desk or work area with a plastic mat or canvas. Gather the materials you will need:
- lump of clay
- tools for carving and pressing designs into the clay
- bowl of water

2. Prepare any unwedged clay by wedging it. Take a large lump of clay and thump it down on the work surface. Press into it with the palms of your hands. Turn the clay and press into it again. Keep turning and pressing until the clay has no more air bubbles in it.

3. Practice connecting clay parts by scoring them. Press a plastic fork onto the connecting points. Add slip, or water-thinned clay, to stick them together. You may keep slip in the bottom of your water bowl.

• • • • •

Forming a Pinch Pot

1. Make a small ball of clay and place it in the palm of your hand.

2. Press your thumb into the middle of the ball. Pinch it with your fingers.

3. Start pinching at the bottom and then move up and out. Keep turning the ball as you pinch.

260 Technique Handbook

Using the Slab Method

1. Using a rolling pin, roll out a piece of clay between two sticks to be approximately 1/2" thick.

2. Cut out slabs for the bottom and sides of a container using a plastic knife or needle tool.

3. Use a moist toothbrush or a toothpick to create score marks, meaning to brush rough grooves or scratches into the surface of the clay.

4. Apply *slip*, a soupy-like mixture of clay and water, to the scored edges.

5. Join the slab pieces together and smooth any irregular places with your fingers.

Portfolios 261

Using the Coil Method

1. Begin with a flat and round slab as the base. Score the edges of your base.

2. Make a coil, or rope, of clay by rolling the clay back and forth between your hands and the work surface. Start rolling in the middle, then move out to the edges. Keep rolling until the coil is the size you want it.

3. Score each coil.

4. Apply slip to the scored areas.

5. Wind the coils into a form. You can stack several coils and shape them.

6. Cut extra coils into pieces to form handles and other parts for your coil form. Score them and apply slip before you press them in place.

262 *Technique Handbook*

Creating a Clay Sculpture

Make a clay sculpture by using these techniques:

- Model parts by coiling, pinching, or making a slab.
- Carve parts by cutting into the clay with a wooden tool or plastic knife. Use the tool to cut shapes and forms from the clay.
- Add features or shapes to the clay. Facial features and other shapes can be modeled by pinching and pressing the fingers, clay tools, drawing tools, or found objects into the clay surface.

Papier Mâché

Making Masks and Animal Sculptures

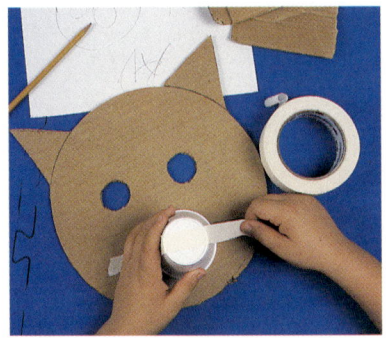

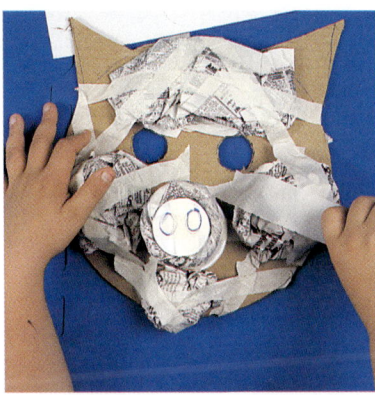

1. Create an armature, or a framework.

- To form the armature for a mask, cut out the shape of the mask, eyes, and other facial features from tagboard, poster board, or another pliable material. Glue or tape pieces of scrap cardboard or foam core to the armature to make the features stand out from the surface.

- To form the armature for a papier mâché animal or another creature, roll newspaper tightly and tape pieces together for neck, trunk, legs and appendages. You may also attach cardboard objects, such as cylinders, spheres, and cubes.

2. Tear and soak newspaper strips and/or paper towels in papier mâché paste. Apply the strips, one over the other, to build up the surface of the armature, allowing each layer to dry. To make the surface smooth, add paper towels as the final two or three layers. Soft tissue paper, soaked in papier mâché paste, can be used to form eyes, eyebrows, and other features.

3. Allow the papier mâché to dry before applying paint. For best results, add color to your mask or creature using an acrylic-based paint. Or apply a water-soluble sealant to the dry surface when tempera paint is used. Yarn, raffia, beads, metallic foils, and other found objects and fabrics can be used to add decoration and interest.

Portfolios **263**

# Repoussé

Creating a Repoussé

1. Cut a sheet of metal foil made of aluminum or copper to your preferred size. Place tape around the edges of the metal for safety.

2. On paper, create a design that will fit the size of the foil.

3. Place the foil on a soft pad, such as an old magazine or a newspaper. Place your drawing on top of the foil, and transfer it to the foil using a blunt pencil.

4. Remove the paper design and deepen the outline in the foil using craft sticks and other wooden tools.

5. Turn the foil over and deepen the other shapes to make them stand out from the front side.

6. Brush waterproof ink, such as India ink, or black shoe polish over the foil design. When the ink or shoe polish is dry, lightly buff, or rub, the raised surfaces with steel wool or a dry paper towel. Mount your repoussé sculpture on wood or heavy cardboard. You may wish to protect your artwork with acrylic spray.

Technique Handbook

Weaving

1. Make a loom to weave on. Cut a piece of cardboard the size you want your loom to be. Use a ruler to draw lines 1/2 inch from the top and from the bottom. Then make a mark every 1/4 inch or so along the lines. Draw slanted lines from the edge of the cardboard to the marks. Then cut along the slanted lines to make "teeth."

2. First, create a warp. Make a loop in one end of a piece of yarn. Hook the loop around the first "tooth" at the top of the loom. Then take the yarn down to the bottom of the loom. Hook it around the first "tooth" there. Take the yarn back up to the second "tooth" at the top, hook it, and so on. Keep wrapping until the loom is filled with vertical lines of yarn.

3. Next, weave the weft. Tie yarn through a hole in a narrow craft stick. Start at the bottom center of the loom. Weave toward one edge by going over and under the yarn. When you get to the last yarn, loop the craft stick around it and start weaving back in the other direction. Keep weaving, over and under, until the loom is covered. Unhook and remove the weaving from the loom. Tie any loose end pieces.

Stitchery

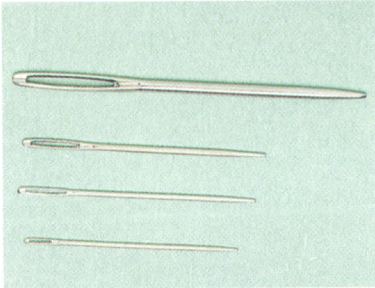

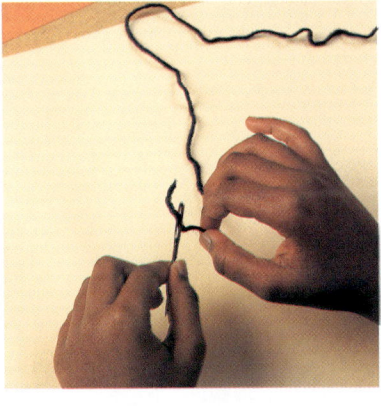

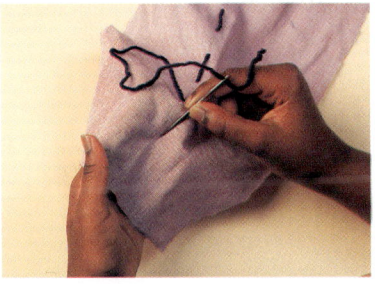

1. Artists use different kinds of needles and threads. A crewel needle is short and has a long eye. It is used for embroidery. A blunt needle is a big needle with a dull point. It can be used for weaving. A darner is a long needle with a big eye. It is used with thick thread like yarn.

⚠️ **WARNING:** Never use a sharp needle without the help of an adult.

2. To thread a needle, cut off a long piece of thread. Dampen your fingers and pinch the end of the thread together between them. This flattens the thread. Push the flattened end through the eye of the needle and pull it through. Make a knot at the other end to keep the thread from coming through cloth.

3. Start a stitch on the back of the cloth. Push the needle through. Then pull the thread up until the knot stops it. Continue pushing and pulling the needle until you have finished your stitching. Finally, push the needle and thread through to the back. Make two small stitches next to each other. Push the needle under these two stitches. Pull thread through, knot it, and cut it off.

Portfolios 265

Computer Art

Drawing and Painting with the Computer

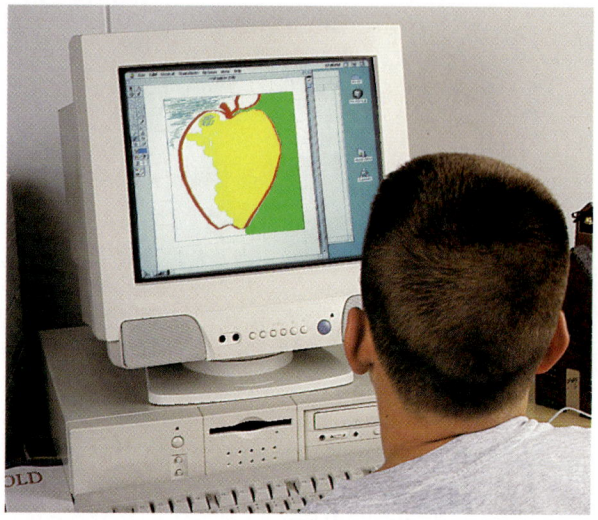

1. Select a new drawing and/or painting document from a software program, such as KidPix™, SuperPaint™, ClarisWorks™, Dabbler™, HyperStudio®, or Corel Draw™. Practice using the drawing tools, such as lines (thick and thin), shapes, paint, spray, eraser, and fill, as well as the text tool. Try shading basic shapes to create forms. Try creating contour and gesture drawings of objects or a classmate. Fill the screen with your experimental designs.

2. Create a contour or gesture drawing using a draw program on your computer or by scanning a contour drawing you created in pencil or black felt-tip pen. Use drawing tools within your program to add form, color, texture, and value to your drawing. Repeat the enhanced drawing several times to create another composition. Add a background by scanning a design you created or by pasting textures, colors, and other drawing and painting tools. A graphics tablet and stylus may be used in place of a mouse.

3. You can create many types of artworks using a computer drawing program. Compose the background by using fill and gradient patterns in your software program. By using the text tool, you can also incorporate a written phrase around the edges, in the foreground or background.

Glossary

abstract A style of art that is not realistic. Abstract art usually contains geometric shapes, bold colors, and lines.

Abstract Expressionism A style of artwork that was developed during the two decades following World War II. The artists often used bold brushstrokes or applied paint by pouring or splattering it onto huge canvases. Also known as action painting.

actual Something that is real, not imaginary.

actual lines Lines that are real and can be seen.

additive method A method of creating sculpture that involves adding to or combining materials.

adobe (uh-DOH-bee) A material used in construction that is formed from straw and wet clay which is then dried in the sun.

adorn To decorate spaces and places with applied artworks.

African art Usually refers to artwork created by African artists living south of the Sahara Desert.

allover design A repeated design that fills a whole area. The designs in some wallpapers and clothing are allover designs.

altered proportion A technique used by an artist to change the size relationship of shapes in an artwork. *See* monumental, miniature, and exaggerated.

alternating rhythm Rhythm created in an artwork by repeating two or more elements on a regular, interchanging basis, such as a triangle-circle, triangle-circle, triangle-circle.

analogous (un-NAL-uh-gus) **colors** Colors that appear next to each other on the color wheel. Analogous colors have one hue in common. For example, blue, blue-green, and blue-violet all contain blue. Also called related colors.

analogous color scheme A color scheme that uses hues that are side by side on the color wheel, and that share a hue.

Anasazi A Navajo name meaning "the ancient one," which refers to the Basket Makers and Pueblo Indians who have lived in North America from about 5500 B.C. to the present.

Ancient Art Artworks created during the years 3500 B.C.–A.D. 400. For example, the ancient monument Stonehenge on Salisbury Plain, England.

animal-style Artworks, such as jewelry and other ornamentation, created during the medieval period that used animals as the subject. For example, carvings of animals adorned Viking ships as a symbol of power.

animated cartoon Motion pictures made from a series of drawings that make the characters appears as though they are moving.

animator A person who creates animation.

animation The art of putting together drawings in a sequence. The pictures are recorded onto film. When the film is run at high speed, the pictures appear to be in motion.

applied art Artworks that are functional. Also known as utilitarian art.

appliqué (AP-li-KAY) An artwork created by sewing small pieces of cloth onto a larger cloth background.

arch A semicircular or curved shape in a building. An arch can frame a doorway or it can support a wall or ceiling.

architect (AR-kih-tekt) Artists who plan buildings and other structures.

architecture (AR-kih-tek-chur) The art and science of designing buildings and other structures.

armature (ARM-uh-chur) The skeletal framework of a sculpture.

art center A group of buildings that relate to art. They may include an art museum, a theatre for performing arts, a fine-arts library, a music building, and a dance studio.

art critic Someone who examines and analyzes art.

art criticism (KRIT-uh-siz-um) The process of looking at, thinking about, and judging an artwork.

art district A section of a community in which art galleries are situated near other art galleries, art museums, theatres, and music halls.

art exhibition A public showing or display of artworks by one or more artists.

art gallery Rooms in an art museum that are devoted to the exhibition of artworks.

art historian Someone who studies art history, as well as cultural and art traditions, such as forms of government, religious beliefs, and social activities.

art history The study of art created in different times and cultures.

art media The materials used by artists to create artworks.

art medium *See art media.* Medium is the singular of the word media.

art museum A structure designed to protect and exhibit artworks.

art studio The place where an artist creates her or his artworks.

art techniques Ways artists use art materials to create certain types of artworks.

artist's intention The artist's purpose or reason for creating an artwork.

assemblage (uh-SEM-blej) An additive sculpture often made of recycled objects that assume new meaning.

assemble To join objects together in order to create an artwork.

assembling A technique that artists use to assemble, or construct new or used objects to make assemblages.

asymmetrical balance (ay-sih-MEH-tri-kul) A type of balance in which the two sides of an artwork look equally important even though they are not alike. Also known as informal balance.

asymmetry (ay-SIH-meh-tree) A type of balance that results when two sides of an artwork are visually balanced even though they are not alike.

atmospheric perspective A technique used to create the illusion of air and space in an artwork. Close-up objects are bright and consist of darker colors; faraway objects and air consist of muted colors and large portions of white.

background The part of an artwork that seems the farthest away.

balance The way an artwork is arranged to make different parts seem equally important. Balance is a principle of design.

base An architectural term for the bottom of a column.

batik (bah-TEEK) An art form in which dye and wax are used to make pictures or patterns on cloth.

binder A material, such as wax, egg, glue, resin, or oil, that bounds together the coloring grains and powder in a pigment.

bird's-eye view A view shown from above. For example, a photograph of a town taken from an airplane.

black-figured A Greek style of vase painting, which depicts moving figures painted in black.

blending A technique that changes the value of a color little by little.

block In printmaking, a piece of flat material, such as wood or metal, with a design on the surface, which is a mirror image of the composition that will appear as a print. The block is used to print the design. (See also *plate*.) In sculpture, a solid material, such as wood or stone, used for carving.

blotto painting A painting created by dropping tempera paint onto one side of a folded sheet of paper, then closing the paper and pressing the two sides together.

blueprint A photographic print used to copy the final drawing of a plan for building something.

border design A design that creates a framelike edge around a shape.

brayer (BRAY-ur) In printing, a rubber roller used to evenly spread ink over a surface.

brush stroke A line, shape, mark, or texture made with a paintbrush.

camcorder Small hand-held video camera.

camera An instrument used to take photographs.

camera obscura An optical device invented by Leonardo da Vinci that is considered the forerunner to the modern camera.

canvas A strong, closely woven fabric, often used as a surface for painting.

capital An architectural term for the top of a column.

caption Explanatory comment accompanying an illustration or cartoon.

career A person's job or profession.

caricature (KAIR-ik-uh-chur) An artwork that exaggerates the features or aspects of a person or object, usually in a way that is funny.

cartoon Drawing intended to be humorous.

cartoonist Artist who creates cartoons.

carve To cut away parts from a block of wood, stone, or other hard material.

carving A subtractive method of sculpting requiring the sculptor to cut or chip away pieces from a block of material, such as wood, stone, or other hard material.

cast An artwork that is created by using a mold form of clay or wax.

casting A technique of building up a sculpture through the additive process, such as a cast bronze sculpture.

castle Fortlike dwelling with high, stone walls and strong towers built during the Middle Ages by wealthy English and European rulers and landowners as protection from invaders.

center of interest The part of an artwork that you notice first.

ceramics (sir-AM-iks) The art of making objects from clay and hardening them with fire. Also artworks made by this process.

charge To fill a brush with paint.

cityscape Artwork that gives a view of a city.

classical architecture A style of modern architecture developed by the ancient Romans, which combines practical features with ideal beauty and proportion.

clavichord (CLA-vuh-cord) An early keyboard from which evolved the harpsichord, pianoforte, piano, electric piano, and synthesizer.

clay A soft, moist material used to create artworks such as sculpture and pottery.

close-up A very near or close view of something.

clothing design The art of planning designs for clothing. Also known as fashion design.

clothing designer An artist who makes drawings for shirts, blouses, skirts, pants, and other garments.

coil method A technique of creating clay pottery and sculpture using long, round, snake like pieces of clay called coils.

collage (kuh-LAZH) A medium in which the artist glues bits of cut or torn paper, photographs, fabric, or other materials to a flat surface.

collagist An artist who creates collages.

color The visual quality of objects caused by the amount of light reflected by them. Color is an element of art. See *hue*.

color family A group of related colors. For example, warm colors and cool colors are each color families.

Color Field A style of painting in which the artist brushes or pours thin paints onto large canvases and uses wet blending of the colors to create soft edges.

colorist An artist who uses color with great skill.

color mixing sheet A reference tool that shows examples of tints and shades, high and low intensity, and a variety of color schemes.

color scheme The plan for combining colors in a work of art.

color wheel Colors arranged in a certain order in the shape of a circle.

colosseum A stadium built by the ancient Romans, which was used as a place of entertainment.

columns The vertical post like structures that carry weight in a building construction.

combine painting A technique of combining cloth and other materials with splattered and smeared paint.

commercial art galleries Places of business that arrange exhibitions of artworks for promoting and selling the works of certain artists.

complementary (kom-pluh-MEN-ter-ee) **colors** Colors that contrast with one another. Complementary colors are opposite one another on the color wheel.

complementary color scheme A color scheme using complementary colors (orange and blue, yellow and violet, green and red).

compose To design or create something by arranging different parts into a whole.

compositions Artists' plans for drawings, paintings, photographs, sculptures, and other artworks to help them communicate their ideas and feelings.

computer A programmable, electronic device that can store, retrieve, and process data.

computer-aided animation Animation, or moving pictures, created with the help of a computer.

concha A shell-shaped form.

Glossary

conservator (kuhn-SUR-vuh-tuhr) A person who works to protect artworks from damage and decay.

construct To make something by putting together materials.

constructed environment An environment containing objects that have been constructed by people.

contemporary (kuhn-TEM-puh-rehr-ee) Current; modern.

contour The edges of an object.

contour drawing A drawing technique in which artists draw contours, or edges of an object, by looking closely at the objects as they slowly move their drawing medium.

contrast A technique for creating emphasis in an artwork by using intensity, the brightness or dullness of a hue.

cool colors The family of colors that includes greens, blues, and violets. Cool colors bring to mind cool things, places, and feelings.

cool color scheme A color scheme made up of cool colors.

costume designer An artist who creates plans for the clothing that actors, dancers, and musicians wear on screen and stage.

crafted Artworks that are skillfully made by hand.

crafts Useful or decorative artworks created by hand, such as quilts, baskets, ceramics, jewelry, and furniture.

craftspeople Artists who create crafts.

crayon etching (EH-ching) A picture made by rubbing wax crayon onto paper and then scratching a design into the wax.

creative Having a skill or talent for making things in a new or different way.

creative process Artists experience the creative process while making their artworks in four stages: saturation, incubation, illumination, and verification.

credit line The information that is given with an artwork. A credit line usually tells the artist, title, date, medium, size, and location of an artwork.

crenations Curved and scalloped edges which appear around the top of a castle tower.

cromlech The circular arrangements of menhirs around a domen, as in Stonehenge, which probably served religious and astrological purposes. These structures may have been the architectural ancestor of modern temples, churches, and mosques.

crosshatching A shading technique using lines that cross each other.

Cubism An abstract style of art characterized by a separation of the subject into cubes and other geometric forms from multiple viewpoints. The style was developed in Paris by a group of artists during the early part of the twentieth century.

cultural style A style of art that shows something about the culture in which the artist lives or lived.

culture The customs, beliefs, arts, and way of life of a group of people.

curator (kyoo-RAY-tuhr) A person who does research for a museum. Curators recommend artworks for the museum to consider purchasing. They also select artworks for display from the museum's permanent collection.

curved line Line that changes direction gradually, expressing movement in a graceful way, such as circles and spirals.

Dark Ages Another name for the medieval period, or Middle Ages.

decorative Artworks that give visual pleasure.

decorative arts Handicrafts that result in beautiful, useful objects. Rug and fabric design, furniture-making, and glassblowing are all decorative arts.

depth A technique to show deep space on a two-dimensional plane.

design A plan for the arrangement of lines, spaces, colors, shapes, forms, and textures in an artwork. Also, the act of arranging the part of an artwork.

de Stijl (duh stil) Dutch term for "the style." The de Stijl artists designed paintings, buildings, and furniture during the early 1900s. They used horizontal and vertical lines with primary colors and neutrals to express a sense of harmony.

detail A small part of a larger artwork. An artist uses crisp and clear lines and shapes to show close-up detail or fuzziness to distant objects.

diagonal line A slanted edge or line.

distance The sense of depth or space between objects in an artwork. (See *perspective*.)

Divisionism A style of artwork, developed by Georges Seurat in nineteenth century, that uses tiny dots of color instead of lines. Also known as Pointillism.

docent (DOH-sent) A person who volunteers in an art museum. Docents give information and conduct tours.

dolmen (DOHL-muhn) Prehistoric monument of two or more upright stones (menhirs) supporting a horizontal stone slab used as an altar or open tomb. For example, Stonehenge on Salisbury Plain, England.

dome A type of form which is like half of a hollow ball or sphere.

dominance The way an artwork shows emphasis in which one element or object in the composition being the strongest or most important part of the work.

drawbridge A bridge that was part of a castle, which could be raised or lowered to allow or hinder passage.

dye A colored liquid used to stain fabric.

earthwork A sculptural form made of natural materials, such as soil, rocks, or plants.

easel (EEZ-ul) A stand with three legs, used to hold a painting while an artist works on it.

Eastern art The artwork of Asia, including China, Japan, Tibet, India, Vietnam, and other countries in the Eastern Hemisphere.

edge The outside line or a shape or form.

edition The total number of impressions made from one plate.

editorial cartoon Cartoons that make a statement about something that is happening in the news.

editorial cartoonist An artist who creates editorial cartoons.

elements of art The basic parts and symbols of an artwork. Line, color, value, shape, texture, form, and space are elements of art.

elevation A drawing that shows one side of a structure.

embroidery The art of forming decorative designs on a textile by using tiny stitches made with needle and thread.

emphasis (EM-fuh-sis) Importance given to certain objects or areas in an artwork. Color, texture, shape, space, and size can be used to create dominance, contrast, or a focal point. Emphasis is a principle of design.

engraving Using sharp tools to carve letters or pictures into metal, wood, or other hard surfaces. Also called etching.

enlargement A copy of a picture that is larger than the original.

environment Things, circumstances, and conditions that surround a person, animal, plant, or object.

exaggerated artworks Artworks that have distorted proportions of objects to show emphasis.

exaggeration (eg-ZADJ-uhr-RAY-shun) Showing something in a way that makes it seem larger or more important than it is.

exhibition A public display of artworks.

expression An artist's use of symbols that holds meaning for them.

Expressionism A style of artwork developed in the twentieth century that expresses a definite or strong mood or feeling through simple designs and brilliant colors.

Expressionists A group of artists who use simple designs and brilliant colors to express feelings. Artists began using this style in Germany in the early 1900s. It gained interest in the United States in the 1940s and 1950s.

exterior The outside of a surface or structure.

fabric Cloth made by knitting or weaving threads together.

facade (fuh-SAHD) The front, or main face, of a building.

fantasy Something that reflects the imaginary.

fashion design The art of planning designs for clothing. Also known as clothing design.

Fauvism A style of artwork, developed by artists in France in the early twentieth century, that used bold color schemes and radical color placement.

femmage A type of collage that includes traditional fabric art made by women.

fiber artist An artist who creates artworks by sewing, weaving, knitting, or stitching fibers together.

fibers Slender, threadlike materials that come from animals (silk, wool), plants (linen, flax, cotton), and chemicals (nylon, rayon).

figure A human form in an artwork.

fine art Artworks that created for the sole purpose of being viewed.

fired Hardened by great heat. Clay objects are sometimes fired to make ceramics.

firing The process of using extreme heat, such as hardening clay objects in a kiln.

flip book A book in which each page shows a part of an action. When the pages are flipped, the viewer sees an animated sequence.

floorplan The arrangement of rooms inside a building.

focal point A way to show emphasis in an artwork in which the artist sets on element apart from the others to set up a center of interest.

Folk art Art made by people who have not been formally trained in art. Folk art usually reflects the artist's culture or tradition.

Folk artist An artist who creates Folk art.

foreground The part of an artwork that seems nearest.

form A three-dimensional object, such as a cube or a ball. Form is an element of art.

found object Something that an artist finds and uses in an artwork. A scrap of metal or a piece of wood could be a found object.

frame One of many pictures in a filmstrip. Also a decorative border or support for an artwork.

free-standing sculpture A type of sculpture that is surrounded on all sides by space.

fresco A technique for creating murals in which colors of paint are applied to wet plaster on a wall.

frontal view The front side of a person, animal, or object in a portrait.

full figure A human form sculpted from head to toe.

functional Designed with a utilitarian purpose in mind.

galleries Places where artwork can be seen and bought.

geometric A word describing shapes and forms such as square, circles, cubes, and spheres.

geometric form A form such as a sphere, cube, or pyramid whose contours represent a circle, square, and triangle, respectively.

geometric shapes Shapes that are precise and mathematical. Circles, squares, triangles, ovals, and rectangles are geometric shapes.

German Expressionism A style of art developed in Germany in the early 1900s. The German Expressionists used simple designs and bright, bold colors to express their feelings in artworks.

gesture drawing A drawing technique in which artists move a drawing medium, such as a pencil, quickly and freely over a surface to capture the form and actions of a subject.

glaze A thin layer of transparent paint made of minerals. A glaze can be applied to a piece of pottery, which is then re-fired.

graphic (GRAF-ik) **design** The art of communicating messages with images and lettering, usually in commercial art such as advertisements, signs, book jackets, and jewel cases.

graphic designer Someone who creates commercial art.

graphics tablet A device by which pictorial information is entered into a computer in a manner similar to drawing, using a stylus.

greenware An object made from clay which, as the clay dries, becomes delicate.

ground-level view The point of view from beneath. Also known as worm's-eye view.

grout A plasterlike substance used to fill in the space around the tesserae in a mosaic.

guideline Artists sometimes fold a sheet of paper and use the fold marks as a guide to place facial features in a portrait. These marks are called guidelines.

gum arabic A water-soluble gum obtained from a variety of the acacia shrubs and trees used as the binder in watercolor paints.

hardware Computer components, such as monitors, keyboards, mouses, CPUs, and modems.

harmony Colors that go together in an artwork. Also, notes that go together in music.

hatching A shading technique using thin parallel lines.

heritage The history, culture, and traditions of a group of people.

horizontal Moving straight across from side to side rather than up and down. For example, the top edge of a piece of paper is horizontal.

horizontal line In an artwork, the line representing the horizon (for example, where the ocean meets the sky). Horizontal lines appear peaceful and calm.

hue (hyoo) Another word for color.

Glossary

illumination The third stage of the creative process when the artist finds a solution to their problem or idea. Also, a handpainted illustration for a book.

illusion (ih-LOO-zhun) An image that tricks the eye or seems to be something it is not.

illustration (ih-luh-STRAY-shun) An informative drawing.

illustrator An artist who creates pictures for books, magazines, or other printed works.

imagination A mental picture of something that may or may not exist.

impasto A technique that uses a thick textured layer of paint.

implied lines Lines that are not real, but implied by the placement of other lines, shapes, and colors.

Impressionism A style of artwork that fills in spaces with hundreds of strokes and dabs to simulate actual reflected light. This style was developed in the nineteenth century by a group of artists in France.

Impressionists A group of artists in the late 19th and early 20th centuries who paid special attention to light and its effect on subjects in their paintings. Also known as Independents.

impressions Multiple prints, or "originals," of the same image, which are individually signed, dated, and numbered by the artist.

incubation The second stage of the creative process in which an artist mulls over options of how to solve the problem.

Independents A group of artists in France in the late 19th and early 20th centuries that developed a style of artwork independent of the Realistic style.

industrial (in-DUS-tree-ul) **design** The design of products manufactured for mass distribution, usually by large companies.

industrial designer An artist who plans the appearance and form of useful objects, such as computers, telephones, cars, toys, and kitchen appliances.

installation (in-stuh-LAY-shun) An artwork that is assembled for an exhibition and removed when the exhibition is over.

intaglio (in-TA-glee-oh) The technique of printing in which the image to be printed is cut or scratched into a surface.

intensity (in-TEN-sih-tee) The brightness or dullness of a hue. A hue mixed with its complement is less intense than the pure color.

interior (in-TEER-ee-ur) The inside of a building or another hollow form, such as a box.

intermediate (in-tur-ME-dee-ut) **colors** Colors that are a mixture of a primary and a secondary color that next to each other on the color wheel. Blue-green, red-orange, and red-violet are examples of intermediate colors.

interpretation A representation of an artist's feelings toward a subject. For example, the medium, style, and colors of an artwork build the artist's interpretation.

keyboard A device, which resembles a typewriter, used to enter information into a computer.

kiln A very hot oven used to harden or dry a substance such as clay.

landmarks Telltale stones or trees, historic buildings, significant hills, or other geographic features associated with legend or fact.

landscape A drawing or painting that shows outdoor scenery such as trees, lakes, mountains, and fields.

landscape architect A person who uses plants, rocks, trees, and other materials to create a pleasing outdoor design.

landscape architecture The planning and design of outdoor areas. (See *landscape architect*.)

layout The arrangement of letters and images on a page.

light source A point of illumination for emphasis, contrast, unity, or dramatic effect in an artwork.

line A thin mark on a surface created by a pen, pencil, or brush. Line is an element of art.

linear perspective An artist uses guidelines (horizon line and vanishing point) to position shapes to appear near or far away. For example, railroads, highways, or other paths that seem to fade into the distance.

line quality The special character of any line, such as thick or thin, smooth or rough, continuous or broken.

lithograph (LITH-oh-graf) A print made by lithography.

logo A design created by a graphic artist as a symbol to visually represent a business, club, city, or other group.

loom A frame or machine used to hold yarn other fibers for weaving, usually at right angles to one another.

lost wax casting technique A process in which a wax form is melted away from a ceramic mold.

Macchia (MOCK-ee-ah) A technique used in creating glass artworks in which one color appears on the inside and another on the outside.

maquette (ma-KET) Small model made of clay that serves as a plan for a larger sculpture.

mascot An animal, object, or a plant that is associated with a group.

mask A cover for the face used as decoration or disguise, which can be a symbol that represents ideas, beliefs, and values of the artist or cultural group with which it is associated.

mass-produce To make many identical products from the same design.

media (MEE-dee-uh) Materials used to create artworks, such as clay or paint. The singular of media is medium.

medieval period The one thousand years (A.D. 400–1400) that followed the fall of the Western Roman Empire. Also known as the Middle or Dark Ages.

melody A pattern of notes in a line of music.

memory A mental image of something that has been learned or experienced.

menhirs (MEN-hirs) The upright stones used in ancient artwork, in which people believed departed spirits lived. For example, Stonehenge on Salisbury Plain, England.

Middle Ages Another name for the medieval period, or Dark Ages.

middle ground In an artwork, the part between the foreground and the background.

miniature artworks Artworks that are of smaller-than-life proportions.

mixed media Artworks that are created from more than one medium.

moat A deep trench around a castle, which was usually filled with water, that add protection.

model Someone or something an artist uses as a subject when creating an artwork. In architecture, a small copy of something that represents the larger version.

modeling A technique using all types of clay, types of additive media, for building up and shaping a sculpture.

Modern Era The period (1800–present) during which artists have experienced the freedom to experiment and express their ideas and feelings.

monitor An electronic device used to view computer information.

monochromatic (mon-oh-kroh-MA-tic) **color scheme** A color scheme that uses different values of a single hue by showing tints and shades of the same hue.

monochrome A color scheme using tints and shades of a single color.

monologue A long speech by one person.

monoprint A print made from a plate that can be used only once.

monumental artworks Artworks that are of larger-than-life proportions.

mood The feeling created in a work of art. For example, light values often suggest a calm, gentle mood, while dark values may seem angry, nervous, and forceful.

mosaic (moh-ZAY-ik) An artwork made by fitting together small pieces of colored glass, stone, paper, or other materials.

motif (moh-TEEF) An element that is repeated often enough to be an important feature of a design.

motion A sense of movement or action in an artwork. Also, a dancer who moves to a rhythm.

motion picture An art form in which pictures are printed on a long strip of film which is shown rapidly to give a sense of motion.

mouse A small, mobile device that manipulates the cursor and assists in the selection of functions on a computer monitor.

movement The sense of motion or action created in an artwork. Also, a trend in art is called a movement.

multimedia A combination of technology-related media used to create a composition.

mural (MYOOR-ul) A large artwork, usually a painting, that is created or placed on a wall or ceiling, often in a public place to convey a theme that has a political or social message.

muralist An artist who creates murals.

museum educators People who work in museums to help visitors explore artworks and art processes.

naja A crescent-shaped silver ornament. At one time, najas decorated the bridles of Navajo horses.

natural environment A natural setting that has not been changed by humans.

needlework Artworks that are created using fabric and some kind of stitchery.

negative space The empty space around and between forms or shapes in an artwork.

neutral color scheme A color scheme of black, white, and various tints and shades of gray which often reflects a calm, quiet mood. Many artists also include brown.

neutrals A word used for black, white, and tints and shades of gray. (Some artists use tints and shades of brown as neutrals.)

niche A nest like enclave.

nonobjective art A type of art that usually shows color, form, and texture, but has no recognizable subject, such as a person or an animal.

Non-Western tradition The art and cultural history of parts of the world other than those included in the Western tradition that include functional art, such as ceremonial masks and costumes, cooking utensils, and tools.

normal proportion A person's height, width, and depth appears normal in size in relation to his surroundings.

observation A process used by an artist to create an artwork by looking at or watching something or someone.

oil-based paint A paint made from a mixture of colored pigment and linseed oil.

opaque (oh-PAKE) The quality of not letting light through; the opposite of transparent.

Op Art A style of art in which artists create the illusion of movement or other optical illusions. Op Art developed in the 1950s.

organic A word describing shapes and forms similar to those in nature.

organic forms "Free forms" which have irregular and uneven edges and are often found in nature, such as apples, trees, and animals.

organic shapes "Free form" shapes that are irregular and uneven, such as leaves, flowers, and clouds.

original A work of art that is created firsthand by an artist; not a copy.

originality An artist's unique way of showing ideas and feelings.

outline The line that forms the edge of any shape or form. Also called the contour.

overlap To partly or completely cover one shape or form with another to show distance in an artwork.

palette (PAL-it) A flat board on which a painter holds and mixes colors.

Palladian (pah-LAY-dee-un) Characteristic of the Renaissance architectural style of Palladio.

papier mâché (PAY-pur muh-SHAY) A process of creating forms by covering an armature or other base with strips of paper that have been soaked in watery paste, and then molding the strips. The form hardens as it dries.

pastel A crayon made of either chalk or oil.

patina Rusted surface on an armature created by natural elements (e.g. rust on iron or a greenish film on copper or bronze).

pattern Repeated colors, lines, shapes, forms, or textures in an artwork. Pattern is a principle of design. Also, a plan or model to be followed when making something.

perception An artist's awareness of the elements in his or her environment by using his or her senses.

permanent collection The group of artworks belonging to a museum.

permanent installation A sculpture that cannot be moved and that is used to adorn an outdoor space.

perspective A way of making a flat artwork look as if it has depth. In a painting, an artist creates perspective by making far away objects smaller and nearby objects larger.

Pharoah (FAY-roh) A ruler of ancient Egypt.

photogram A print made on light-sensitive paper used for blueprints.

photograph An image made with a camera by recording light on film.

photographer A camera artist.

photographic collage A collage made by combining parts of different photographs. Also known as photomontage.

photography The art of taking pictures with a camera and film.

pictographs (PIK-toh-grafs) Ancient drawings, often found on cave walls, that tell stories or record a culture's beliefs and practices.

pigment A coloring material made from crushed minerals and plants or chemicals, usually held together with a binder.

pinch method A way of shaping a ball of clay into pottery by pinching, pulling, and pressing it with the hands.

pitch The high or low quality of a musical sound.

plasticity A technique using altered proportions in which an artist shows round and full figures of people, creating a similar—almost toylike—appearance for people of all walks of life. This technique was used by Fernando Botero.

plate In printmaking, a piece of flat material, such as wood or metal, with a design on the surface, which is a mirror image of the composition that will appear as a print. The plate is used to print the design. (See also *printing block*.)

Pointillism A style of artwork, developed by Georges Seurat in the nineteenth century, that uses tiny dots of color instead of lines. Also known as Divisionism.

point of view Angle from which the viewer sees an object or a scene. The three angles are straight-on view, bird's-eye view, and ground-level or worm's-eye view.

Pop Art A style of art developed during the 1950s. Pop artists show people, objects, or scenes from popular culture and use graphics similar to those found in advertisements or comic strips.

porcelain (POR-suh-luhn) A translucent ceramic developed by the Chinese that is used for dishes and vases.

portable structures Outdoor sculptures that can be moved from one location to another.

portfolio (port-FOH-lee-oh) A portable container used to hold and organize artworks, especially drawings and paintings. Also the artworks collected in this container.

portrait A work of art created to show a person, animal, or group of people, usually focusing on the face.

pose The way a subject sits or stands while an artist sketches or paints a portrait.

positive space Shapes, forms, or lines that stand out from the background in a work of art.

potter An artist who makes pottery.

potter's wheel A flat, spinning disc used by potters. Potters place soft clay on a spinning wheel and then use their hands to shape the clay in to a form.

pottery Objects made of clay, which can be useful and/or decorative.

Pre-Columbian Artworks created in the Americas before Christopher Columbus and other Europeans arrived in the area.

Prehistoric Art Artworks created during the years 30,000-3500 B.C., when people were nomadic and lived mainly by hunting and gathering food. These artworks are usually found on cave walls.

primary colors The colors which cannot be mixed from other colors, but from which other colors are made. The primary colors are red, yellow, and blue.

principles of design Guidelines that artists use to organize the elements in a composition. Unity, variety, emphasis, balance, proportion, pattern, and rhythm are the principles of design.

print An artwork made by covering a textured object or a carved design with ink and then pressing it onto paper or pressing paper onto it.

printing ink A type of ink that is thicker and stickier than the ink for fountain pens and that is used in the printmaking process.

printmaker An artist who uses the process of printmaking.

printmaking The process of transferring an image from an inked surface to another surface to create an artwork.

profile The side view of a subject.

progressive rhythm Rhythm created in an artwork by showing regular changes in a repeated element, such as a series of circles that progressively increase in size from small to large. The changes may also progress from light to dark, or bottom to top.

prop In an artwork, an object held or used by the subject.

properties Color attributes, such as hue, value, tint, shade, and intensity.

proportion The relation of the parts of an artwork to each other and to the whole. Proportion is a principle of design.

prototype A working model of a product that will be mass-produced.

pulled threadwork An artwork created by pulling threads from a piece of fabric in a way that creates a design.

punch A metal tool used for stamping a design on a surface.

quilting A type of stitchery in which the artist stitches together two layers of cloth with padding between the layers.

radial balance A type of balance in which lines or shapes spread out from a center point.

Realism A style of art that represents people, places, objects, or events as they are perceived by the senses.

Realistic art An artwork using Realism.

regular rhythm Rhythm in an artwork created by repeating the same element, such as a shape, without variation.

related colors Colors such as yellow, yellow-orange, and orange that are next to each other on the color wheel. Also called analogous colors.

relief print The technique of printing in which an image raised from a background is inked and printed.

relief sculpture A type of sculpture in which forms project from a background and are meant to be seen from one side.

Renaissance (re-nuh-ZAHNS) The period between A.D. 1300–1600, during which new ideas and technological advances, as well as renewed interest in the classical styles of the Romans and Greeks, laid the foundation for modern art and society.

renovated (REN-oh-vay-ted) Remodeled or restored.

repertoire (REP-uhr-twahr) The skills and knowledge of a particular person or group.

replica An exact reproduction.

repoussé (re-pooh-SAY) A technique of hammering a sheet of gold over a wooden form.

resist medium A material, such as wax, used to protect parts of a surface from paint or dye.

rhythm (RIH-thum) The repetition of elements, such as lines, shapes, or colors, that creates a feeling of visual motion in an artwork. Rhythm is a principle of design. In music, the pattern of a melody.

saturation The first stage of the creative process in which an artist is caught up with an idea or a problem that seems unsolvable.

scale The size of an object in relation to an ideal or normal size.

scanner A device used to transfer text or graphics into a computer.

scenario In a video production, all the action that takes place before the camera changes angles or positions.

score To scratch a surface with a tool.

sculpting The process of taking away from a form or adding to it.

sculptor An artist who creates sculptures.

sculpture An artwork made by modeling, carving, or joining materials into a three-dimensional form. Clay, wood, stone, and metal are often used to make sculptures.

seascape An artwork that includes in the scene a sea, ocean, or shore.

secondary colors Colors made by mixing two primary colors. The secondary colors are orange, violet, and green.

self-portrait An artwork that shows the likeness of the artist.

self-taught Having taught oneself without formal training.

set designer An artist who designs spaces and props for theatre, motion pictures, or television.

sfumato (sfoo-MAH-toh) A technique of painting soft, blurry, smoke like edges in the background of a painting.

shade A color made by adding black to a hue. For example, adding black to green results in dark green. Also, the darkness of a color value. (See *value*.)

shading A way of showing gradual changes in lightness or darkness in a drawing or painting. Shading helps make a picture look more realistic.

shading stump An artist's tool usually made of soft paper felt, generally used for blending and shading with pencils, charcoals, conté crayons, chalks, and pastels. (See also *tortillon*)

shaft An architectural term for the cylindrical pillar between the capital and base of a column.

shape A flat, two-dimensional area with height and width, which might have an edge, or outline, around it. Shape is an element of art.

shrine A sanctuary to honor gods and goddesses of a culture.

silversmith An artist who make articles of silver.

site-specific Refers to an artwork that must be viewed in a certain place. The place often is a part of the artwork.

size relationships A technique that alters the proportions of compositions. The three categories are monumental, miniature, and exaggerated.

sketch (skech) A quick drawing. A sketch can be used to record what an artist sees, explore an idea, or plan another artwork.

sketchbook A book or pad of blank paper used for drawing and keeping sketches.

slip A creamlike mixture of clay and water that acts as glue to join scored pieces of clay.

software Computer applications used for various functions, such as editing text, creating graphics, or programming.

solvent A liquid, such as turpentine or water, used to control the thickness or thinness of paint.

space Areas that are empty or full, far away or nearby, or huge or small. Space is an element of art.

spokes The warp materials in basketweaving.

stained glass A type of artwork composed of brightly colored pieces of glass joined by lead to create designs or scenes.

stamp A tool used to shape the surface of the material, such as silver, to which it is applied.

still life An artwork showing an arrangement of nonliving objects, such as fruit, foods, bottles, books, or cut flowers.

still photographer Someone who takes still rather than moving photographs using a camera and film.

still photography The art and science of making a picture with a camera and film.

stippling A shading technique creating dark values by applying a dot pattern.

stitchery A term for artwork created with a needle, thread or yarn, and cloth, such as a quilt.

storyboard A series of drawings on small cards that represents the visual plan of a video production.

straight-on view Point of view that encourages a viewer to focus on other aspects of the composition.

studio A room or building where an artist creates artworks.

style An artist's individual way of expressing his or her ideas. Also, a technique used by a group of artists in a particular time or culture.

stylus A pen-shaped pointing device used for entering positional information (as from a graphics table) into a computer.

subject What an artwork is about. A person, animal, object, or scene can be the subject of an artwork.

subtractive (sub-TRAK-tiv) A word describing sculpture that is made by taking away, or subtracting, material from a larger piece or block.

subtractive method A method of creating sculpture by taking away, or subtracting, material from a larger piece or block. Carving is an example of the subtractive method.

surface The outside layer of a material, an object, or another form.

Surrealism (suh-REE-uh-liz-uhm) A style of art developed during the 1920s that combines realistic images and dream like ideas. Many Surrealist artworks contain illusions.

symbol A letter, color, sign, or picture that represents words, messages, or ideas, such as thoughts and feelings. For example, a red heart is often used as a symbol for love.

symmetrical (sih-MEH-tri-kul) **balance** A type of balance in which both sides of an artwork look the same or almost the same. Also known as formal balance.

symmetry (SIH-muh-tree) Balance created by making both sides of an artwork the same or almost the same.

syndicated The sale of cartoons by an organization to many newspapers for publication.

tactile texture A texture you can feel with your hands. Also called actual texture.

technique (tek-NEEK) The way an artist uses art materials to create a certain type of artwork.

technique sheet A reference tool showing each element of art and principle of design.

technology The way human beings use machines and other tools to make or do something.

tempera paint A chalky, water-based paint that is thick and opaque. Also called poster paint.

Glossary

tessellation A pattern of shapes that fits together in a way that leaves no space in between, as in the artworks of M.C. Escher.

tesserae (TEH-sur-ray) Small pieces of material, such as paper, stone, tile, or glass used to make a mosaic.

textile An artwork made from cloth or fibers, such as yarn.

texture The way something feels to the touch or how it may look. Texture is an element of art.

theme In an artwork, the artist's message about the subject of the work.

three-dimensional Having height, width, and thickness. Forms are three-dimensional.

three-quarter view The subject of an artwork that is positioned between a front view and a profile, so that you can usually see both eyes, the nose, and the mouth.

thumbnail sketch A sketch of what is seen through a viewfinder.

tint A color, such as pink, that is created by mixing a hue with white. Also, the lightness of a color value. (See *value*.)

tooling A technique in which an artist places a sheet of gold metal over a relief of a motif on a block of wood and hammers gently to define the motif.

tortillon An artist's tool usually made of soft, tightly wound paper, generally used for blending and shading with pencils, charcoals, conté crayons, chalks, and pastels. (See also *shading stump*)

totems Symbols that represent clans and other subgroups of a culture.

totem pole A carved post that is representative of a clan or subgroup of a culture.

tradition Knowledge, beliefs, and activities handed down from one generation to the next.

transparent The quality of letting light pass through; the opposite of opaque.

traveling exhibition A group of artworks that travels to many museums.

triptych (TRIP-tik) A picture or carving in three panels.

twin-handled vase A vase which has two handles—one on each side.

two-dimensional Having height and width. A drawing is two-dimensional.

unity (YOO-ni-tee) The quality of seeming whole and complete, with all parts looking right together. Unity is a principle of design.

utilitarian art Artworks that are designed for a specific purpose. Also known as applied art.

value The lightness or darkness of a color. Tints have a light value. Shades have a dark value. Value is an element of art.

value scale A series of blocks showing the gradual increase of shading of a color.

variety (vuh-RY-ih-tee) The combination of elements of art, such as line, shape, or color, to provide interest in an artwork. Variety is a principle of design.

verification The fourth stage of the creative process in which the artist puts the solution into concrete form while checking it for error and usefulness.

vertical Running up and down rather than side to side. For example, the side edge of a piece of paper is vertical.

vertical line In an artwork, the line that runs up and down, such as a flagpole or a giant redwood tree. Vertical lines appear strong and powerful.

vessel A functional and decorative container made from clay used to hold solids or liquids.

video art A medium for creating motion pictures, such as motion picture films or videotaped television programs.

videographer An artist who operates a video camera.

videotape A recording of visual images and sound made on magnetic tape.

viewfinder A device used by an artist to show the area of a composition.

visual (VIH-zhoo-ul) **rhythm** In an artwork, rhythm created by repeating elements, such as colors and lines. Visual rhythm might remind a viewer of music or dance rhythm.

visual texture The way a surface appears through the sense of vision. For example, the surface of a sculpture may be shiny or dull. Also called simulated texture.

warm colors The family of colors that includes reds, yellows, and oranges. Warm colors bring to mind warm things, places, and feelings.

warm color scheme A color scheme made up of warm colors.

warp In weaving, the vertical threads attached to the top and bottom of a loom.

water-based paint Water-soluble paints, such as tempera, watercolor, or acrylic, that use different binders and have different qualities.

watercolor paint A water-based paint that uses gum arabic as its binder and has a transparent quality.

weave A process of interlocking thread, yarn, or other fibers to create a fabric, usually on a loom.

weaver The weft in basketweaving.

weft The threads that cross over and under the warp fibers on a loom.

Western tradition Art and cultural history which began in Egypt, Greece, and Rome, then spread to all of Europe and North America.

wet wash A way to prepare a surface for watercolor paints by sweeping a clean brush across the surface with water.

woodcut A type of relief print made by cutting away the surface of a block of wood.

worm's-eye view The point of view from beneath. Also known as ground-level view.

zigzag lines A series of diagonal lines moving in different directions (vertically, horizontally, or diagonally) that come together at sharp angles. These lines can create feelings of confusion, nervousness, or excitement.

Color Wheel

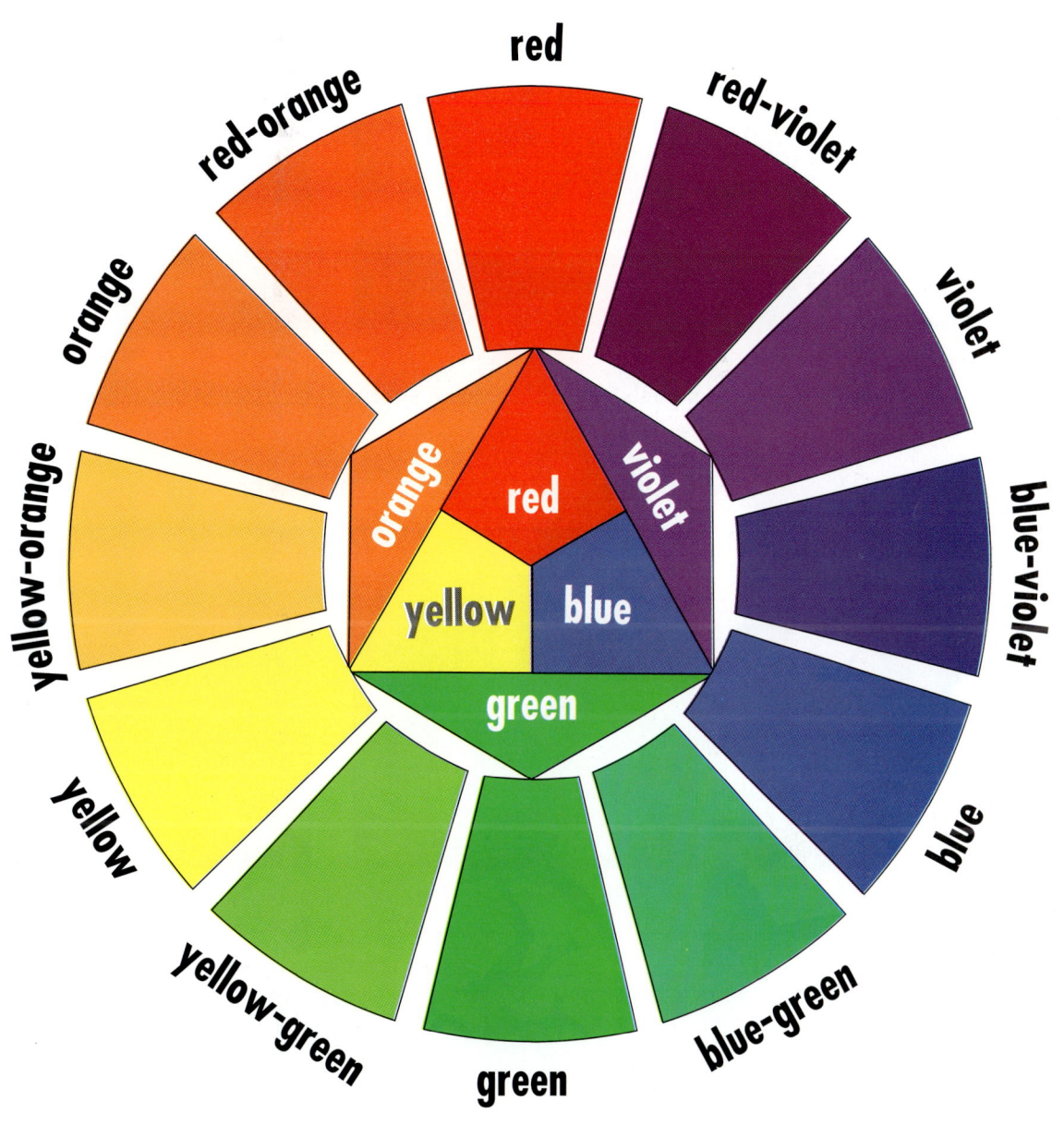

Elements of Art

Line

Color

Value

Form

Texture

Shape

Space

Richard T. Sibert, *Il Chiesa*, 1998. Oil on canvas, 24 by 36 inches. ©1998 RTS.

Principles of Design

Balance

Pattern

Variety

Unity

Proportion

Emphasis

Rhythm

Artist unknown. *Nataraja: Siva as King of Dance.* South India, Chola Period, 11th century. Bronze, height 44 1/2 inches. © The Cleveland Museum of Art, 1996, purchase from the J. H. Wade Fund, 1930.331.

List of Art and Artists

Unknown Artists

Beaded Zemi, ca. 1515 205
Breastplate, ca. A.D. 1000–1470 (Peruvian) 202
Caerlaverock Castle, ca. A.D.1270 111
Ceremonial Knife, Pre-Columbian (Peruvian) 204
Cliff Palace, ca. A.D. 600 (Anasazi culture) 115
Colosseum, ca. A.D. 70–82 (Roman) 108
The Court of Empress Theodora, A.D. 547 130
Dancing Figure, 16th century (Italian) 58
Dragon's Head, ca. A.D. 820 (Scandinavian) 110
Duck-shaped Earrings, 18th dynasty (Egyptian) 204
Ducks and Ducklings, 1st century B.C.–A.D. 1st century (Roman) 107
Egyptian Rulers and Their Crowns, date unknown (Egyptian) 100
Figure (Drummer), date unknown (Nkanu culture) 96–97, 125
Fishing Scene: Attendants with harpoons and string of fish, 1436–1411 B.C. (Egyptian) 101
The Flying Horse, A.D. 2ND century 176
Funerary Mask, ca. A.D. 400–600 (Teotihuacán culture) 230
Hall of Bulls and Horses, (date unknown) 60
Head of Queen Tiy, ca. 1391–1353 B.C. (Egyptian) 140
Horned Toad Mask, ca. 1996 (North American) 232
Inca Mask, date unknown (Peruvian) 230
Kente Cloth, 20th century (Asante people) 70
Kifwebe Mask, date unknown (African) 231
Lokapala, the Guardian King, ca. A.D. 700–755 (Chinese) 72
Nataraja: Siva as King of Dance, 11th century 132
Nuihaku, ca. 18th century (Japanese) 200
Olmec Head, 1200–900 B.C. (Olmec culture) 34
Pectoral, ca. A.D. 600–800 (Tolima culture) 30
Peplos Kore, ca. 530 B.C. (Greek) 138
Pictograph, ca. 30,000 B.C. 98
Portrait Bust, ca. 54–117 (Roman) 106
(Detail) Queen Tiy from the Tomb of Userhat, 18th dynasty 132
Restoration Model of the Acropolis, 5th century B.C. (Greek) 78
Rock Painting, date unknown 98
Rose de France, ca. A.D. 1200 (French) 112
Spartan Woman, 6th century B.C. (Greek) 104
Stirrup Jar with Octopus, ca. 1200–1100 B.C. (Mycenaean culture) 198

Artworks

808A End of Waters on the Roof (1985), Friedensreich Hundertwasser .224
Anna and David (1987), Miriam Schapiro 94
Apartment Hill (1980), Wayne Thiebaud 215
Apples and Oranges (ca. 1900), Paul Cézanne 148
Arrival of the Normandy Train, Gare Saint-Lazare (1877), Claude Monet 156
The Artist's Father (1866), Paul Cézanne 53
At the Theatre (Woman in a Loge) (ca. 1879), Mary Cassatt 158
August and the Red Glass (1976), Janet Fish 95
Baile (Dance) (1970), Elizabeth Catlett 94
Beaded Zemi (ca. 1515) 205
Bed (1955), Robert Rauschenberg 196
Big Star (ca. 1962), Stanislawa Dawid 30
Birthday (l'Anniversaire) (1915), Marc Chagall 248
Birthday Party (1989), Carmen Lomas Garza 248
Block Lamp (1996), Harri Koskinen 192
Boys 'n cat (notes of a mad girl) (1996), Karin Broker 65
Breastplate (ca. A.D. 1000–1470), Peruvian 202
Breezing Up (1873–1876), Winslow Homer 31
The Brueghel Series (A Vanitas of Style) (1982–1984), Pat Steir 174
Buffalo (1992), Holly Hughes 28
Buffaloes in Combat (late 16th century), Attributed to Miskin 118
Caerlaverock Castle (ca. A.D. 1270) 111
Case Alien (1991), David Strickland 195
Cat and Spider (ca. 1868–1911), Toko 144
Cataract III (1967), Bridget Riley 40
Celebration (1983–1985), Thana Lauhakaikul 248
Ceremonial Knife (Pre-Columbian), Peruvian 204
A Certain Smile (1994), William Wegman 145
The Chess Game (1555), Sofonisba Anguissola 52
Cliff Palace (ca. A.D. 600), Anasazi culture 115
Clothespin (1976), Claes Oldenburg 166
Clowns (1983), Melissa Miller 164
Color Shapes (1914), Paul Klee 26
Colosseum (ca. A.D. 70–82), Roman 108
Couch Potato (1994), Nam June Paik 249
The Connoisseur (1962), Norman Rockwell 234
The Court of Empress Theodora (A.D. 547) 130
CSI, Inc. (1997), Seppo Aarnos 185
Dancing Figure (16th century), Italian 58
Dancing in Colombia (1980), Fernando Botero 36

Danza de la Alegria (Dance of Joy) (1950), Rufino Tamayo 94
Dawn (1962), Louise Nevelson 194
Deco Chair (1997), Barbara Brozik 188
Dome of the Florence Cathedral (1420–1436), Filippo Brunelleschi .76
Domino Players (1943), Horace Pippin 50
Dragon's Head (ca. A.D. 820), Scandinavian 110
Drawing XIII (1915), Georgia O'Keeffe 22
Duck-shaped Earrings (18th dynasty), Egyptian 204
Ducks and Ducklings (1st century B.C.–A.D. 1st century), Roman .107
Dürer at Thirteen (1484), Albrecht Dürer 142
Edward Ruscha Monument (1978–1987), Kent Twitchell 180
Egyptian Rulers and Their Crowns (date unknown), Egyptian 100
The Elephants (1961), Salvador Dali 164
Enclosed Field with Rising Sun (1889), Vincent van Gogh 6–7, 45
Energy Apples (1980), Audrey Flack 29
Eugene McDermott Concert Hall of the Morton H. Meyerson Symphony Center
    (1989), I.M. Pei, architect, and Russell Johnson, acoustician 77
The Family (1962), Marisol Escobar 177
Family Tree (1986), Jaune Quick-to-See Smith 176
Figure (Drummer) (date unknown), Nkanu culture 96–97, 125
Fishing Scene: Attendants with harpoons and string of fish (1436–1411 B.C.), Egyptian 101
The Flying Horse (A.D. 2nd century) 176
Frida and Diego Rivera (1931), Frida Kahlo 134–135, 169
From the Lake No. I (1924), Georgia O'Keeffe 216–217, 241
Funerary Mask (ca. A.D. 400–600), Teotihuacán culture 230
A Game of Hand Sumo in the New Yoshiwara (ca. 1740), Furuyama Moromasa 20
Genesis (1932), John Storrs 12
George Went Swimming at Barnes Hole, But It Got Too Cold (1957), Joan Mitchell 161
Georgia O'Keeffe (1953), Laura Gilpin 240
Girl with Doll (1908–1909), Gabriele Münter 33
Girl with Gold Necklace (1944), Henri Matisse 10
Grandmother Series: July Cone Hat (1982), Viola Frey 138
The Green House (1990), Sandy Skoglund 25
Guernica (1937), Pablo Picasso 133
Hall of Bulls and Horses (date unknown) 60
Head of Queen Tiy (ca. 1391–1353 B.C.), Egyptian 140
Horned Toad Mask (ca. 1996), North American 232
The Horse Fair (1853), Rosa Bonheur 120
The Hunter (1943), Andrew Wyeth 222
Hydria with Running Figures (date unknown), Painter of Micali 105
I and the Village (1911), Marc Chagall 246
Improvisation 19a (1911), Wassily Kandinsky 121

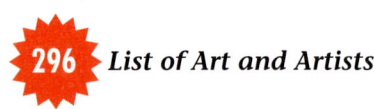

Inca Mask (date unknown), Peruvian 230
Interior with Egyptian Curtain (1948), Henri Matisse 178–179, 207
Intruder in the Port (1993), Lee N. Smith III 163
"It's just the architect's model, but I'm very excited." (1997), Leo Cullum 234
Isola di San Giacomo in Palude Chandelier (1996), Dale Chihuly 16
Ivy in Flower (1953), Henri Matisse 122
Judy Baca with one of her murals 181
Kara (1983), Janet Fish 95
Man and Boy (Edo period, 1658–1868), Katsushika Hokusai 8
Kente Cloth (20th century), Asante people 70
Kifwebe Mask (date unknown), African 231
Lady Wearing a Gauze Headdress (ca. 1435), Rogier van der Weyden 141
Lamb, Mask, Venus, Universal Man, Snail, and Covenant Tablets (1979), Francisco Matto 229
The Lawrence Tree (1929), Georgia O'Keeffe 223
Le Moulin de la Galette (1876), Pierre-Auguste Renoir 19
Letter to the World–The Kick (1986), Andy Warhol 39
The Lighthouse at Honfleur (1886), Georges Seurat 154
Lobby of The Morton H. Meyerson Symphony Center (1989), I.M. Pei 77
Lokapala, the Guardian King (ca. A.D. 700–755), Chinese 72
Love Is In the Hare (1998), Chuck Jones 236
Man and Boy (Edo period, 1658–1868), Katsushika Hokusai 8
Master of Ceremonies (1985), Miriam Schapiro 92
Men Shoveling Chairs (date unknown), Attributed to Rogier van der Weyden 56
Merryn (1962), Barbara Hepworth 18
Miriam Schapiro with her artwork 221
Modem: Close Encounter of the Computer Kind (1983), Barbara Nessim 80
Modern Art (1895), Arthur Wesley Dow 227
Mona Lisa (1503–1506), Leonardo da Vinci 116
Mont Sainte-Victoire Seen from the Bibemus Quarry (1897), Paul Cézanne 62
Morning of the Rooster (1980), Romare Bearden 212
Moveable Blue (1973), Helen Frankenthaler 60
My History (1997), Miriam Schapiro 220
The Mysteries of the Horizon (1955), René Magritte 162
Nataraja: Siva as King of Dance (11th century) 132
November Sun Emerging (1956–1959), Charles Burchfield 153
Nuihaku (ca. 18th century), Japanese 200
Nurse (1964), Roy Lichtenstein 166
Oiseau sur l'arche (1993), Niki de Saint-Phalle 184
The Old King (1916–1936), Georges Rouault 132
Olmec Head (1200–900 B.C.), Olmec culture 34
Passage (1987), Bill Viola 84
Pectoral (ca. A.D. 600–800), Tolima culture 30

(Detail) *Pemberton Street Mosaic* (1997), Isaiah Zagar 182
Peplos Kore (ca. 530 B.C.), Greek 138
Pianist and Checker Players (1924), Henri Matisse 42, 52
Pictograph (ca. 30,000 B.C.) 98
The Place du Havre, Paris (1893), Camille Pissarro 157
Polychrome Ceramic Pottery (ca. 1900–1980), Nampeyo, Fannie Nampeyo,
    and Dextra Quotskuyva 198
Poppies (ca. 1950), Victor Joseph Gatto 218
Portrait Bust (ca. 54–117), Roman 106
Portrait of a Kenyan Elder (1997), Judy Walgren 82
Portrait of Amilcare, Minerva, and Astrubale Anguissola (ca. 1559),
    Sonfonisba Anguissola 117
Portrait of Marianne von Werefkin (1909), Gabriele Münter 160
(Detail) *Queen Tiy from the Tomb of Userhat* (18th dynasty) 132
Red Cow (1989), Leonora Carrington 32
Red Poppy (1927), Georgia O'Keeffe 218
Red Relief with Mask and Animals (1960), Francisco Matto 72, 74
The Red Tree (1908), Piet Mondrian 222
Restoration Model of the Acropolis, 5th century B.C., Greek 78
The Riches of California (1931), Diego Rivera 35
Rind (1955), M.C. Escher 64
Rock Painting (date unknown) 98
Rose de France (ca. A.D. 1200), French 112
Roy II (1994), Chuck Close 140
Running Fence, Sonoma and Marin Counties, California (1972–1976),
    Christo and Jeanne-Claude 214
Sand Brought to an Edge to Catch the Light (August 1991), Andy Goldsworthy 214
Sculptured Roof Garden (1997), Isaiah Zagar 183
Seasons Greetings from WGBH Design (1985), Chris Pullman, and Gaye Korbet 190
Sebastian's Beast (1997), Isabel De Obaldía 17
Self-Portrait (1873), Camille Pissarro 157
Self-Portrait (1943), M.C. Escher 86
Self-Portrait (ca. 1900), Henri Matisse 206
Self-Portrait (The Frame) (ca. 1938), Frida Kahlo 168
Self-Portrait with Straw Hat (1887), Vincent van Gogh 44
Spartan Woman (6th century B.C.), Greek 104
Stephen Spender, Mas St. Jerome II (1985), David Hockney 82
Stirrup Jar with Octopus (ca. 1200–1100 B.C.), Mycenaean culture 198
Stirrup Spout Vessel in the Form of a Seated Deer (3rd–6th century), Moche culture 146
Stonehenge (ca. 1800–1700 B.C.) 99
Street Show (ca. 1868), Honoré Daumier 58
Study of a Sleeping Woman (1921), Diego Rivera 23

(Detail) *Study for Portugal* (ca. 1937), Sonia Terk Delaunay 14
Sunset and Moonrise with Maudell Sleet (1978), Romare Bearden 68
System Drawing E66 (1945), M.C. Escher 38
The Table (1928), Georges Braque 150
Tahitian Landscape (1891), Paul Gauguin 152
Telephone Explosion (1983), James Rosenquist 167
Temple I (ca. A.D. 300–900), Mayan culture 114
Temple of Athena Nike (427–424 B.C.), Callicrates 78
The Third-Class Carriage (ca. 1863), Honoré Daumier 137
Three Quilters (Quilting Party) (1952), John Biggers 136
Throne of Tutankhamen (ca. 1340 B.C.), Egyptian 102
Tlingit House Post (date unknown), Tlingit culture 228
Triangle System I A3 Type I (1938), M.C. Escher 54–55, 87
Tutankhamen, mask from mummy case (ca. 1340 B.C.), Egyptian 101
(Detail) *Une Femme d'Alger* (19th century), Eugène Delacroix 57
Untitled (1978), Tony Palladino 226
Untitled (Eclipse) (1986), Deborah Butterfield 176
Vessel (Effigy in the form of a deer) (14th–15th century), Chimu culture 146
Vietnam Women's Memorial (1993), Glenna Goodacre 186
Watts Towers (1921–1954), Simon Rodia 214
Wedding Blouse: Gaj (early 20th century), Pakistani 200
Weighing Fish (1919), Antonio Frasconi 66
Wenceslaus Psalter (ca. 1250–1260), French 112
West Facade of The Morton H. Meyerson Symphony Center (1989), I.M. Pei 77
The White Soup Bowl (1771), Anne Vallayer-Coster 149
Winged Tiger (19th century), Chinese 119
Women Gathering Fruit (ca. 5th century B.C.), Greek 105
Yellow Pad (1997), Janet Fish 24

Careers in Art

Architecture

Architects create plans for buildings and other structures. They design the interior and exterior of homes, office buildings, museums, churches, and theaters. Architects have a keen sense of space and how to design structures to best utilize a space. Architects may employ wood artisans and sculptors to establish a pleasing, aesthetic environment. Architects receive special training from colleges specializing in architecture.

The Morton H. Meyerson Symphony Center, Dallas, Texas. p. 77

I.M. Pei is a Chinese-American architect known for his designs of public buildings and urban complexes. Many of Pei's creations are buildings he designed especially for the arts.

Art Historian

Art historians are people who study, analyze, and examine art history. They record discoveries and changes in the world of art. They also conduct research about the artists who created the found artworks and the setting in which they lived and worked. Art historians study cultural and artistic traditions, such as forms of government, religious beliefs, and social activities. Art historians are usually teachers or professors in universities and may be employed by an art museum or gallery.

Art Teacher

Art teachers are usually artists with a desire to share their knowledge and skills with students of art. An art teacher must have a college education in the areas of art history and the use of art materials and techniques. An art teacher can work in schools, museums, hospitals, retirement homes or any environment where learning occurs.

Joaquín Torres-García (1874–1949) was a well-known art educator from Uruguay. He and Francisco Matto started an art school known as El Taller Torres-García.

Cartoonist

A cartoonist is an artist who creates drawings and captions that show people or things in a humorous situation. Cartoons are created for comic strips, adventure books, greeting cards, and animations for television and movies. Some drawings are produced for advertisements and editorial cartoons found in newspapers and magazines. Cartoonists illustrate stories in an amusing way to help the reader understand what the story is about. Cartoonists may work for publishers of magazines or newspapers. Many are freelance artists who sell their work to various publications.

Chuck Jones, Animated Cartoonist, p. 236

Chuck Jones is a well-known cartoonist who animates cartoon characters. His work is known throughout the world in the animations of Bugs Bunny, Daffy Duck, Porky Pig, Roadrunner, and Wile E. Coyote.

Leo Cullum, Cartoonist, p. 234

Fashion Designer/Costume Designer

Fashion designers create drawings of shirts, blouses, skirts, pants, and other garments. Some designs are selected to be sewn as an outfit and presented at a fashion show for clothing manufacturers. If a manufacturer likes the outfit, the design is purchased and manufactured for department stores and fashion boutiques. A few fashion designers might be lucky enough to create "one-of-a-kind" garments for famous individuals who can afford such a luxury.

Costume designers create the clothing you see for screen and stage actors, dancers, and musicians. The costume is created from a sketch drawn by hand or on the computer.

Glass Blower/ Glass Sculptor

Neon glassblowing is a technique used to create glass artworks. This kind of sculpture is first heated until the glass softens or melts. The artist then blows the glass and manipulates it into tube forms. These forms are often filled with gases that are lit electronically to produce neon lights for commercial signs or advertisements.

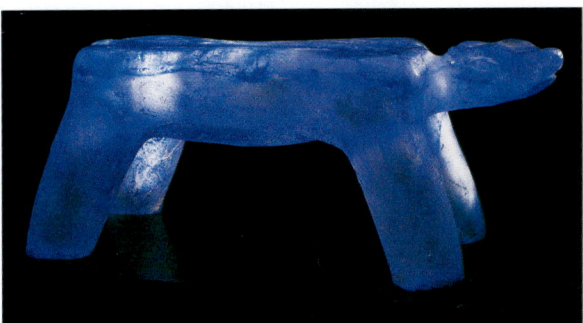

Dale Chihuly and Isabel De Obaldía are artists who use glass as a medium to create organic glass forms. Chihuly directs a team of artists in the traditional glassblowing tradition. De Obaldía creates casts or forms to be filled with glass chips which are heated in a kiln until melted.

Graphic Designer

A graphic designer creates artistic messages with images and lettering that are often used in advertisements and commercial signs. Most graphic designers use high-powered computers to create the graphics for video games, layouts and illustrations for magazines, and designs and illustrations for books and textbooks. Graphic designers are in demand in today's commercial art market.

Arthur Wesley Dow, Poster Artist, p. 227

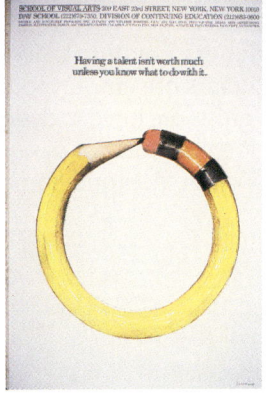

Tony Palladino, Poster Artist, p. 226

Isabel De Obaldía, Glass Sculptor, p. 17

Illustrator

Illustrators create pictures for books, magazines, or other printed works. They draw or paint visual expressions of printed texts. Illustrators work for publishers of magazines, newspapers, trade and textbooks, and film companies. They also work as freelance artists. Many illustrators use a computer as a design tool. Today's commercial art industry relies heavily on the speed and techniques of the computer.

Norman Rockwell, Illustrator/Painter, p. 234

Industrial Designer

An industrial designer is an artist who plans the appearance and form of useful objects. Industrial designers work with scientists and engineers to design objects, such as computers, telephones, cars, toys, and kitchen appliances which are made in factories. These products are mass-produced from the same design. After the products have been used by the consumer, industrial designers create plans to improve the products. Designers are employed by every industry; for example, artists are hired to design jewelry for a jewelry manufacturer. Interior designers create plans for the interiors of offices and homes.

Harri Koskinen, Industrial Designer, p. 192

Museums

Art educators, classroom teachers, and volunteers with an appreciation of fine art work in art museums and art galleries. Museums and galleries hire people to work behind the scenes to display, protect, and preserve the artworks within their buildings.

Conservator A conservator explores and studies ways to protect artworks from damage and decay. The work of a conservator can be tedious, requiring detailed records and studies of new ways to preserve artworks for future generations.

Curator A curator selects artworks to be displayed at the museum. This person may travel the world looking for artwork to purchase for the museum's permanent collection or for an interesting exhibition. The curator arranges for exhibitions to be brought to the museum for an extended period of time.

Docent A docent guides visitors through the museum and answers questions about the artworks, artists, and the museum itself. A docent may be employed by the museum or work as a volunteer. Many docents are art historians or teachers.

Gallery Owner/Art Dealer An art gallery promotes and sells the works of selected artists. Artists are invited by the gallery owner or art dealer to display their works in a gallery. Many artists strive to have their artworks sold from a gallery. Gallery owners are usually artists themselves or have studied art history in college.

Careers in Art

Painter

Artists who express their thoughts and feelings through painting are called painters. Professional painters are hired to create murals, billboards, or fine-art, such as portraits and landscapes.

Lee N. Smith III, Surrealist Painter, p. 163

Chuck Close, Portrait Painter, pp. 140, 141

Kent Twitchell, Muralist, p. 180

Frida Kahlo, Painter, pp. 134, 168

John Biggers, Painter, p. 136

Paul Cézanne, Still Life Painter, pp. 53, 62, 148

Anne Vallayer-Coster, Still Life Painter, p. 149

Georges Braque, Cubist Painter, p. 150

Paul Gauguin, Painter, p. 152

Charles Burchfield, Watercolor Painter, p. 153

Georges Seurat, Pointillist Painter, p. 154

Claude Monet, Impressionist Painter, p. 156

Camille Pissarro, Impressionist Painter, p. 157

Mary Cassatt, Impressionist Painter, p. 158

Gabriele Münter, German Expressionist Painter, pp. 33, 160

Joan Mitchell, Abstract Expressionist Painter, p. 161

René Magritte, Surrealist Painter, p. 162

Judy Baca, Muralist, p. 181

Salvador Dali, Surrealist Painter, p. 164

Melissa Miller, Surrealist Painter, p. 164

James Rosenquist, Pop Artist, p. 167

Roy Lichtenstein, Pop Artist, p. 166

Robert Rauschenberg, Combine Painter, p. 196

Georgia O'Keeffe, Painter, pp. 216, 218, 223

Victor Joseph Gatto, Folk Art Painter, p. 218

Piet Mondrian, Painter, p. 222

Andrew Wyeth, Realist Painter, p. 222

Friedensreich Hundertwasser, Abstract Painter, p. 224

Norman Rockwell, Illustrator, p. 234

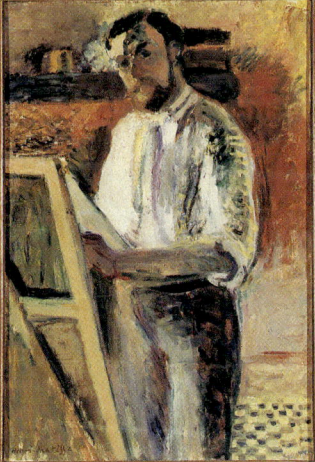

Henri Matisse, Fauvist Painter, pp. 42, 178, 206

Photographer/Photojournalist

A photographer is an artist skilled in creating photographs with a still camera, or recording video with a video camera. Photographers are visual reporters, and they often follow a career in photojournalism. Photographers are hired by newspapers, magazines, and television stations to report news, create advertisements, or tell a story.

David Hockney, Photographer, p. 82

Judy Walgren, Photographer, pp. 82, 83

Bill Viola, Videographer, p. 84

William Wegman, Photographer, p. 145

Potter

A potter is an artist who creates pottery from wet clay. Potters create functional objects such as vases, bowls, pots, and dishes, as well as decorative objects.

M.C. Escher, Printmaker, p. 64

Some printmakers work as commercial artists for advertising or printing companies, while others create prints for art galleries and museums.

Sculptor

A sculptor can model, carve, cast, or join materials into a three-dimensional form. Sculptors commonly use wood, clay, stone or metal to create their artworks. Sculptors are commissioned by architects and landscape designers to create forms to add meaning, beauty, or function to the design of a building or grounds.

Viola Frey sculpts ceramic figures of both men and women, some being more than 11 feet high. Her monumental figures command attention. The artist began her career in art as a painter and expanded to clay, which allowed her to combine painting and drawing with sculpture.

Fannie Nampeyo, Potter, p. 198

Printmaker

Printmaking is the process of transferring an image from an inked surface to another surface to create artwork. Multiple copies can be made by re-inking the surface and repeating the process. Many techniques are used for creating various types of prints. Engraving or etching in wood or linoleum, transfering images on paper, and making a print from a photographic negative are some examples. Artists who make prints are called printmakers.

Claes Oldenburg, Pop Sculptor, p. 166

Niki de Saint-Phalle, Sculptor, p. 184

Seppo Aarnos, Metal Sculptor, p. 185

Glenna Goodare, Clay Sculptor, p. 186

Viola Frey, Ceramist Sculptor, pp. 138, 139

Careers in Art

Louise Nevelson, Assemblage Sculptor, p. 194
David Strickland, Assemblage Sculptor, p. 195
Francisco Matto, Wood Sculptor, pp. 72, 74, 229

Textile/Fiber Designer/Weaving Artist

Fiber arts are considered craft art, or artworks made by hand that are either useful or functional. Examples of fiber art are quilting, embroidery, crochet, lace, and fabric. These artists are highly skilled, often creating original designs or patterns for fabric to be sold to fashion designers. These designs can then be mass-produced and sold throughout the world.

Miriam Schapiro refers to each of her mixed-media collages as a femmage. It is a type of collage that includes traditional fabric art made by women. Aprons, handkerchiefs, hotpads, lace, and other needlework fabrics add meaning to her femmages.

Miriam Schapiro, Femmages, pp. 92, 220, 221

Theater/Stage Design Sets/Prop Designer

Artists who are stage designers plan spaces and props for the theater. Stage designers are skilled in architecture as well as drawing, painting, and sculpture. Stage designers usually work with a crew that builds the sets and moves the sets between play acts or intermission.

Woodworker/Furniture Builder

Most furniture is manufactured in factories, however, hand-crafted furniture is designed and built by artists. Woodworking, a technique often used by furniture designers, is a crafted skill resulting from practice and technique building.

Barbara Brozik, Furniture Designer, pp. 188, 189

Barbara Brozik creates one-of-a-kind furniture sculptures. Each item has its own design, form, and pattern. Brozik often receives commissions from customers to design and build artworks to their specifications. She also creates furniture to sell in shops and galleries.

Art History Timeline

Cave Painting France

2570 B.C.–2500 B.C.
Pyramids of Giza and the Great Sphinx built

Ancient Period

2050 B.C.–1786 B.C.
Middle Kingdom

3000 B.C.　　　2500 B.C.　　　2000 B.C.

Prehistoric | Ancient Egypt

3000 B.C.–2686 B.C.
Old Kingdom

Indus (Ancient Indian) Civilization

1800 B.C.–1700 B.C.
Stonehenge built on what is now Salisbury Plain, England

Every artwork is the product of an artist's particular knowledge and experiences as well as the larger historical and cultural contexts in which the artist lives. The following notes provide broad descriptions of the artwork of selected cultures and periods in history. They are not intended as a definitive characterization of any one artist's work.

ART IN WESTERN CIVILIZATION

Prehistoric Art (25,000–3500 B.C.)

The earliest known artworks were created during the **Paleolithic Age** (the Old Stone Age, 25,000–8000 B.C.), a time in which people were nomadic and lived mainly by hunting and gathering food. Bone and ivory carvings of animals and fertility deities are common during this period. Cave paintings of hunting scenes appeared during the **Mesolithic Age** (the Middle Stone Age, 8000–6000 B.C.) in what are now Spain and France. These paintings are crude yet powerful representational depictions, created with red, yellow, and black paints made out of clay and other natural substances. Between 6000 and 3500 B.C., the **Neolithic Age** (the New Stone Age) ushered in a radical shift in lifestyle as people moved from hunting and gathering cultures to more settled agricultural ones. The artworks of this period are mainly functional, including pottery, cloth, and buildings.

Ancient Art (3500 B.C.–A.D. 400)

Centers of civilization arose almost simultaneously in areas that are now Europe, the Middle East, India, Asia, and the Americas.

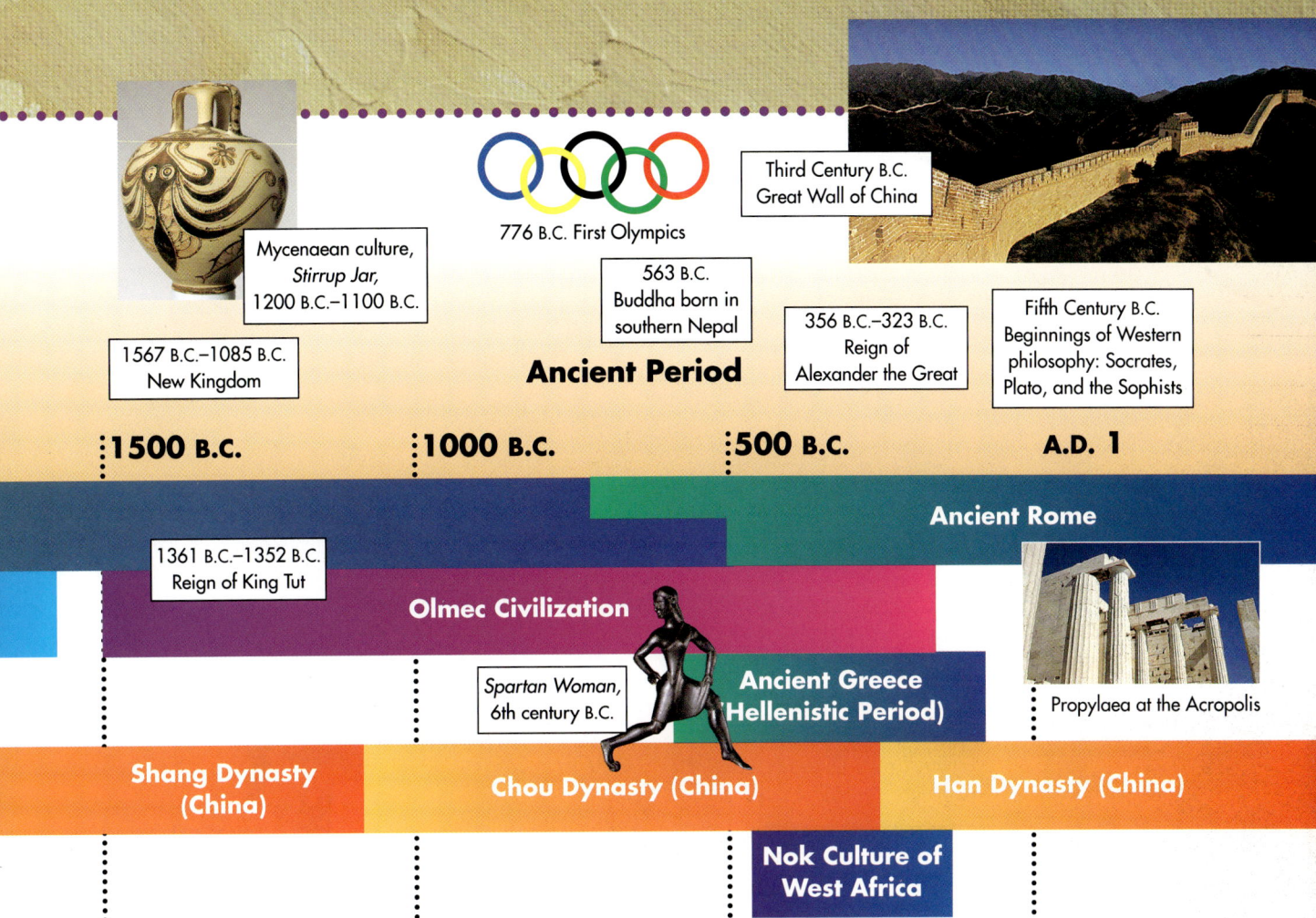

Rapid population expansion in each of these areas created a need for shelters and for religious and civic buildings. Cross-culturally, the art of this period conveys an intense respect for the spiritual and political aspects of humanity. In **Ancient Egypt** (3000–500 B.C.), pyramids and fresco paintings reflect the Egyptian belief in an afterlife and an appreciation of proportion and symbolism in art. The art of both **Ancient Greece** (600–150 B.C.) and **Ancient Rome** (753 B.C.–A.D. 476) emphasizes perfection of form, proportion, and balance. These elements, later recognized as central components of the classical style, are seen in Greek temples such as the Parthenon and in Roman civic buildings such as the Colosseum. In contrast to the abstract, symbolic qualities of Greek art, however, Roman art was characterized by an interest in naturalistic detail.

Medieval Art (400–1400)

The single most important influence on European art during the Medieval period was Christianity, which became the official religion of the Roman Empire in 313 and which remained the central political and cultural force in Europe after the Roman Empire's collapse in 476. The dominant characteristic of Medieval art is its rich symbolism, most evident in the great cathedrals of the period as well as in paintings, mosaics, tapestries, and illuminated, or elaborately decorated, manuscripts. **Byzantine art** (330–1500), which evolved out of Roman, Greek, and Asian art styles and flourished in the Near East, often featured stilted, abstract human forms on backgrounds of rich gold. **Romanesque art** (1050–1200) grew mainly out of the classical Roman style and is marked by the rounded arches of massive cathedrals and by complex, stylized sculpture. Pointed arches and stained

Portfolios

Moche culture, *Stirrup Spout Vessel* A.D. 3rd–6th century

Roman, *Portrait Bust*, ca. A.D. 54–117

A.D. 313 Christianity becomes official religion of Roman Empire

Ancient Period

A.D. 64 Rome burns

A.D. 1 | 100 | 200 | 300

Ancient Rome

Han Dynasty (China)

753 B.C.– A.D. 476
The Roman Empire
- development of republican form of government
- birth of Jesus of Nazareth
- roads and aqueducts (plumbing) invented

Roman aqueducts pictured at right

Roman aqueducts

glass windows characterize cathedrals built in the **Gothic art** style (1100–1400). The fluid, graceful lines of Gothic paintings and sculpture reflect a return to and refinement of Ancient Roman naturalism.

Renaissance Art (1400–1600)

The Renaissance, which means "rebirth," was a period enkindled by the rediscovery of the art and philosophy of Ancient Greece and Ancient Rome. Like the art of classical antiquity, Renaissance art is characterized by exact proportion, idealized forms, symmetry, simplicity, and naturalistic detail. Although religious themes were common, secular subjects also became popular. Art was greatly influenced by radical developments in the sciences and in math as formal rules for linear perspective and other kinds of spatial representation were established.

Enlightenment Art (1600–1800)

Two major styles of art emerged during the Enlightenment, or the Age of Reason. The 1600s, a century marked by religious and political revolution, produced a style of art known as **Baroque** (meaning "irregular"). Although Baroque art retained the Renaissance interest in the classical forms of unity and order, it was strongly expressive, featuring dramatic lighting and coloring, rich textures, elaborate swirls and curves, and dynamic, sometimes violent movement. The 1700s—a century preoccupied with manners, good taste, and the privileges of aristocracy—saw the rise of **Rococo**, an art style that was playful and highly decorative but that conveyed the delicacy and elegance associated with society's upper classes.

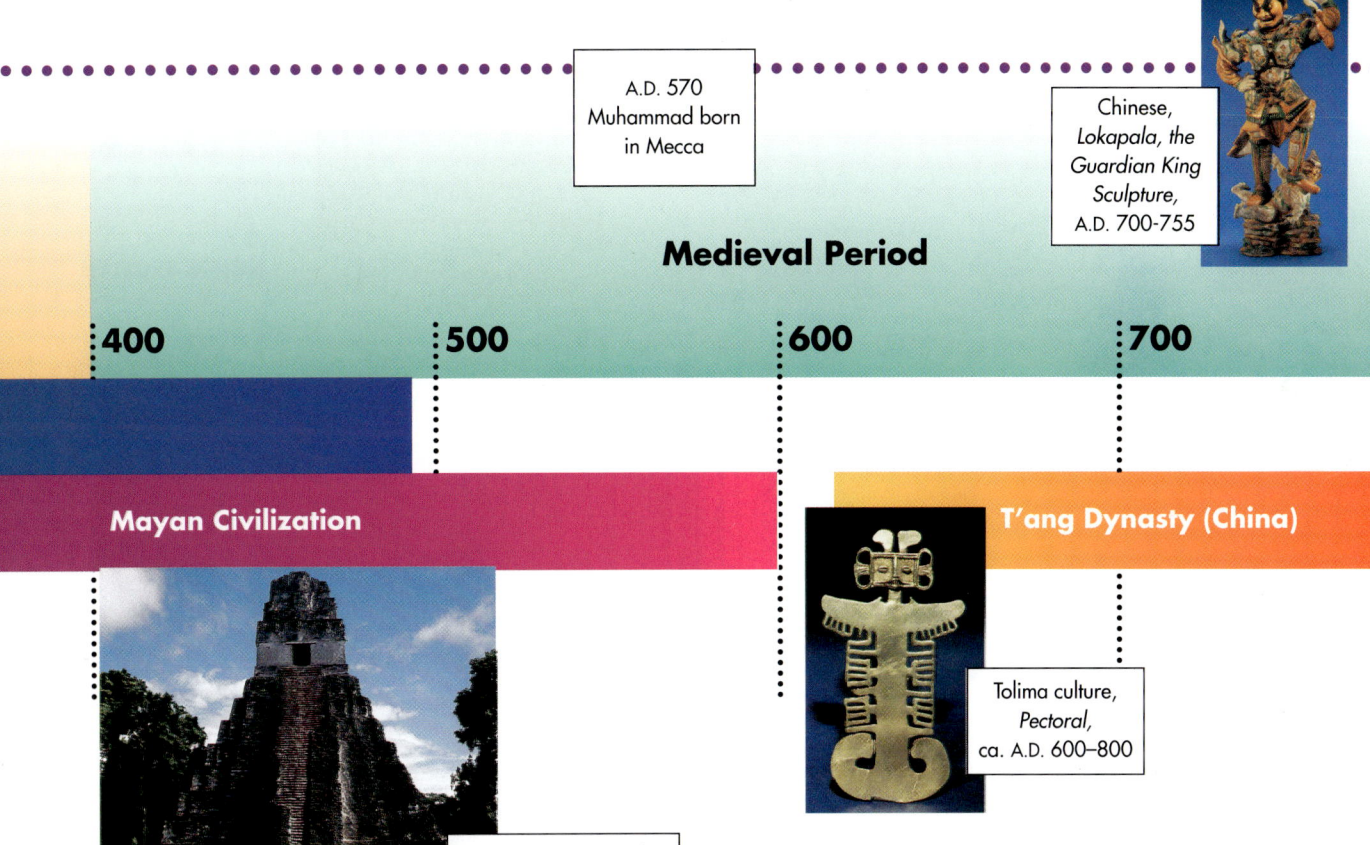

Art of the Modern Era
(1800–Present)

The art of the Modern Era has been influenced most heavily by the rise of industry and, more recently, technology. Individualism and subjectivity are the dominant themes in the art of this period, with an increasing emphasis on psychology and multiple perspectives.

Neoclassicism (1750–1875) reacted against the excesses of the Baroque and Rococo movements by reviving and imitating classical art forms and techniques.

Romanticism (1800–1850) celebrated the imagination, the supernatural, and freedom for individual expression. Romantic art expressed these ideals through the use of bold lighting, deep shadows, and exotic subject matter.

Realism (1850–1900), also known as **Naturalism**, was a rationalist response to the mysticism of Romanticism. Realistic art attempted to portray life as it was—to describe accurately the world as it was perceived by the senses.

Impressionism (1875–1910) sought to capture on canvas the impressions received by a glance of the eye: light reflecting off surfaces, pure colors, imprecise forms. The Impressionists believed that art should not convey political, moral, or emotional meanings.

Post-Impressionism (1880–1915) employed the techniques developed by the Impressionists (visible brushstrokes, heavily textured surfaces) but infused art with emotional and symbolic significance. The Post-Impressionists also experimented with stronger brushwork and higher intensities of color.

Expressionism (1890–1930) attempted to use art to give form to strong inner feelings. The Expressionists located truth and beauty in the mind rather than in the eye and rejected the idea that art's primary purpose was to represent nature. They used distorted,

Portfolios **309**

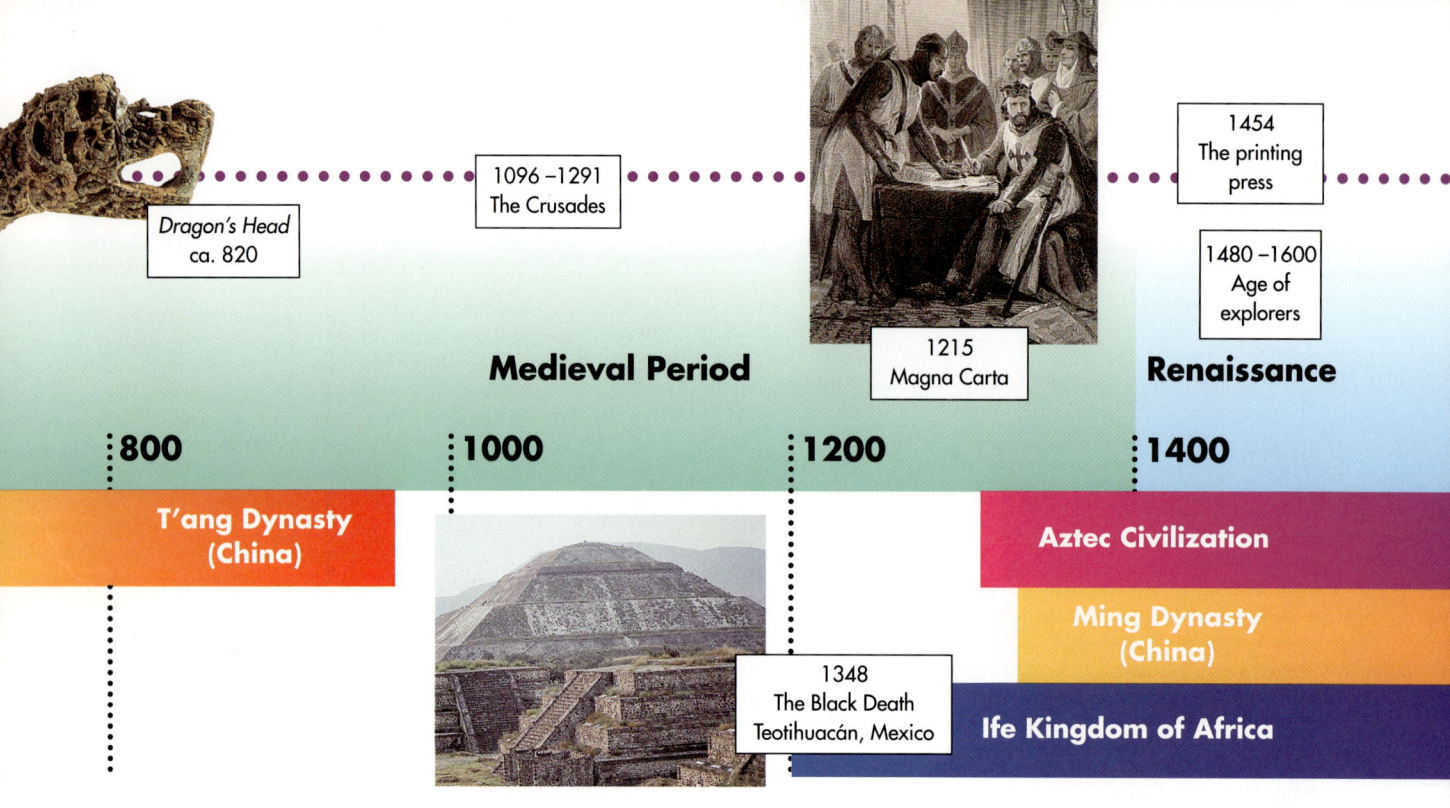

exaggerated forms, vivid colors, and heavy brushstrokes. **Fauvism (1899–1906)**, an influential movement within Expressionism, exalted pure, high-intensity color.

ART IN THE TWENTIETH CENTURY

Most twentieth-century (also known as Modern Art) styles continue to be explored and modified; thus in most cases no ending dates are given.

Cubism (1907–) is characterized by the fragmentation and reorganization of shapes and forms, as well as the unconventional treatment of space. Futurism (1909–) aims to break strongly with the past. Futuristic art glorifies the speed and energy of the machine age, using multiple overlapping images and fragments of color to convey these qualities.

Dadaism (1916–) grew out of a protest movement in the arts whose agenda was to shock and provoke the public out of its complacency. Art in the Dada style is playful, highly experimental, and nonsensical.

Nonobjective Art (1917–) is a general term for extremely abstract art characterized by geometric forms and no identifiable subject matter.

The Harlem Renaissance (1919–1929) was a cultural and artistic movement during which African American painters, sculptors, writers, and musicians living in Harlem, New York City, celebrated their heritage and expressed their identity through art, introducing African American themes into American Modernism.

Surrealism (1924–), like Dadaism, was a protest movement that attempted to use art to reform society. Unlike Dadaism, though, Surrealism sought to broaden "reality" to include the subconscious, instinctual level of human existence, using highly symbolic, dreamlike imagery.

Abstract Expressionism (1950–) celebrates the process of creating art. It experiments with color, the physical properties of paint, and the power conveyed by very large artworks. In general, Abstract Expressionism takes the form of nongeometric abstract art.

Op Art (1950–) aims to startle and disorient the viewer through optical illusion, often creating the sensation of movement through innovative uses of pattern and color.

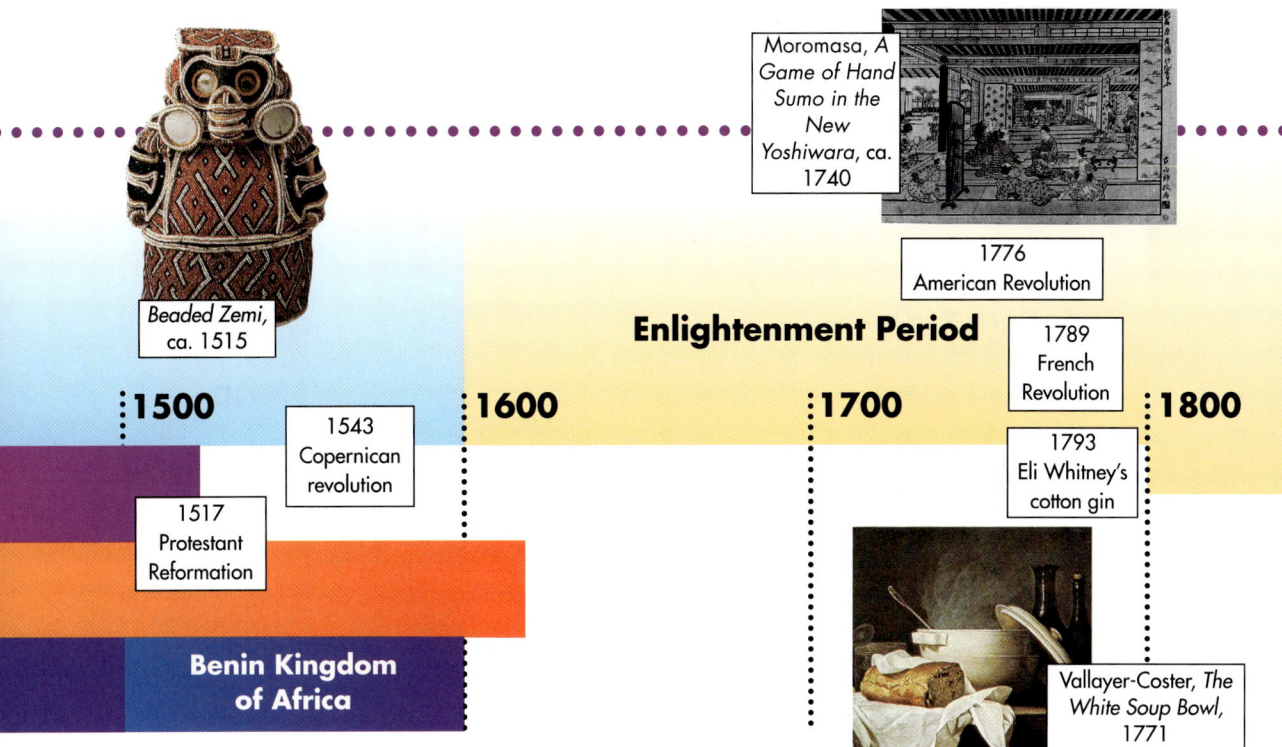

Pop Art (1950–) uses forms and themes from mass culture, frequently in a satirical or playful manner. Pop artists seek to demystify the obscure or elusive aspects of traditional art.

Postmodernism (1960–) refers to a broad movement in philosophy, literature, and the arts that questions the assumptions underlying inherited traditions, art forms, and bodies of knowledge.

 NATIVE ARTS OF THE AMERICAS

Pre-Columbian Art

Pre-Columbian art refers to art originating in the Americas before they were colonized by Europeans beginning in the 15th century. Three important pre-Columbian civilizations were the Olmec, the Maya, and the Aztec, each of which produced impressive bodies of art.

Olmec (ca. 1500–200 B.C.) This ancient civilization is known for its monumental, free-standing stone carvings of human figures and for its relief sculptures on themes such as fertility, the powers of nature, and religion.

Mayan (ca. A.D. 250–600) The Mayan civilization probably had an Olmec origin, and seems to have inherited from Olmec an intense interest in sculpture. Mayan sculpture was primarily architectural, however. The remains of massive, intricately decorated limestone structures at Mayan centers such as Copán and Uaxactún reveal the Mayan preference for ornament, ritual, and symbolism.

Aztec (ca. 1325–1520) The people of this extensive empire practiced a fierce, militaristic religion that required elaborate, decorative costumes and accessories. The most renowned artworks of the Aztecs are their monumental sculptures depicting gods, goddesses, and other organic forms such as snakes, grasshoppers, and cacti.

Native North American Art. The history of Native American art is as rich and diverse as the American Indian cultures producing it. These cultures share a fundamental belief in the close link between humanity, the natural world, and the spirit world, a belief that is reflected in their art. While many Native American cultures were permanently transformed by the arrival of the Europeans in the 1400s, some aspects of these

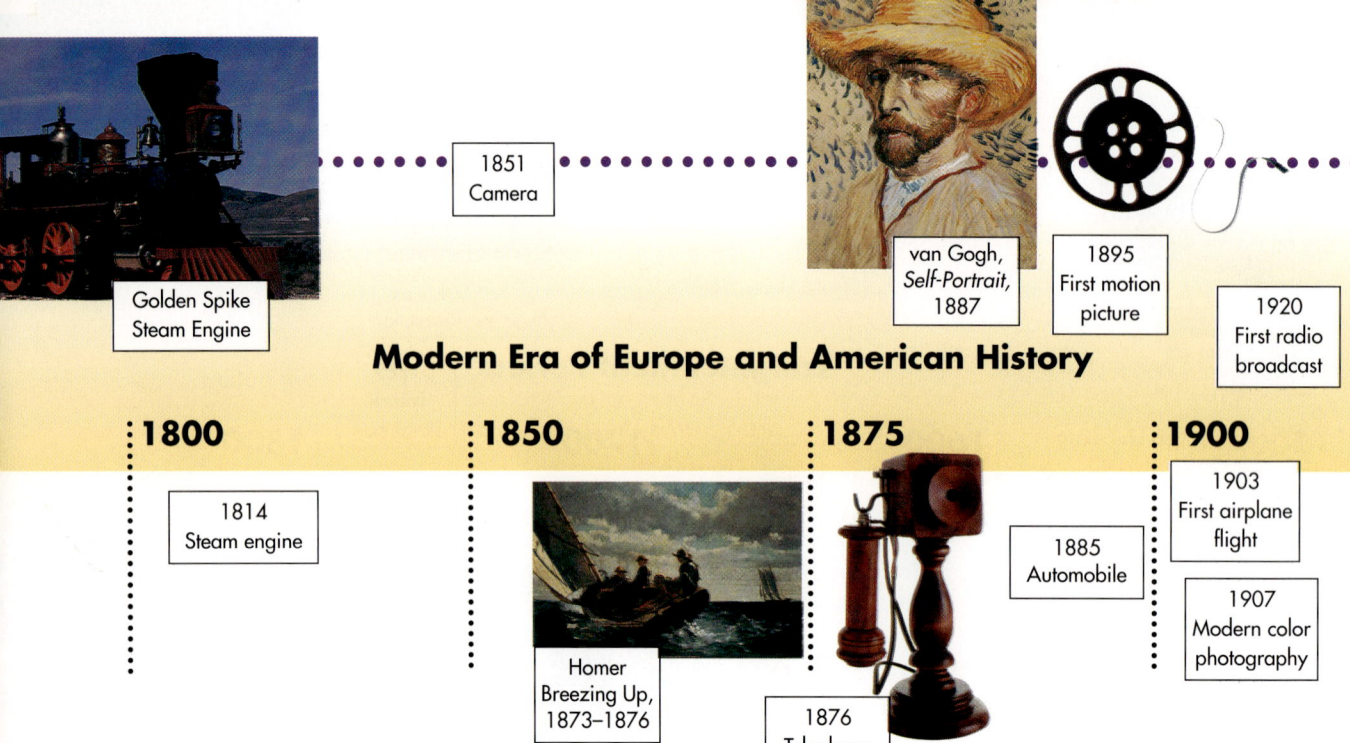

Modern Era of Europe and American History

1800 — 1814 Steam engine
1850 — 1851 Camera; Homer *Breezing Up*, 1873–1876
1875 — 1876 Telephone; 1885 Automobile; van Gogh, *Self-Portrait*, 1887; 1895 First motion picture
1900 — 1903 First airplane flight; 1907 Modern color photography; 1920 First radio broadcast

Golden Spike Steam Engine

cultures did survive intact. In what is now the Southwest United States, for example, American Indian traditions still thrive among remote or culturally similar peoples such as the Pueblo, including the Hopi of Arizona. Pueblo sculptors continue to fashion traditional kachina dolls, models of spirits dressed in ceremonial costumes. Well into the 1800s, the nomadic Plains cultural groups of central North America sustained their traditions, including the carving of sacred pipes, pipe bowls, spoons, and flutes from stone and wood. To this day, American Indians of the Northwest have an extravagant sculptural tradition. From massive totem poles to spoons and figurines, almost all of these artworks—like most American Indian artworks of the past—feature animal themes that signify the mythology and history of the cultural group that creates them.

SUB-SAHARAN AFRICAN ART

Sub-Saharan Africa has many regions well known for their artworks, particularly for sculpture. From as early as 500 B.C., African peoples such as the Nok were creating clay sculptures of human and animal figures, thought to be symbolic of the spirit world. The Nok also used terra cotta clay to fashion earthenware and other pottery. Later, the Ife (1200–1500) and Benin (1500–1600) kingdoms produced bronze and wooden sculptures that were increasingly naturalistic, often representing divine kings and other royal personages. Besides sculpture, traditional sub-Saharan African arts also include masquerade (a complex, performance-based art involving sculpted masks, elaborate costuming, music, and dance); a wide variety of decorative utilitarian objects such as chairs and pipes; and finely crafted cloths, leather goods, and basketry.

ASIAN ART

The Art of India

The earliest Indian artworks were naturalistic, anatomical sculptures created by people of the Indus civilization (2500–1700 B.C.). Along with the advent of Buddhism (563 B.C.) came a host of new art forms, including monumental polished sandstone pillars and columns; cave temples carved out of the faces of cliffs; and symbolic and anthropomorphic sculp-

312 Art History Timeline

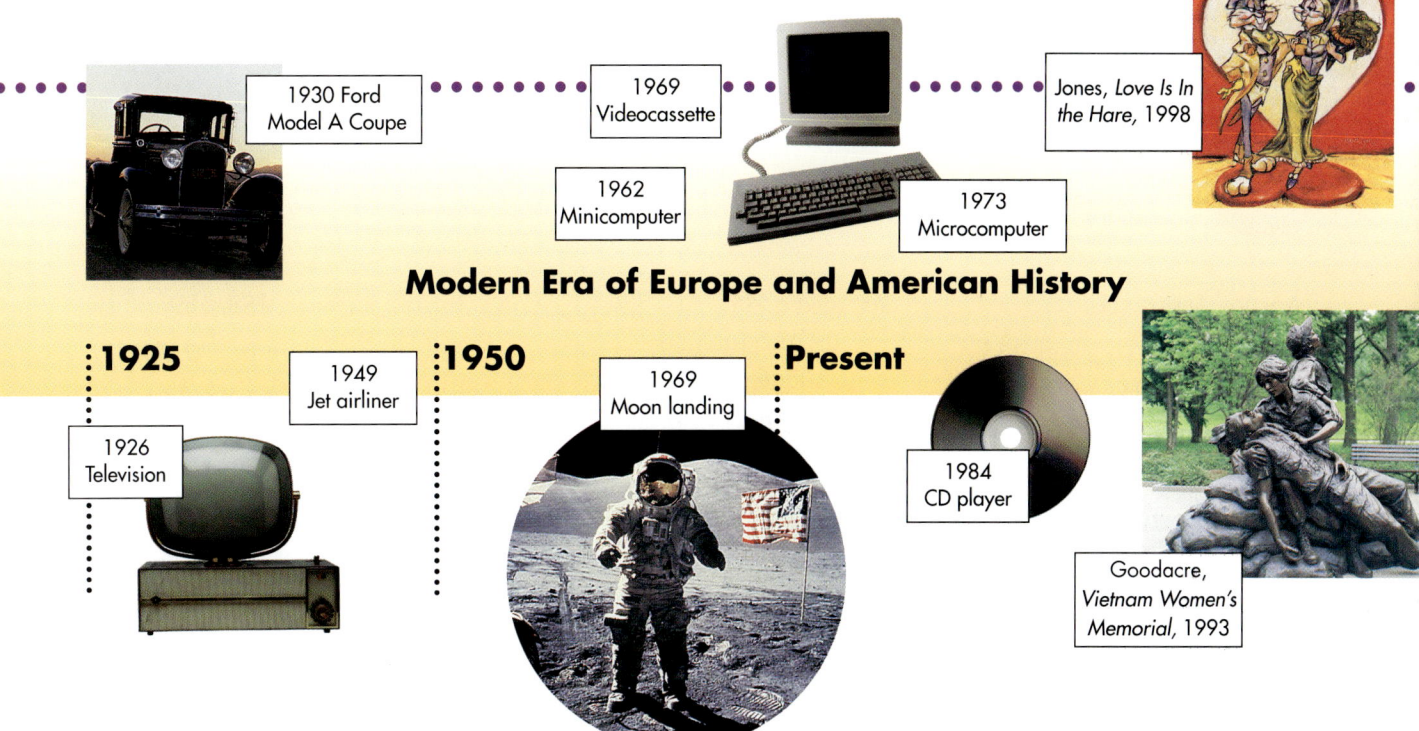

tures of the Buddha. Between 100 and 200 B.C., a new religion, Hinduism, appeared; by A.D. 500–600 it had flourished, quashing Indian Buddhism. Then, with the Muslim invasions of the 700s, a second major religion was added to Indian culture. Much Indian artwork since that time has been either Hindu or Muslim in theme. Murals and reliefs painted on and carved into massive stone temples depict stories from traditional Hindu literature, and Muslim mosques are decorated with intricate designs, often inlaid in white marble with semiprecious stones.

The Art of China

Painting is one of the oldest Chinese art forms. As early as 5000 B.C. the Chinese were painting sophisticated designs on pottery, and painting on silk dates to around 400 B.C. The earliest Chinese sculptures were small bronze and jade figures made to be placed in tombs during the Shang (1766–1122 B.C.) and Zhou (1120–250 B.C.) dynasties The arrival of Buddhism from India during the Han dynasty (206 B.C.–A.D. 220) inspired the building of elaborate, highly ornate temples. During the Tang dynasty (620–936) the Chinese developed some of the world's first porcelain. The dishes and vases made out of this translucent ceramic during the Tang, Ming (1368–1644), and Qing (1644–1912) dynasties are among the most treasured of Chinese artworks.

The Art of Japan

Ancient Japanese art consisted primarily of pottery vessels and figurines, the techniques for which were developed by a culture known as Jomon as early as 4000 B.C. From the A.D. 200s to 500s, small clay sculptures known as *haniwa* were placed in the burial mounds of important Japanese citizens. With the arrival of Buddhism in A.D. 552, Japanese artists turned their energies toward building and decorating Buddhist temples using wood, clay, and bronze. Early Japanese painting dealt mostly with Buddhist subjects; from the 1100s to the 1300s, many painters created long picture scrolls that told historical and religious stories. Between 1300 and 1550 ink painting flourished; after that, painting became more decorative, featuring bright colors and gold-leaf ornamentation. During the 1600s to 1800s, Japanese artists created colorful woodblock prints. Printing is still a popular art form in Japan today.

Portfolios

Index

Aarnos, Seppo, 184, 185
Abstract Expressionism, 135, 160, 161, 196
action painting, 160 (*See also* Abstract Expressionism)
African art, 70, 124, 231
African sculpture, 150
alternating rhythm, 38
Anasazi architecture, 114, 115
analogous color scheme, 27
Ancient art, 98–99
Ancient Egypt, 100–01
Ancient Greece, 104–05, 198
Ancient Rome, 106
Angelou, Maya, 136, 137
Anguissola, Sofonisba, 117
animal style, 110
animated cartoons, 236
applied art, 146, 204 (*See also* functional art)
architectural model, 78–79, 108–09
architecture, 76–77
    Anasazi, 114, 115
    Eastern, 118
    Mayan, 114
    Medieval, 111
    Roman, 108
armature, 232
art careers (*See* careers)
art galleries, 238–39
art history, 97

art media, 55
    architecture, 76
    collage, 68–69
    drawing, 56–57
    painting, 60–61
    photography, 82
    printmaking, 64–65
    sculpture, 72–73
    textiles, 70–71
art museums, 238–39
assemblage, 73, 194–95
assembling, 73
asymmetrical balance, 31
atmospheric perspective, 19, 157 (*See also* perspective)

Baca, Judy, 181
Bach, Johann Sebastian, 128
background, 18
balance, 30–31
Bearden, Romare, 68, 69
Biggers, John, 136, 137
binder, 60
bird's-eye view, 222
block, 64
blotto paintings, 25
blueprint, 76
Blue Rider, 160–61 (*See also* Münter, Gabriele)
Bonheur, Rosa, 120
Botero, Fernando, 36
Braque, Georges, 150
brayer, 65, 66

Brozik, Barbara, 188, 189
Brunelleschi, Filippo, 20, 76, 77
Burchfield, Charles, 152–53

Callicrates, 78
caption, 234
caricature, 236–37
careers
    architect, 77
    cartoonist, 234, 235
    clothing designer, 201
    collagist, 69
    computer artist, 81
    conservator, 239
    costume designer, 29
    curator, 239
    docent, 239
    furniture designer, 189
    graphic designer, 226
    industrial designer, 190–92
    muralist, 181
    painter, 141, 157, 163
    photographer, 83
    poster artist, 227
    sculptor, 17, 139, 229
Carrington, Leonora, 32
cartooning, 234–36
carving, 73
Cassatt, Mary, 158
casting, 73, 146
castles, 111
cave painting, 99, 118, 129, 144
ceramics, 146–47, 198–99
Cézanne, Paul, 62, 148, 149, 157

Chihuly, Dale, 16, 17
China, 118, 119
Chopin, Frederic, 128
chorus, 129 (See also theatre)
cityscapes, 152, 224–25
clay, 198 (See also pottery)
Close, Chuck, 140, 141
clothing design, 200–201
collage, 37, 68–69, 82, 122–23, 150, 220
color
    cool, 25
    expression, 219
    intermediate, 25
    mixing sheet, 27
    primary, 24, 25
    properties, 26–27
    secondary, 24–25
    schemes, 27, 42
    warm, 25
colorist, 26
color wheel, 24, 26
Columbus, Christopher, 114
columns, 78
combine painting, 196–97, 220
combine sculpture, 197
comedy, 173
commercial art, 167, 224–25
commercial art galleries, 238
complementary color scheme, 27, 152
composition, 7
    abstract, 122
    balance, 31
    checklist, 43
    color, 24
    contrast, 33
    emphasis, 33

    object placement, 35
    point of view, 220–22
    principles of design, 7
    proportion, 34–35
    shapes, 14–16
    size relationships, 14
    space, 18
    three-dimensional, 17
    two-dimensional, 17
    unity, 42
computer art, 41, 80–81, 220, 226
conservator, 239
contour drawing, 10–11, 17 (See also drawing)
contrast, 22, 32, 33
cool colors, 25
costume designers, 201
craft, 70, 204
creative process, 55
Cubism, 150–51
Cullum, Leo, 234
curator, 239

Dali, Salvador, 164
dance, 48, 90, 128, 172, 210, 244
Daumier, Honoré, 58, 137
da Vinci, Leonardo, 116
Dawid, Stanislawa, 30
decorative art, 205
deep space, 19 (See also space)
Degas, Edgar, 158
Delaunay, Sonia Terk, 14
De Obaldía, Isabel, 17
depth, 18–19, 20, 35
de Saint-Phalle, Niki, 184, 185

design, 7, 30–31, 32, 34, 39, 42
detail, 14, 18
Dickinson, Emily, 49
divisionism, 154 (See also pointillism)
docent, 239
dome, 76
dominance, 32
Dow, Arthur Wesley, 226, 227
drama, 49 (See also theatre)
drawing, 10–11, 17, 56, 58–59
Dürer, Albrecht, 142

Eastern art, 118–19, 120
edition, 64
Egypt, 100–01
elements of art, 7
elevation, 76
embroidery, 118 (See also stitchery)
emotion, 40–41, 219 (See also mood)
emphasis, 32–33
Escher, M.C., 38, 54, 55, 64, 86–87
exaggerated art, 35
experimental literature, 129 (See also literature)
expression, 217, 219
Expressionism, 160–61 (See also Abstract Expressionism; German Expressionism)
exterior, 76

facial proportions, 37, 140, 232 (See also proportion)

fashion design, 200–01
Fauvism, 161, 206
femmage, 221 (See also mixed media)
fiber art, 70–71
figures, 138
film, 173 (See also theatre)
fine art, 146
Fish, Janet, 24, 25
Flack, Audrey, 29
floorplan, 76, 238
focal point, 32–33
Folk art, 218
form, 16–17
Frankenthaler, Helen, 60, 61
Frasconi, Antonio, 66
Frey, Viola, 138, 139
front view, 140
functional art, 97 (See also utilitarian art)
furniture, 188–89

galleries, 238–39
Gauguin, Paul, 152
geometric forms, 16, 150
geometric shapes, 12–13
German Expressionism, 120–21, 160–61
gesture drawing, 58–59 (See also drawing)
glazes, 199 (See also pottery)
gold-leaf decoration, 200
Goodacre, Glenna, 186
graphic design, 226–27
graphics tablet, 80

Greece, 104–105
greenware, 198 (See also pottery)
Grosz, George, 69
ground-level view, 223

Hammer, Jan, 128
Hancock, Herbie, 128
Hanson, Duane, 211
Harlem Renaissance, 69
Hepworth, Barbara, 18
history, 97
Hockney, David, 82
Hokusai, Katsushika, 8
Homer, Winslow, 31
horizon line, 9, 18–19 (See also perspective)
hue, 24, 26, 33
Hughes, Holly, 28–29
Hundertwasser, Friedensreich, 224

illuminations, 112
illustration, 227
impasto, 44–46
impression, 64
Impressionism, 156–59
Incas, 204–05, 231 (See also Pre-Columbian art)
India, 118
industrial design, 190–92
Industrial Revolution, 188, 190
intaglio, 65
intensity, 26–27

intermediate color, 25
interior, 76

Japanese art, 20, 200
Jones, Chuck, 236
Joseph Gatto, Victor, 218, 219

Kahlo, Frida, 134, 135, 168, 169, 220
Kandinsky, Wassily, 121
Kelly, Ellsworth, 30
Kennedy, Richard, 49
kente cloth, 70
King Mene, 100
King Tut, 100–101, 102
Klee, Paul, 26, 27
Korbet, Gaye, 190
Koskinen, Harri, 192

landmark painting, 62–63
landscape architect, 76
landscapes, 45, 152–53
Lichtenstein, Roy, 166, 167
light source, 137
line, 7
    actual, 9
    emphasis, 32
    horizon, 18–19, 20, 21
    implied, 9
    quality, 8–9
    types of, 8–9
linear perspective, 18–19, 20 (See also perspective)
literature, 49, 91, 129, 173, 211, 245
lithograph, 227

logos, 226
loom, 71
Love, Kenna, 218

Magritte, René, 162
maquette, 122, 186
masks, 230–31, 233
Matisse, Henri, 10, 42, 43, 74, 122, 178, 179, 206–07
Matteucci, Nedra, 239
Matto, Francisco, 72, 74, 228, 229
Mayan architecture, 114
Medieval art, 110, 112
medium, 55
Middle Ages, 110–12
middle ground, 18
Miller, Melissa, 164
miniature art, 34
Miskin, 118
Mitchell, Joan, 161
mixed media, 220, 221 (*See also* collage)
model (architectural), 78–79, 108–09, 239
modeling, 73
Modern Art, 120, 144, 167
Mona Lisa, 116
Mondrian, Piet, 222
Monet, Claude, 156–57, 158
monochromatic color scheme, 27
monoprint, 65
Mont Sainte-Victoire, 62
monumental art, 34

mood, 23 (*See also* emotion)
Moromosa, Furuyama, 20
mosaics, 107, 118
motif, 202
movies, 49 (*See also* theatre)
multimedia, 226
Münter, Gabriele, 33, 160–61
muralist, 181
murals, 22, 117, 118, 180, 182
museums, 236–37
music, 48, 90, 172, 210, 244
musical instruments, 128

Nampeyo, 198, 199
Nampeyo, Fannie, 198
Native Americans, 115, 228
negative space, 18
Nessim, Barbara, 80, 81
neutral color scheme, 27
Nevelson, Louise, 194, 195, 220
Newton, Sir Isaac, 24
Nonobjective Art, 60, 121
normal proportion, 34 (*See also* proportion)

objects, 35
observation, 30
oil paint, 61
O'Keeffe, Georgia, 22, 23, 217, 218, 219, 223, 240–41
Oldenburg, Claes, 166
opaque, 61
organic forms, 16–17
organic shapes, 13

originality, 217
overlapping, 18, 35

painting, 217
    action, 160
    art media, 60
    blotto, 25
    combine, 196–97, 220
    Greek style, 105
    landmarks, 62–63
    sfumato, 116
    swirl, 241
    techniques, 61
    textured, 63
Pakistan, 200
palette, 25, 61
Palladino, Tony, 224
paper sculpture, 73
papier mâché, 232–33
patina, 185
pattern, 7, 38–41
Pei, I.M., 76, 77
perception, 56
perspective, 18–19, 20–21, 157
Peru, 204–05, 231
photographic collage, 82, 83
photography, 82
photojournalism, 83
Picasso, Pablo, 150
pigment, 60
Pissarro, Camille, 156–57, 158
pixels, 80
plasticity, 36
plays, 49 (*See also* theatre)
pointillism, 135, 154–55
point of view, 222–23

Pollock, Jackson, 245
Pop art, 166–67
porcelain, 119
portraits, 106, 141 (*See also* self-portraits)
pose, 140
positive space, 18
posters, 226, 227
pottery, 198–99
Pre-Columbian architecture, 114
Pre-Columbian art, 74, 229
prehistoric art, 98–99
prehistoric cave paintings, 99, 118, 129, 144
primary color, 24–25
principles of design, 7, 30, 39, 42, 43, 139
printer, 80
printing ink, 64
printing plate, 64, 66
printmaking, 64–65, 86–87
profile view, 140
progressive rhythm, 38
proof, 64
proportion, 34–37, 138–39, 140, 230
prototype, 192–93
Pueblo Indians, 115
Pullman, Chris, 190

Quechuan Indians, 231 (*See also* Native Americans)
quilting, 71
Quotskuyva, Dextra, 198

radial balance, 31
Rauschenberg, Robert, 196, 220
Realistic art, 120, 121, 157, 160
regular rhythm, 38
relic, 97
relief prints, 65, 66–67
relief sculpture, 72, 74, 75
Renaissance, 116, 117
Renoir, Pierre Auguste, 18, 19
repoussé, 202–03
rhythm, 7, 38–41
Riley, Bridget, 40
Rivera, Diego, 22, 23, 35, 134, 168
Rockwell, Norman, 234
Roman art, 106–08
Rosenquist, James, 167
Ruscha, Edward, 180

scale, 166 (*See also* size relationships)
scanner, 80
Schapiro, Miriam, 220, 221
sculpture, 146, 229
    African, 124–25, 150
    animals, 144–45, 146
    art media, 72–73
    assemblage, 194–95
    bronze, 186
    combine, 197
    Eastern art, 118
    in the round, 72
    lost wax, 186
    maquette, 186–87
    outdoor, 184–85
    paper, 73
    patina, 185
    permanent installation, 184
    portable structures, 184
    relief, 72, 74, 75
    techniques, 73
seascapes, 152, 154–55
secondary color, 24–25
self-portraits, 44, 142, 169, 221 (*See also* portraits)
Seurat, Georges, 135, 154
sfumato, 116
shade, 26
shading, 22, 57
shape, 7, 12–13, 18, 32, 219
silk, 119
size relationships, 34–35, 166
sketchbook, 9
Skoglund, Sandy, 25
Smith, Lee N. III, 163
software applications, 80
solvent, 60
space, 18–19, 32
stained glass, 112, 113
Stein, Gertrude, 129
Stieglitz, Alfred, 240
still life, 148–51
still photography, 82 (*See also* photography)
stitchery, 71 (*See also* embroidery)
Stonehenge, 99
Storrs, John, 12
straight-on view, 222
Strickland, David, 195, 220
style, 36, 135, 218
stylus, 80
subject, 60, 135
    animals, 107, 118, 144–47

    landscapes, 152–54
    light source, 137
    people, 136
    still life, 148–51
Surrealism, 135, 162–65
swirl painting, 241
symbols, 74, 164, 215–16, 220, 228, 230–31
symmetrical balance, 30, 31

tactile texture, 28, 29
tessellation, 86, 88
tesserae, 107, 118, 182
textiles, 70–71, 118
texture, 28–29, 32, 49
textured painting, 63
theatre, 49, 91, 129, 173, 211, 245
three-quarter view, 140
tint, 26
Toko, 144
tomb paintings, 100–01, 102
tooling, 202, 203

Torres-García, 229
totems, 228, 229
transparent, 61
Triptych, 208
Tutankhamen, 100–101, 102
Twitchell, Kent, 180, 181

unity, 42–43, 221
utilitarian art, 146, 204 (See also functional art)

Vallayer-Coster, Anne, 149
value, 22–23, 26
van der Weyden, Rogier, 141
van Gogh, Vincent, 6, 44–45
vanishing point, 19–20 (See also perspective)
variety, 42–43, 221
vessels, 198, 199
Vikings, 110
Viola, Bill, 220
visual texture, 28–29 (See also texture)

Walgren, Judy, 82, 83
wall hanging, 202
Warhol, Andy, 39
warm colors, 25
warp, 71
water-based paint, 61
weaving, 71
weft, 71
Wegman, William, 145
Western tradition, 97
worm's-eye view, 223
writers, 49 (See also literature)
Wyeth, Andrew, 222

Zagar, Isaiah, 182

Portfolios 319

Acknowledgments

Contributors

The author and publisher wish to thank the following teachers for their expertise, wisdom, and wholehearted good will during the field testing of this textbook:

Laurie Adams, Nita Adams, Kim Allread, Jane Brass, Judy Cluck, Carolyn Daniels, Marti Fox, Becky Hernandez, Terry Hrehocik, Sally Kemble, Jody Moore, Beth Moss, Tammy Obar, Robin Scott Papathanasiou, Diane Rohman, Vicki Shaw, Shirley Smith, Nita Ulaszek, Carol Webb, Iris Williams, Jean Yant.

We gratefully acknowledge the following schools for allowing us to work with their teachers and students in the development of this textbook:

Agnew Middle School, Mesquite Independent School District; Honey Grove Middle School, Honey Grove Independent School District; Cannaday Elementary, Mesquite Independent School District; Northwood Hills Elementary, Richardson Independent School District; J.H. Florence Elementary, Mesquite Independent School District; Dover Elementary, Richardson Independent School District; Porter Elementary, Mesquite Independent School District; Webb Middle School, Austin Independent School District; Spring Valley Middle School, La Mesa–Spring Valley School District; Allen Elementary, Chula Vista School District; Poole Middle School, Stafford County School District; Drew Middle School, Stafford County School District; Collins Intermediate, Conroe Independent School District; Austin Elementary School, Mesquite Independent School District; Chisholm Trail Intermediate, Keller Independent School District; Bear Creek Intermediate, Keller Independent School District; Spring Ridge Elementary, Richardson Independent School District; Math/Science/Technology Magnet School, Richardson Independent School District; Wilkinson Middle School, Mesquite Independent School District; Applied Learning Academy, Fort Worth Independent School District; Beasley Elementary School, Mesquite Independent School District; Prairie View Intermediate, Northwest Independent School District; Price Elementary School, Mesquite Independent School District.

A special acknowledgment to the founders of the SHARE program in San Antonio, Texas, Pamela Valentine and Sue Telle, who graciously allowed us to share with the world their prized and inspirational student artworks. The SHARE *(Students Help Art Reach Everyone)* program is a foundation dedicated to students and their art, and develops opportunities for students to interact with and enlighten their communities.

Photo Credits

Key: (t) top, (c) center, (b) bottom, (l) left, (r) right.

UNIT 1. Page 6, 7(br), 45(t) Private collection/SuperStock; 8(tr) Courtesy of the Freer Gallery of Art, Smithsonian Institution, Washington, D.C. 04.232; 9(tl) © Telegraph Colour Library 1997; 10(tr) Collection of The University of Arizona Museum of Art, Tucson. Gift of Edward J. Gallagher, Jr.(Acc# 55.7.7). © 1999 Succession H. Matisse, Paris/Artists Rights Society (ARS), New York; 14(tr) The National Museum of Women in the Arts, Gift of Wallace and Wilhelmina Holladay; © L&M Services B.V. Amsterdam 990506; 16(tr) © Chihuly Studio. Photo by Russell Johnson; 18(tr) The National Museum of Women in the Arts. Gift of Wallace and Wilhelmina Holladay. © Copyright Alan Bowness Hepworth Estate; 19(t) Musée d'Orsay, Paris/SuperStock; 20(t) The Metropolitan Museum of Art, New York, Frederick C. Hewitt Fund, 1911. (JP655); 22(tr) The Metropolitan Museum of Art, Alfred Stieglitz Collection, 1950. (50.236.2). Photograph © 1997 The Metropolitan Museum of Art. © 1999 The Georgia O'Keeffe Foundation/Artists Rights Society (ARS), New York; 23(tr) Courtesy of the Fogg Art Museum, Harvard University Art Museums, bequest of Meta and Paul J. Sachs. Photographic Services, © President and Fellows of Harvard College, Harvard University. © Banco de México, Av. 5 de Mayo No. 2, Col. Centro 06059, México, D.F. Reproduction authorized by Banco de México, Trustee of the Trust relating to the Museums Diego Rivera and Frida Kahlo; 24(b) Photo by Beth Phillips, courtesy DC Moore Gallery, NY; 25(t) © Sandy Skoglund. Photo courtesy Sandy Skoglund/SuperStock; 26(tl) Barnes Foundation, Merion, Pennsylvania/SuperStock; 28(tr) Courtesy of the artist; 28(bl) Courtesy of the artist; 29(t) Photo by Steven Lopez; 30(tr) Courtesy Dr. Peter T. Furst; 30(br) Girard Foundation Collection at the Museum of International Folk Art, a unit of the Museum of New Mexico, Santa Fe. Photo by Michel Monteaux; 31(t) National Gallery of Art, Washington, D.C. Gift of the W. L. and May T. Mellon Foundation. Photograph by Bob Grove, © 1998 Board of Trustees, National Gallery of Art, Washington; 32(t) Courtesy Brewster Arts Ltd. © 1999 Leonora Carrington/Artists Rights Society (ARS), New York; 33(tl) © 1999 Artists Rights Society (ARS), New York/VG Bild-Kunst, Bonn; 34(tr) ©1998 H. Huntly Hersch/D. Donne Bryant Stock Photography; 35(tr) Photo © 1982 by Don Beatty. © Banco de México, Av. 5 de Mayo No. 2, Col. Centro 06059, México, D.F. Reproduction authorized by Banco de México, Trustee of the Trust relating to the Museums Diego Rivera and Frida Kahlo; 36(t) The Metropolitan Museum of Art. Anonymous gift, 1983(1983.251). Photograph © 1983 The Metropolitan Museum of Art. © Fernando Botero, courtesy Marlborough Gallery, NY; 38(t) All M.C. Escher works © Cordon Art B.V., Baarn, Holland. All rights reserved; 39(t) © 1999 Andy Warhol Foundation for the Visual Arts/Artists Rights Society (ARS), New York; 42(t), 52(tr) Collection of Mr. and Mrs. Paul Mellon. Photograph © 1996 Board of Trustees, National Gallery of Art, Washington, D.C. © 1998 Succession H. Matisse, Paris/Artists Rights Society (ARS), New York; 43(tl) Barrett Kendall photo by Laurie O'Meara; | 44 © Rijksmuseum Vincent van Gogh, Amsterdam/Vincent van Gogh Foundation; 50(t) © The Phillips Collection, Washington, D.C.; 53(l) National Gallery of Art, Washington, D.C. Collection of Mr. and Mrs. Paul Mellon. © 1998 Board of Trustees, National Gallery of Art, Washington, D.C.

UNIT 2. Page 54, 55(br), 87(t) All M.C. Escher works © Cordon Art B.V., Baarn, Holland. All rights reserved; 56(t) The Metropolitan Museum of Art, Robert Lehman Collection, 1975(1975.1.848). Photograph © 1985 The Metropolitan Museum of Art; 57(tr) Courtesy of The Metropolitan Museum of Art, Harris Brisbane Dick Fund, 1928; 58(tr) The Metropolitan Museum of Art, gift of Cornelius Vanderbilt, 1880 (80.3.72).

Photograph © 1998 Metropolitan Museum of Art; 58(br) The Metropolitan Museum of Art, Rogers Fund, 1927 (27.152.2). Photograph © 1992 The Metropolitan Museum of Art; 60(tr) © FPG International; 60(b) © Helen Frankenthaler; 62(t) The Baltimore Museum of Art, The Cone Collection, formed by Dr. Claribel Cone and Miss Etta Cone of Baltimore, Maryland BMA 1950.196; 64(tr) All M.C. Escher works © Cordon Art B.V., Baarn, Holland. All rights reserved; 65(tr) © Karin Broker; 66(tr) Norton Simon Museum, Pasadena, CA. Gift of the Weyhe Gallery, New York, NY, 1953; 69(tl) Courtesy of VAGA, NY; 70(t) Courtesy of the Trustees of the British Museum, © British Museum; 71(tr) Courtesy of Frances Moore, Piscataway, NJ; 71(cl),(bl) Barrett Kendall photos by Laurie O'Meara; 72(tr) The Nelson-Atkins Museum of Art, Kansas City, Missouri. Acquired through the Joyce C. Hall Estate and various Hall Family Funds; 72(br) Courtesy of Fundación Museo de Arte Americano de Maldonado. Photo by Acosta Bentos; Courtesy of Cecelia de Torres, Ltd., New York; 73(bl) Barrett Kendall photo by Laurie O'Meara; 74(tr) Courtesy of Fundación Museo de Arte Americano de Maldonado. Photo by Acosta Bentos; Courtesy of Cecelia de Torres, Ltd., New York; 76(tr) Alinari/Art Resource, NY; 76(br) Photo by J. Griffis Smith, courtesy of Texas Highways Magazine; 77(tl) Owen Franken/Corbis; 77(bl) Photo by J. Griffis Smith, courtesy Texas Highways Magazine; 77(br) Photo courtesy of The Morton H. Meyerson Symphony Center; 78(t) Erich Lessing/PhotoEdit; 78 (br) Photograph courtesy of the Royal Ontario Museum, © ROM; 81(tl) © Seiji Kakizaki; 82(t) Courtesy of Judy Walgren; 83(t) © Nan Coulter; 84(t) Collection: Edition 1, San Francisco Museum of Modern Art. Edition 2, Musée National d'art Moderne, Centre Georges Pompidou, Paris. Photo by Kira Perov; 86(t) All M. C. Escher works © Cordon Art B.V., Baarn, Holland. All rights reserved; 95 (tl), 95 (bl) © Janet Fish, Abudefduf, Inc., New York. Photos courtesy of Janet Fish.

UNIT 3. Page 96, 97(br),125(tl) © Africa-Museum Tervuren, Belgium. Photograph by R. Asselberghs; 98(t) © Jean Clottes, Ministere de la Culture/Sygma; 98(b) Holton Collection/SuperStock; 99(t) S. Vidler/SuperStock; 100(t) Wernher Krutein/Liaison International; 101(tr) Erich Lessing/Art Resource, NY; 101(tl) Egyptian Expedition of The Metropolitan Museum of Art, Rogers Fund, 1930(30.4.67). Photograph © 1984 The Metropolitan Museum of Art; 102(tr) © Boltin Picture Library; 104(t) Courtesy of the Trustees of the British Museum, © The British Museum; 105(tl) Erich Lessing/Art Resource, NY; 105(tr) Scala/Art Resource, NY; 106(tr) Alinari/Art Resource, NY; 107(tl) The Metropolitan Museum of Art, gift of Mrs. W. Bayard Cutting, 1932(32.141). Photograph © 1980 The Metropolitan Museum of Art; 108(tr) Scala/Art Resource, NY; 110(t) Werner Forman/Art Resource, NY; 111(tl) Manley/SuperStock; 112(br) Photograph © Adam Woolfitt/Robert Harding Picture Library; 114(b) M. Hunn/SuperStock; 115(tl) D. Dietrich/SuperStock; 116(tr) Musée de Louvre, Paris/A.K.G. Berlin/SuperStock; 117(tl) Erich Lessing/Art Resource, NY; 118(t) The Metropolitan Museum of Art. Harris Brisbane Dick Fund, 1983(1983.258). Photograph © 1984 The Metropolitan Museum of Art; 119(tl) The Metropolitan Museum of Art, gift of Mrs. John H. Ballantine, 1947.(47.75.1). Photograph © 1990 The Metropolitan Museum of Art; 120(t) The Metropolitan Museum of Art, Gift of Cornelius Vanderbilt, 1887.(87.25). Photograph copyright © 1997 The Metropolitan Museum of Art; 122(t) © 1999 Succession H. Matisse, Paris/Artists Rights Society (ARS), New York; 124 SuperStock.

UNIT 4. Page 134, 135, 168, 169 San Francisco Museum of Modern Art, the Albert M. Bender Collection. Photograph by Ben Blackwell. 36.6061. © Banco de México, Av. 5 de Mayo No. 2, Col. Centro 06059, México, D.F. Reproduction authorized by Banco de México, Trustee of the Trust relating to the Museums Diego Rivera and Frida Kahlo; 136(tr) © John Biggers. Photograph by Earlie Hudnall; 137(tl) The Metropolitan Museum of Art, H.O. Havemeyer Collection, bequest of Mrs. H.O. Havemeyer, 1929(29.100.129). Photograph by Schecter Lee, © 1986 The Metropolitan Museum of Art; 138(l) Nimatallah/Art Resource, NY; 138(r) The Nelson-

Atkins Museum of Art, Kansas City, Missouri. Gift of Byron and Eileen Cohen; 139(tr) © 1998 M. Lee Fatherree; 140(tl) Ägyptisches Museum und Papyrussammlung, © BPK, Berlin, 1998. Photo by M. Büsing; 140(tr) Hirshhorn Museum and Sculpture Garden, Smithsonian Institution, Washington, D.C. Regents Collections, Acquisition Program with matching funds from the Joseph H. Hirshhorn Purchase Fund, 1995. Photo by Ellen Page Wilson, courtesy of PaceWildenstein; 141(tl) Fratelli Alinari/SuperStock; 141(br) Photo by Ellen Page Wilson, courtesy of PaceWildenstein; 142(tr) Foto Marburg/Art Resource, NY; 144(b) The Metropolitan Museum of Art, Charles Stewart Smith Collection, gift of Mrs. Charles Stewart Smith, Charles Stewart Smith, Jr., and Howard Caswell Smith, in memory of Charles Stewart Smith, 1914(14.76.61.73). Photograph © 1980 The Metropolitan Museum of Art; 146(tl) The Metropolitan Museum of Art, gift of Nathan Cummings, 1963(63.226.7). Photograph © 1988 The Metropolitan Museum of Art; 146(tr) The Metropolitan Museum of Art, the Michael C. Rockefeller Memorial Collection, gift of Nelson A. Rockefeller, 1969(1978.412.160). Photograph © 1981 The Metropolitan Museum of Art; 148(t) Musée d'Orsay, Paris/Lauros-Giraudon, Paris/SuperStock; 150(r) © 1999 Artists Rights Society (ARS), New York/ADAGP, Paris; 152(t) The Minneapolis Institute of Arts, The Julius C. Eliel Memorial Fund; 153(tl) © Charles E. Burchfield Foundation, courtesy of Kennedy Galleries, NY; 154(t) © 1999 Board of Trustees, National Gallery of Art, Washington, D.C. Collection of Mr. and Mrs. Paul Mellon; 156(t) The Art Institute of Chicago, Mr. and Mrs. Martin A. Ryerson Collection, 1933.1158. Photograph © 1998 The Art Institute of Chicago. All rights reserved; 157(tl) The Art Institute of Chicago, Mr. and Mrs. Potter Palmer Collection. Photograph © 1998 The Art Institute of Chicago. All rights reserved; 157(cr) Giraudon/Art Resource, NY; 158(tr) The Nelson-Atkins Museum of Art, Kansas City, Missouri. Purchase: acquired through the generosity of an anonymous donor; 160(tr) Städtische Galerie im Lenbachhaus, Munich. GMS 656. © 1999 Artists Rights Society (ARS), New York/VG Bild-Kunst, Bonn; 161(tl) © Estate of Joan Mitchell; 162(tr) Christie's Images/SuperStock. © 1999 Charly Herscovici, Brussels/Artists Rights Society (ARS), New York; 163(tl) Courtesy of Lyons Matrix Gallery, Austin, Texas; 163(bl) © Shirlee Smith; 164(t) © 1999 Artists Rights Society (ARS), New York; 164(b) Photo by Bill Kennedy; 166(br) © Al Michaud/FPG International; 166(tr) Photograph by Robert McKeever.

UNIT 5. Page 176, 177(br), 207(tl) © 1999 Succession H. Matisse, Paris/Artists Rights Society (ARS), New York; 180 © Kent Twitchell; 181(t) © Kenna Love; 182(tr), 183(tl) Courtesy of Snyderman Gallery. Photo by Barry Halkin; 184(tr) Photo by Laurent Condominas, courtesy of Archives Niki de Sainte-Phalle, Paris; 185(tl) Courtesy Seppo Aarnos; 186(tr) © 1993 Vietnam Women's Memorial Project, Inc. Photo by Gregory Staley, courtesy of Goodacre Studio, Santa Fe; 186(cr) © Summer Pierce; 188 Photo by Bart Karsten; 189(tl) Courtesy Robyn Montana Turner; 190 Jonathan Kantor; 194 © 1999 Estate of Louise Nevelson/Artists Rights Society (ARS), New York. Photograph courtesy of PaceWildenstein; 195(tl) Photograph courtesy of PaceWildenstein; 195(tr) Photo by George Holmes, © 1998 Blanton Museum of Art, University of Texas; 198(tr), 199 (tl) © Jerry Jacka, All rights reserved; 196(br) The Metropolitan Museum of Art, Purchase, Louisa Eldridge McBurney Gift, 1953(53.11.6). Photograph © 1996 The Metropolitan Museum of Art; 200(b) Girard Foundation Collection at the Museum of International Folk Art, a unit of the Museum of New Mexico, Santa Fe. Photo by Michel Monteaux; 202(t) The Art Institute of Chicago, gift of the Antiquarian Society, Mrs. Harold T. Martin, and Mrs. H. Alex Vance funds, 1978.144. Photograph © 1998 The Art Institute of Chicago. All rights reserved; 204(tl) © Boltin Picture Library; 204(tr) Robert Frerck/The Stock Market; 205(t) Photo by Daniela Masci, courtesy El Museo del Barrio, NY; 206 © 1999 Succession H. Matisse, Paris/Artists Rights Society (ARS), New York. Photograph by Jacqueline Hyde.

UNIT 6. Page 216, 217(br), 241(t) Purchased with funds from the Coffin Fine Arts Trust, Nathan Emory Coffin Collection of the Des Moines Art Center, 1984.3. Photo by Michael Tropea, Chicago, © 1997 Des Moines Art Center. © 1999 The Georgia O'Keeffe Foundation/Artists Rights Society (ARS), New York; 218(t) Art Resource, NY. © 1999 The Georgia O'Keeffe Foundation/Artists Rights Society (ARS), New York; 221(tl) © Kenna Love; 222(tl) © 1999 Artists Rights Society (ARS), New York/ADAGP, Paris; 223(t) Wadsworth Atheneum, Hartford. The Ella Gallup Sumner and Mary Catlin Sumner Collection Fund. Photo by Malcolm Varon, NY. © 1999 The Georgia O'Keeffe Foundation/Artists Rights Society (ARS), New York; 226(b) National Museum of American Art, Washington, D.C./Art Resource, NY; 228 University of Pennsylvania Museum (Neg# T4-614); 230(b) © Boltin Picture Library; 230(tl) National Museum of Anthropology, Mexico City/Explorer, Paris/SuperStock; 234(tr) Printed by permission of the Norman Rockwell Family Trust. Copyright © 1962 the Norman Rockwell Family Trust; 236(tr) Courtesy of Linda Jones Enterprises; 236(cr) Dean Diaz, © 1997 Chuck Jones Enterprises; 238(tr) SuperStock; 239(tl) Courtesy of Nedra Matteucci Galleries; Tony Walton, set designer. Set model for *Death of a Salesman*, 1985. A Roxbury and Punch Production. From the Collection of the American Museum of the Moving Image, Gift of Tony Walton.

Diego Rivera and Frida Kahlo image reproductions authorized by the Bank of Mexico, Av. 5 de Mayo No. 2, Col. Centro 06059, Mexico, D.F. © Fiduciaro en el Fideicomiso relativo a los Museos Diego Rivera y Frida Kahlo.

ILLUSTRATION CREDITS

Holly Cooper: 11, 21, 41, 63-65, 67, 88, 113, 123, 143, 147, 155, 170, 197, 208, 225, 237

Leslie Kell: 13, 16, 19, 43, 210

Mike Krone: 15, 37, 46, 57, 59, 73, 75, 79, 85, 99, 100, 103, 108, 109, 126, 139, 151, 159, 165, 187, 193, 203, 233, 242

Jane Thurmond: 26, 137, 172

Rhonda Warwick: 50, 78, 81, 92, 130, 174, 213, 247